The Municipal Year Book 2012

ICMA PRESS

The authoritative source book of local government data and developments

The Municipal Year Book 2012

Washington, DC

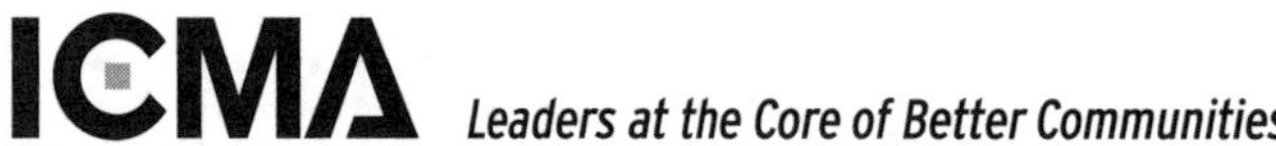

ICMA advances professional local government worldwide. Its mission is to create excellence in local governance by developing and advancing professional management of local government. ICMA, the International City/County Management Association, provides member support; publications, data, and information; peer and results-oriented assistance; and training and professional development to more than 9,000 city, town, and county experts and other individuals and organizations throughout the world. The management decisions made by ICMA's members affect 185 million individuals living in thousands of communities, from small villages and towns to large metropolitan areas.

Volume 79, 2012

ISBN: 978-0-87326-770-0

ISSN: 0077-2186

43675

Library of Congress Catalog Card Number: 34-27121

The views expressed in this Year Book are those of individual authors and are not necessarily those of ICMA.

Suggested citation for use of material in this Year Book: Jane S. Author [and John N. Other], "Title of Article," in *The Municipal Year Book 2012* (Washington, D.C.: ICMA, 2012), 00–000.

Design and composition: Charles E. Mountain

12-100

Contents

Directories

Acknowledgments

The Municipal Year Book, which provides local government officials with information on local government management, represents an important part of ICMA's extensive research program. Each year, ICMA surveys local officials on a variety of topics, and the data derived from their responses constitute the primary information source for the *Year Book*. Authors from local, state, and federal government agencies; universities; and public interest groups as well as ICMA staff prepare articles that describe the data collected and examine trends and developments affecting local government.

We would like to express our appreciation to the thousands of city and county managers, clerks, finance officers, personnel directors, police chiefs, fire chiefs, and other officials who patiently and conscientiously responded to ICMA questionnaires. It is only because of their time-consuming efforts that we are able to provide the information in this volume.

In addition, I would like to thank the ICMA staff who have devoted countless hours to making the *Year Book* so valuable. Ann I. Mahoney is the director of publishing and Jane C. Cotnoir is the *Year Book* editor. Other ICMA staff members who contributed to this publication are Evelina Moulder, director of survey research and information management; Valerie Hepler, director of publications production; Erika Abrams, graphic designer; Sebia Clark, program analyst; and Nedra James, executive assistant.

Robert J. O'Neill Jr.
Executive Director
ICMA

Inside the *Year Book*

Local government concerns are increasingly complex and sophisticated, and the need for familiarity with a broad range of issues is unsurpassed. Furthering the knowledge base needed to better manage local government is one of ICMA's top goals.

Management Trends and Survey Research

1 The Politics of Apolitical Leadership: Professional Management in a Digital and Divided Society

The United States today appears deeply divided. Politically, the nation seems roughly split between the right and the left. Surveys show that two-thirds of Americans believe there is too much income disparity, a topic that is dominating election year politics. Local governments have shed over 440,000 positions, yet issues of pensions and benefits still loom as economic issues for many. Digital technologies are facilitating communication in unprecedented ways, exerting a major influence on social movements but also exacerbating the divide between those with access and those without. Through all of this, political rhetoric and civic discourse seem to have hit a new low, and the trends do not bode well for 2012. As the growing polarization of the external environment and elected bodies increases the pressures on the professional manager, this article asks: To be effective today, does the professional manager have to be more "political" to be effective? *Can* a professional manager be "political"—that is, directly engaged with the community—and still be perceived as nonpartisan?

2 311/CRM Systems: A Potential Path to Service Improvement, Budget Savings, and Citizen Satisfaction

Constituent relationship management (CRM) systems (with or without a dedicated 311 number) are in place in more than 100 cities and counties across the United States, and have become a critical point of contact between citizens and local government. In addition to improving customer service, 311/CRM systems can generate valuable business intelligence that can be used to reengineer local government processes and procedures—and potentially increase efficiency, realize cost savings, and improve overall citizen satisfaction. This article examines preliminary evidence on the extent to which 311/CRM systems are achieving their potential to transform local government. Using case studies from Indianapolis, San Francisco, and Knoxville, the first section describes how these three local governments use 311/CRM systems to increase efficiency and strive for continuous improvement. The second section, which relies on available data to explore how 311/CRM systems may affect overall citizen satisfaction, concludes that the relationship between 311/CRM systems and citizen satisfaction is a priority area for future research.

3 Local Government Use of Development Impact Fees: More Fallout from a Poor Economy?

Development impact fees are one-time fees assessed against new development—commercial, industrial, or residential—to generate funds for the new or expanded infrastructure and services that such development will require, such as water, sewer, roads, schools, parks, libraries, emergency service facilities, fire stations, and police stations. Contributing to their viability as a way for local government to finance off-site infrastructure are taxpayer refusal to approve general obligation bonds and incur higher taxes, reductions in state and federal funds earmarked for local infrastructure, and environmental concerns related to sprawl. However, impact fees are often criticized for their exclusionary effect—by increasing the price of development, they make housing more expensive for lower-income residents—and for reducing the amount of multifamily housing constructed. This article reviews two and a half decades of research into the use, policy implications, and effects of development impact fees. It then presents findings from the third in a series of random surveys of local governments to investigate trends in the use of development impact fees, especially in light of the current economic climate, and what those trends suggest about the use of this mechanism in the future.

4 Local Government Employee Health Insurance Programs, 2011

Providing health care coverage to support a healthy workforce makes sense for local governments, just as it does for all employers. To assess the range of options of health care coverage as well as of health and wellness programs, ICMA partnered with CIGNA HealthCare to conduct a national survey. Preliminary results of the survey were presented in a session at the 2011 ICMA Annual Conference in Milwaukee, Wisconsin, and CIGNA prepared a summary report. Subsequently, close to 350 additional local governments responded to the survey. This article discusses survey results as they address, among other things, local governments' workforce health concerns and programs; health insurance benefits and payment arrangements for current employees, early (pre-65) retirees, and retirees 65 and older; obstacles to developing a healthy workforce; approaches to reducing health care expenses; the impact of federal health care reform legislation; and considerations in selecting health care plans and carriers.

5 Off the Beaten Path: Sustainability Activities in Small Towns and Rural Municipalities

Judging by all the attention they receive in the media, one would assume that the adoption of environmental sustainability policies is spreading like wildfire across the country. But in reality, local government adoption of such policies has been proceeding slowly. One reason for the misperception could be the publicity generated by successful initiatives undertaken by big cities such as Boston, Chicago, and New York, but the achievements of these cities paint an incomplete picture. Small cities and rural towns face capacity challenges, both fiscal and technical, that are not faced by larger places with higher levels of civic activism and more progressive political environments, and so they have been slower to adopt sustainability policies. In 2010, ICMA conducted a national survey of municipalities in conjunction with Arizona State University to gauge their adoption of sustainability policy actions. This article provides further analysis of the data produced in that survey by focusing primarily on smaller communities—cities, villages, and towns with fewer than 25,000 residents.

6 CAO Salary and Compensation: The Big Picture

Compensation for municipal employees became a national issue in 2009 when the *Los Angeles Times* broke the story of the pay scandal in Bell, California, where the city manager, city council members, and at least two senior staff were exploiting the city for outrageous sums. ICMA guidelines state that compensation for local government chief administrative officers (CAOs) should be "fair, reasonable, transparent, and based on comparable public salaries nationally and regionally." They further recommend that compensation benchmarks be established in accordance with comparable local government and/or public sector agencies. However, there is no consensus to date on what external positions are appropriate for benchmarking CAO pay, and ICMA guidelines are broad. This article looks at compensation issues for CAOs by examining new data from a 2011 national survey of local government CAOs in the context of the "ICMA Guidelines for Compensation," the *ICMA Model Employment Agreement,* and the ICMA Code of Ethics.

7 E-Government 2011: Trends and Innovations

Electronic government (e-government) has been with us for nearly two decades and has spread rapidly across the globe. Today, all national, most if not all subnational, and nearly all local governments now offer information and services electronically every hour of every day throughout the year through official government websites. Reporting on the findings from a 2011 U.S. local government survey that used a modified version of the survey instrument used in 2004, this article examines local e-government functionality, including social media and cloud computing; reasons for and barriers to adopting e-government; changes as a result of e-government; and local e-government management and financing to present a snapshot of the place of e-government in the nation as of 2011.

8 Award-Winning Innovations in 2011: Exploring the Boundaries of Transformation

Five years into the "Great Recession," local governments continue to struggle with reduced sales and income tax revenues and a slowly recovering housing market. In a 2009 survey, a majority of responding local government managers reported having taken short-term steps—for example, making across-the-board cuts, imposing furloughs, and eliminating vacant positions—rather than significantly changing their organizations, rethinking their approaches to service delivery, or revising their long-term strategic plans. Others, however, sought creative and new approaches intended to make government more effective in addressing community problems, more efficient in delivering services, and better able to ensure that the workforce of today and tomorrow will be ready to serve. This article highlights 21 of the most noteworthy approaches, organized according to five broad categories: new connections to leverage results, citizens as volunteers, organization and finance, sustainability, and solving uncommon local problems. It then examines key features of the highlighted cases and reviews lessons learned from them.

9 Public Pensions Face Record Pace of Change

Local governments face growing challenges in funding their pension obligations, in large part because of the ongoing economic downturn. Nevertheless, the aggregate assets of public pensions are substantial ($2.7 trillion, versus $0.8 trillion in unfunded liabilities), and most local governments have enough time to make the necessary changes to improve their financial footing. Using several case examples, this article compares successful and less successful approaches to pension funding, and provides recommendations that are designed not only to improve funding, but also to help ensure that the public sector can continue to recruit and retain qualified, dedicated staff.

10 Police and Fire Personnel, Salaries, and Expenditures for 2011

Continuing the trend identified in 2010 when police and fire departments, like other local government departments, saw their budgets reduced, police and fire pensions in 2011 have been on the table in some communities while other communities have considered increasing the police and fire personnel share of health insurance premiums. Some local governments have also reduced the numbers of police and fire personnel, and some are exploring shared and contracted services to save costs. This article, a longtime staple of the *Municipal Year Book*, is based on the results of an annual survey that is meant to provide a general picture of police and fire personnel and expenditures for each year. It presents the following information for both police and fire departments in tabular form: total personnel, the number of uniformed personnel, minimum crew per fire apparatus, entrance and maximum salaries, information on longevity pay, and a breakdown of departmental expenditures. Data from the 2011 survey are compared with those from 2010.

Directories

Directory 1 consists of eight lists providing the names and websites of U.S. state municipal leagues; provincial and territorial associations and unions in Canada; state agencies for community affairs; provincial and territorial agencies for local affairs in Canada; U.S. municipal management associations; international municipal management associations; state associations of counties; and U.S. councils of governments recognized by ICMA.

Directory 2 presents "Professional, Special Assistance, and Educational Organizations Serving Local and State Governments." The 79 organizations that are included this year provide educational and research services to members and others, strengthening professionalism in government administration.

Organization of Data

Most of the tabular data for *The Municipal Year Book 2012* were obtained from public officials through questionnaires developed and administered by ICMA. ICMA maintains databases with the results of these surveys. All survey responses are reviewed for errors. Extreme values are identified and investigated; logic checks are applied in the analysis of the results.

Government Definitions

A municipality, by census definition, is a "political subdivision within which a municipal corporation has been established to provide general local government for a specific population concentration in a defined area." This definition includes all active governmental units officially designated as cities, boroughs (except in Alaska), villages, or towns (except in Minnesota, New York, New England, and Wisconsin), and it generally includes all places incorporated under the procedures established by the several states.

Counties are the primary political administrative divisions of the state. In Louisiana these units are called parishes. Alaska has county-type governments called boroughs. There are certain unorganized areas of some states that are not included in the *Year Book* database and that have a county designation from the Census Bureau for strictly administrative purposes. These comprise 11 areas in Alaska, 5 areas in Rhode Island, 8 areas in Connecticut, and 7 areas in Massachusetts.[1]

According to the U.S. Bureau of the Census, in January 2007 there were 89,476 governments in the United States (Table 1).

Table 1 U.S. Local Governments, 2007

Local governments	89,476
County	3,033
Municipal	19,492
Town or township	16,519
School district	13,051
Special district	37,381

Municipality Classification

Table 2 details the distribution of all municipalities of 2,500 and over in population by population, geographic region and division, metro status, and form of government.

Population This edition of the Year Book generally uses the 2000 Census Bureau figures for placing local governments in the United States into population groups for tabular presentation. The population categories are self-explanatory.

Geographic Classification Nine geographic divisions and four regions are used by the Bureau of the Census (Figure 1). The nine divisions are *New England:* Connecticut, Maine, Massachusetts, New Hampshire, Rhode Island, and Vermont; *Mid-Atlantic:* New Jersey, New York, and Pennsylvania; *East North-Central:* Illinois, Indiana, Michigan, Ohio, and Wisconsin; *West North-Central:* Iowa, Kansas, Minnesota, Missouri, Nebraska, North Dakota, and South Dakota; *South Atlantic:* Delaware, the District of Columbia, Florida, Georgia, Maryland, North Carolina, South Carolina, Virginia, and West Virginia; *East South-Central:* Alabama, Kentucky, Mississippi, and Tennessee; *West South-Central:* Arkansas, Louisiana, Oklahoma, and Texas; *Mountain:* Arizona, Colorado, Idaho, Montana, Nevada, New Mexico, Utah, and Wyoming; and *Pacific Coast:* Alaska, California, Hawaii, Oregon, and Washington.

The geographic regions are consolidations of states in divisions: *Northeast:* Connecticut, Maine, Massachusetts, New Hampshire, New Jersey, New York, Pennsylvania, Rhode Island, and Vermont; *North Central:* Illinois, Indiana, Iowa, Kansas, Michigan, Minnesota, Missouri, Nebraska, North Dakota, Ohio, South Dakota, and Wisconsin; *South:* Alabama, Arkansas, Delaware, the District of Columbia, Florida, Georgia, Kentucky, Louisiana, Maryland, Mississippi, North Carolina, Oklahoma, South Carolina, Tennessee, Texas, Virginia, and West Virginia; and *West:* Alaska, Arizona, California, Colorado, Hawaii, Idaho, Montana, Nevada, New Mexico, Oregon, Utah, Washington, and Wyoming.

Metro Status Metro status refers to the status of a municipality within the context of the U.S. Office of Management and Budget (OMB) definition of a statistical area. The OMB has redefined metropolitan statistical areas, metropolitan divisions, micropolitan statistical areas, combined statistical areas, and New England city and town areas in the United States. ICMA is in the process of updating its local government records to correspond to these new definitions, but the updates are not available at this time.

Form of Government Form of government relates primarily to the organization of the legislative and executive branches of municipalities and townships.

In the *mayor-council* form, an elected council or board serves as the legislative body. The head of government is the chief elected official, who is generally elected separately from the council and has significant administrative authority.

Many cities with a mayor-council form of government have a city administrator who is appointed by the elected representatives (council) and/or the chief elected official and is responsible to the elected officials. Appointed city administrators in mayor-council governments have limited administrative authority: they often do not directly appoint department heads or other key city personnel, and their responsibility for budget preparation and administration, although significant, is subordinate to that of the elected officials.

Under the *council-manager* form, the elected council or board and chief elected official (e.g., the mayor) are responsible for making policy. A professional administrator appointed by the council or board has full responsibility for the day-to-day operations of the government.

The *commission* form of government operates with an elected commission performing both legislative and executive functions, generally with departmental administration divided among the commissioners.

The *town meeting* form of government is a system in which all qualified voters of a municipality meet to make basic policy and elect officials to carry out the policies.

Table 2 Cumulative Distribution of U.S. Municipalities with a Population of 2,500 and Over

	Population								
Classification	2,500 and over	5,000 and over	10,000 and over	25,000 and over	50,000 and over	100,000 and over	250,000 and over	500,000 and over	Over 1,000,000
Total, all cities	7,506	5,249	3,309	1,457	668	248	68	32	9
Population group									
Over 1,000,000	9	9	9	9	9	9	9	9	9
500,000-1,000,000	23	23	23	23	23	23	23	23	...[1]
250,000-499,999	36	36	36	36	36	36	36	...	...
100,000-249,999	180	180	180	180	180	180	...	...	...
50,000-99,999	420	420	420	420	420	...	...	...	...
25,000-49,999	789	789	789	789	...	...	...	...	...
10,000-24,999	1,852	1,852	1,852	...	...	...	...	...	...
5,000-9,999	1,940	1,940	...	...	...	...	...	...	...
2,500-4,999	2,257	...	...	...	...	...	...	...	...
Geographic region									
Northeast	2,022	1,478	901	328	114	33	8	4	2
North-Central	2,181	1,481	932	376	150	45	14	5	1
South	2,182	1,408	847	357	178	77	23	13	3
West	1,121	882	629	396	226	93	23	10	3
Geographic division									
New England	752	554	352	138	46	12	1	1	...
Mid-Atlantic	1,271	924	549	190	68	21	7	3	2
East North-Central	1,461	1,049	684	270	105	30	8	5	1
West North-Central	721	433	249	106	45	15	6		...
South Atlantic	938	609	387	170	86	34	9	4	...
East South-Central	467	310	169	56	23	12	3	2	...
West South-Central	778	488	290	131	69	31	11	7	3
Mountain	410	281	163	94	52	27	8	3	1
Pacific Coast	708	601	466	302	174	66	15	7	2
Form of government									
Mayor-council	3,292	2,051	1,203	495	241	99	40	21	6
Council-manager	3,656	2,798	1,884	911	413	144	26	10	3
Commission	143	110	70	25	9	5	2	1	...
Town meeting	351	235	106	5	...	...	...	...	...
Rep. town meeting	64	55	46	21	5	...	...	...	...

Note: This table comprises *only* city-type local governments with populations of 2,500 and above.

1 (...) indicates data not applicable or not reported.

Under the *representative town meeting* form of government, the voters select a large number of citizens to represent them at the town meeting(s). All citizens can participate in the meeting(s), but only the representatives may vote.

County Classification

Counties are the primary political administrative divisions of the states. The county-type governments in Alaska are called boroughs. Using the same geographic

Figure 1 U.S. Bureau of the Census Geographic Regions and Divisions

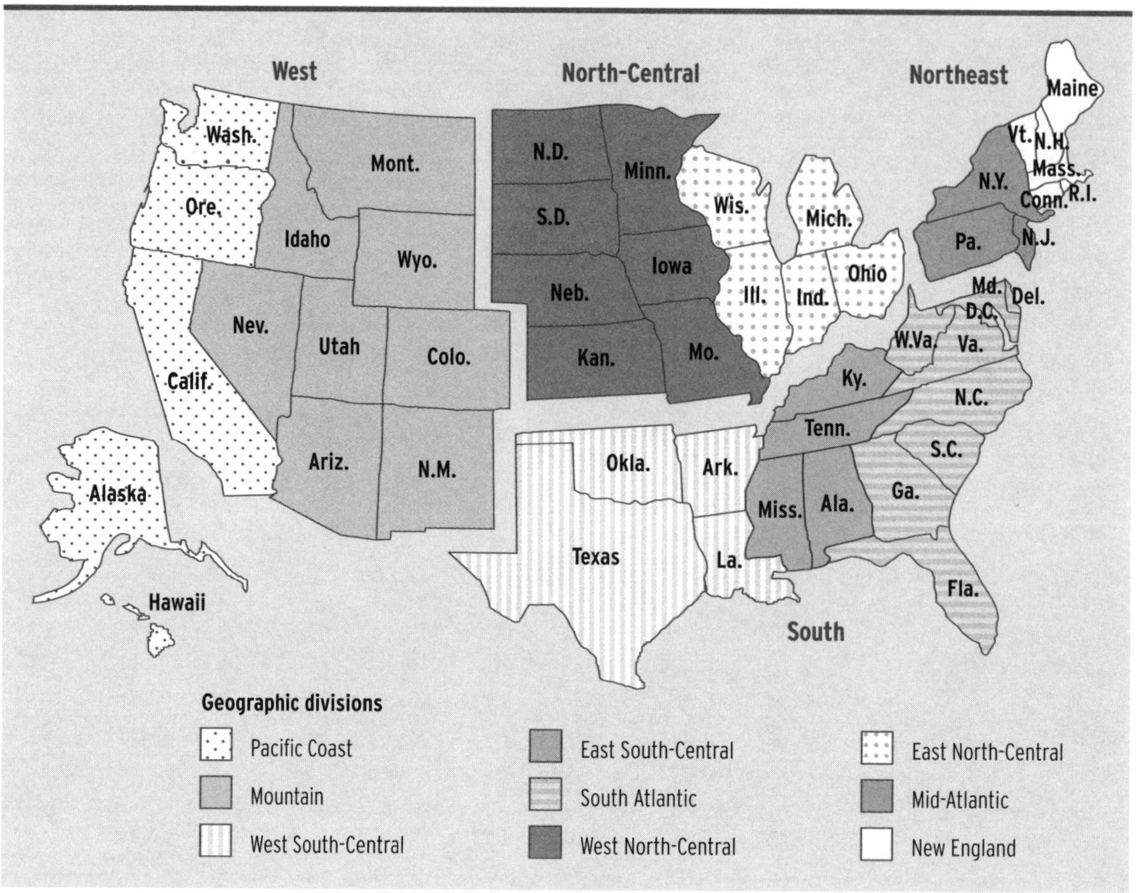
West
North-Central
Northeast
South
Wash.
Ore.
Calif.
Alaska
Hawaii
Mont.
Idaho
Wyo.
Nev.
Utah
Colo.
Ariz.
N.M.
N.D.
S.D.
Neb.
Kan.
Minn.
Iowa
Mo.
Wis.
Mich.
Ill.
Ind.
Ohio
Maine
Vt.
N.H.
Mass.
Conn.
R.I.
N.Y.
Pa.
N.J.
Md.
D.C.
Del.
W.Va.
Va.
Ky.
N.C.
Tenn.
S.C.
Okla.
Ark.
Texas
La.
Miss.
Ala.
Ga.
Fla.
Geographic divisions
Pacific Coast
Mountain
West South-Central
East South-Central
South Atlantic
West North-Central
East North-Central
Mid-Atlantic
New England

and population categories as Table 2, Table 3 reflects the distribution of counties throughout the nation.

Metro Status Metro status refers to the status of a municipality within the context of the OMB definition of a statistical area. The OMB has redefined metropolitan statistical areas, metropolitan divisions, micropolitan statistical areas, combined statistical areas, and New England city and town areas in the United States. ICMA is in the process of updating its local government records to correspond to these new definitions, but the updates are not available at this time.

Form of Government For counties, form of government relates to the structural organization of the legislative and executive branches of counties; counties are classified as being with or without an administrator. There are three basic forms of county government: commission, council-administrator, and council–elected executive.

The *commission* form of government is characterized by a governing board that shares the administrative and, to an extent, legislative responsibilities with several independently elected functional officials.

In counties with the *council-administrator* form, an administrator is appointed by, and responsible to, the elected council to carry out directives.

The *council–elected executive* form features two branches of government: the executive and the legislative. The independently elected executive is considered the formal head of the county.

The use of varying types of local government is an institutional response to the needs, requirements, and articulated demands of citizens at the local level. Within each type of local government, structures are developed to provide adequate services. These structural adaptations are a partial result of the geographic location, population, metropolitan status, and form of government of the jurisdiction involved.

Consolidated Governments

The Bureau of the Census defines a consolidated government as a unit of local government in which the functions of a primary incorporated place and its county or minor civil division have merged.[2] There

Table 3 Cumulative Distribution of U.S. Counties

Classification	All counties	Population: 2,500 and over	5,000 and over	10,000 and over	25,000 and over	50,000 and over	100,000 and over	250,000 and over	500,000 and over	Over 1,000,000
Total, all counties	3,033	2,921	2,748	2,362	1,494	857	474	200	90	27
Population group										
Over 1,000,000	27	27	27	27	27	27	27	27	27	27
500,000-1,000,000	63	63	63	63	63	63	63	63	63	...[1]
250,000-499,999	110	110	110	110	110	110	110	110	...	...
100,000-249,999	274	274	274	274	274	274	274	...	...	...
50,000-99,999	383	383	383	383	383	383	...	...	...	...
25,000-49,999	637	637	637	637	637	...	...	...	...	...
10,000-24,999	868	868	868	868	...	...	...	...	...	...
5,000-9,999	386	386	386	...	...	...	...	...	...	...
2,500-4,999	173	173	...	...	...	...	...	...	...	...
Under 2,500	112	...	...	...	...	...	...	...	...	...
Geographic region										
Northeast	189	189	188	183	174	129	85	45	19	3
North-Central	1,052	1,005	912	745	444	228	124	45	19	7
South	1,371	1,345	1,300	1,151	683	364	177	65	27	6
West	421	382	348	283	193	136	88	45	25	11
Geographic division										
New England	45	45	45	43	40	24	14	6	2	...
Mid-Atlantic	144	144	143	140	134	105	71	39	17	3
East North-Central	437	436	433	407	298	165	94	33	15	5
West North-Central	615	569	479	338	146	63	30	12	4	2
South Atlantic	544	542	534	481	313	191	100	38	16	2
East South-Central	360	358	356	323	175	73	27	7	2	...
West South-Central	467	445	410	347	195	100	50	20	9	4
Mountain	276	245	215	159	93	54	32	14	7	2
Pacific Coast	145	137	133	124	100	82	56	31	18	9
Form of government										
County commission	1,728	1,639	1,501	1,215	665	303	130	46	17	4
Council-manager/administrator	817	805	788	736	545	357	216	87	43	15
Council-elected executive	488	477	459	411	284	197	128	67	30	8

1 (...) indicates data not applicable or not reported.

are several categories of consolidations: city-county consolidations that operate primarily as cities (Table 4), metropolitan governments operating primarily as cities (Table 5), and areas that maintain certain types of county offices but as part of another city or township government (Table 6). In addition, the District of Columbia is counted by the Census Bureau as a city, a separate county area, and a separate state area. To avoid double counting in survey results, ICMA counts the District of Columbia only as a city.

The Census Bureau defines independent cities as those cities operating outside of a county area and administering functions commonly performed by counties (Table 7). The bureau counts independent cities as counties. For survey research purposes, ICMA counts them as municipal, not county governments.

Uses of Statistical Data

The *Municipal Year Book* uses primary and secondary data sources. ICMA collects and publishes the primary source data. Secondary source data are data collected by another organization. Most of the primary source data are collected through survey research. ICMA develops questionnaires on a variety of subjects during a given year and then pretests and refines them to increase the validity of each survey instrument. Once completed, the surveys are sent to officials in all cities above a given population level (e.g., 2,500 and above, 10,000 and above, etc.). For example, the city managers or chief administrative officers receive the *ICMA Economic Development Survey*, and finance officers receive the *Police and Fire Personnel, Salaries, and Expenditures* survey.

ICMA conducts the *Police and Fire Personnel, Salaries, and Expenditures* survey every year. Other research projects are conducted every five years, and some are one-time efforts to provide information on subjects of current interest.

Table 4 Legally Designated Consolidated City-County Governments Operating Primarily as Cities, 2007

State	Consolidated government
Alaska	City and Borough of Anchorage
	City and Borough of Juneau
	City and Borough of Sitka
California	City and County of San Francisco
Colorado	City and County of Broomfield
	City and County of Denver
Hawaii	City and County of Honolulu
Kansas	Kansas City and Wyandotte County
Montana	Anaconda-Deer Lodge
	Butte-Silver Bow

Table 5 Metropolitan Governments, 2007

State	Consolidated city
Tennessee	Hartsville-Trousdale County
	Lynchburg-Moore County
	Nashville-Davidson

Note: The Census Bureau treats these as consolidated cities.

Table 6 Areas That Maintain Certain Types of County Offices but as Part of Another Government, 2007

State	County	Other government
Florida	Duval	City of Jacksonville
Georgia	Chattahoochee	Cusseta-Chattahoochee County unified
	Clarke	Athens-Clarke County unified
	Georgetown-Quitman County	Georgetown-Quitman County unified
	Muscogee	City of Columbus
	Richmond	City of Augusta
	Webster and cities of Preston and Weston	Webster County unified
Hawaii	Kalawao	State of Hawaii
Indiana	Marion	City of Indianapolis
Kentucky	Lexington-Fayette Urban County	Lexington-Fayette
	Louisville-Jefferson County	Louisville-Jefferson
Louisiana	Parish of East Baton Rouge	City of Baton Rouge
	Parish of Lafayette	City of Lafayette
	Parish of Orleans	City of New Orleans
	Terrebonne Parish	Terrebonne Parish consolidated
Massachusetts	County of Nantucket	Town of Nantucket
	County of Suffolk	City of Boston
New York	County of Bronx	New York City
	County of Kings	New York City
	County of New York	New York City
	County of Queens	New York City
	County of Richmond	New York City
Pennsylvania	County of Philadelphia	City of Philadelphia

Table 7 Independent Cities

State	Independent city
Maryland	Baltimore City
Missouri	St. Louis
Nevada	Carson City
Virginia	Alexandria
Virginia	Bedford
Virginia	Bristol
Virginia	Buena Vista
Virginia	Charlottesville
Virginia	Chesapeake
Virginia	Colonial Heights
Virginia	Covington
Virginia	Danville
Virginia	Emporia
Virginia	Fairfax
Virginia	Falls Church
Virginia	Franklin
Virginia	Fredericksburg
Virginia	Galax
Virginia	Hampton
Virginia	Harrisonburg
Virginia	Hopewell
Virginia	Lexington
Virginia	Lynchburg
Virginia	Manassas
Virginia	Manassas Park
Virginia	Martinsville
Virginia	Newport News
Virginia	Norfolk
Virginia	Norton
Virginia	Petersburg
Virginia	Poquoson
Virginia	Portsmouth
Virginia	Radford
Virginia	Richmond
Virginia	Roanoke
Virginia	Salem
Virginia	Staunton
Virginia	Suffolk
Virginia	Virginia Beach
Virginia	Waynesboro
Virginia	Williamsburg
Virginia	Winchester

Limitations of the Data

Regardless of the subject or type of data presented, data should be read cautiously. All policy, political, and social data have strengths and limitations. These factors should be considered in any analysis and application. Statistics are no magic guide to perfect understanding and decision making, but they can shed light on particular subjects and questions in lieu of haphazard and subjective information. They can clarify trends in policy expenditures, processes, and impacts and thus assist in evaluating the equity and efficiency of alternative courses of action. Statistical data are most valuable when one remembers their imperfections, both actual and potential, while drawing conclusions.

For example, readers should examine the response bias for each survey. Surveys may be sent to all municipalities above a certain population threshold, but not all of those surveys are necessarily returned. Jurisdictions that do not respond are rarely mirror images of those that do. ICMA reduces the severity of this problem by maximizing the opportunities to respond through second and (sometimes) third requests. But although this practice mitigates the problem, response bias invariably appears. Consequently, ICMA always includes a "Survey Response" table in each article that analyzes the results of a particular survey. This allows the reader to examine the patterns and degrees of response bias through a variety of demographic and structural variables.

Other possible problems can occur with survey data. Local governments have a variety of recordkeeping systems. Therefore, some of the data (particularly those on expenditures) may lack uniformity. In addition, no matter how carefully a questionnaire is refined, problems such as divergent interpretations of directions, definitions, and specific questions invariably arise. However, when inconsistencies or apparently extreme data are reported, every attempt is made to verify these responses through follow-up telephone calls.

Types of Statistics

There are basically two types of statistics: descriptive and inferential.

Descriptive

Most of the data presented in this volume are purely descriptive. Descriptive statistics summarize some characteristics of a group of numbers. A few numbers represent many. If someone wants to find out something about the age of a city's workforce, for example, it would be quite cumbersome to read a list of several hundred numbers (each representing the age of individual employees). It would be much easier to have a few summary descriptive statistics, such as the mean (average) or the range (the highest value minus the lowest value). These two "pieces" of information would not convey all the details of the entire data set, but they can help and are much more useful and understandable than complete numerical lists.

There are essentially two types of descriptive statistics: measures of central tendency and measures of dispersion.

Measures of Central Tendency These types of statistics indicate the most common or typical value of a data set. The most popular examples are the mean and median. The mean is simply the arithmetic average. It is calculated by summing the items in a data set and dividing by the total number of items. For example, given the salaries of $15,000, $20,000, $25,000, $30,000, and $35,000, the mean is $25,000 ($125,000 divided by 5).

The mean is the most widely used and intuitively obvious measure of central tendency. However, it is sensitive to extreme values. A few large or small numbers in a data set can produce a mean that is not representative of the "typical" value. Consider the example of the five salaries above. Suppose the highest value was not $35,000 but $135,000. The mean of the data set would now be $45,000 ($25,000 divided by 5). This figure, however, is not representative of this group of numbers because it is substantially greater than four of the five values and is $90,000 below the high score. A data set such as this is "positively skewed" (i.e., it has one or more extremely high scores). Under these circumstances (or when the data set is "negatively skewed" with extremely low scores), it is more appropriate to use the median as a measure of central tendency.

The median is the middle score of a data set that is arranged in order of increasing magnitude. Theoretically, it represents the point that is equivalent to the 50th percentile. For a data set with an odd number of items, the median has the same number of observations above and below it (e.g., the third value in a data set of 5 or the eighth value in a data set of 15). With an even number of cases, the median is the average of the middle two scores (e.g., the seventh and eighth values in a data set of 14). In the example of the five salaries used above, the median is $25,000 regardless of whether the largest score is $35,000 or $135,000. When the mean exceeds the median, the data set is positively skewed. If the median exceeds the mean, it is negatively skewed.

Measures of Dispersion This form of descriptive statistics indicates how widely scattered or spread out the numbers are in a data set. Some common measures of dispersion are the range and the interquartile range. The range is simply the highest value minus the lowest value. For the numbers 3, 7, 50, 80, and 100, the range is 97 (100 – 3 = 97). For the numbers 3, 7, 50, 80, and 1,000, it is 997 (1,000 – 3 = 997). Quartiles divide a data set into four equal parts similar to the way percentiles divide a data set into 100 equal parts. Consequently, the third quartile is equivalent to the 75th percentile, and the first quartile is equivalent to the 25th percentile. The interquartile range is the value of the third quartile minus the value of the first quartile.

Inferential

Inferential statistics permit the social and policy researcher to make inferences about whether a correlation exists between two (or more) variables in a population based on data from a sample. Specifically, inferential statistics provide the probability that the sample results could have occurred by chance if there were really no relationship between the variables in the population as a whole. If the probability of random occurrence is sufficiently low (below the researcher's preestablished significance level), then the null hypothesis—that there is no association between the variables—is rejected. This lends indirect support to the research hypothesis that a correlation does exist. If they can rule out chance factors (the null hypothesis), researchers conclude that they have found a "statistically significant" relationship between the two variables under examination.

Significance tests are those statistics that permit inferences about whether variables are correlated but provide nothing directly about the strength of such correlations. Measures of association, on the other hand, indicate how strong relationships are between variables. These statistics range from a high of +1.0 (for a perfect positive correlation), to zero (indicating no correlation), to a low of –1.0 (for a perfect negative correlation).

Some common significance tests are the chi square and difference-of-means tests. Some common measures of association are Yule's Q, Sommer's Gamma, Lambda, Cramer's V, Pearson's C, and the correlation coefficient. Anyone seeking further information on these tests and measures should consult any major statistics textbook.

Inferential statistics are used less frequently in this volume than descriptive statistics. However, whenever possible, the data have been presented so that the user can calculate inferential statistics whenever appropriate.

Summary

All social, political, and economic data are collected with imperfect techniques in an imperfect world. Therefore, users of such data should be continuously cognizant of the strengths and weaknesses of the information from which they are attempting to draw conclusions. Readers should note the limitations of the data published in this volume. Particular attention should be paid to the process of data collection and potential problems such as response bias.

Notes

1. The terms *city* and *cities*, as used in this volume, refer to cities, villages, towns, townships, and boroughs.
2. See U.S. Census Bureau, *Consolidated Federal Funds Report for Fiscal Year 2009: State and County Areas* (August 2010), Appendix A, census.gov/prod/2010pubs/cffr-09.pdf.
3. For additional information on statistics, see Tari Renner's *Statistics Unraveled: A Practical Guide to Using Data in Decision Making* (Washington, D.C.: ICMA, 1988).

Management Trends and Survey Research

1 The Politics of Apolitical Leadership: Professional Management in a Digital and Divided Society

2 311/CRM Systems: A Potential Path to Service Improvement, Budget Savings, and Citizen Satisfaction

3 Local Government Use of Development Impact Fees: More Fallout from a Poor Economy?

4 Local Government Employee Health Insurance Programs, 2011

5 Off the Beaten Path: Sustainability Activities in Small Towns and Rural Municipalities

6 CAO Salary and Compensation: The Big Picture

7 E-Government 2011: Trends and Innovations

8 Award-Winning Innovations in 2011: Exploring the Boundaries of Transformation

9 Public Pensions Face Record Pace of Change

10 Police and Fire Personnel, Salaries, and Expenditures for 2011

e • Innovations • Pensions • Health Insurance Pro
pact Fees • 311/CRM Systems • Police and Fire • Di
ation • Innovations • Sustainability • CAO Compensatio
Pensions • CAO Compensation • Sustainability • Dire
s • Innovations • Police and Fire • Health Insurance Pro
Directories • Police and Fire • Pensions • CAO Compen
s • E-Government • Sustainability • Directorie
Insurance Programs • CAO Compensation • Pensio
ation • Development Impact Fees • 311/CRM Systems • F
ent • Sustainability • Police and Fire • Directo
Fire • Innovations • Health Insurance Programs • Pen
s • 311/CRM Systems • Pensions • E-Government
Sustainability • CAO Compensation • Health I
surance Programs • 311/CRM Systems • Pen

1

The Politics of Apolitical Leadership: Professional Management in a Digital and Divided Society

Ron Carlee
ICMA

The world was supposed to end on October 21, 2011. The new date is December 21, 2012. It may or may not happen. What has and will occur is life ending and beginning literally every day in communities all across the world.

In 2011, the Federal Emergency Management Agency issued 99 major disaster declarations, more than in any year since 1953.[1] The United States set a record with 14 separate $1 billion weather disasters, with aggregate damage of over $55 billion from tornados, floods, and blizzards.[2] Among the most devastating events were the series of tornados in April that hit Alabama, Tennessee, and numerous other communities in the Southeast, killing 368 people; these were followed by the May twister that hit Joplin, Missouri, killing at least 160 people—the largest single tornado event since 1950. August brought Hurricane Irene, causing severe flooding in the Northeast that killed at least 45 people. And at times during the year it seemed as though most of Texas was on fire.[3]

Internationally, life and death events were even more dramatic. The United States ended its military involvement in Iraq with 4,487 service members dead and 32,226 wounded.[4] In Afghanistan, the death toll among coalition military forces is over 2,800, with another 14,300 U.S. military personnel injured.[5] Getting an accurate number of civilian deaths and injuries in

SELECTED FINDINGS

Social movements fueled by social media can occur anywhere with little warning, as exemplified by the Arab Spring and the Occupy movement.

Income and digital disparities require new awareness and new local strategies. A Pew Research Center survey found that 66% of the public "believes there are 'very strong' or 'strong' conflicts between the rich and the poor–an increase of 19 percentage points since 2009." And as of the end of 2011, 32% of U.S. households *did not* subscribe to broadband communications, which puts them at risk of becoming digitally excluded.

Local governments have lost more jobs than other sectors–443,000 workers (3%) from January 2009 to June 2011–but defaults on municipal bonds in 2011 were a quarter of those in 2010 and only 1% of all defaults in 2011.

Managers are most respected when they are seen as apolitical, but that does not mean they have to avoid difficult policy issues. Professional managers must have the political skills to actively navigate the policy continuum without a perception of partisanship.

Iraq and Afghanistan is difficult, but by most reports the number is in the tens of thousands. Nature has been even more brutal: in Japan, the one-two punch of a tsunami/flood resulting in failure of nuclear power plants left over 22,000 people dead or missing and over 160,000 people still displaced at the end of the year.[6] The continuing drought in Africa has put a staggering 13 million people at risk of starvation.[7] And the list goes on: a cyclone in Australia, flooding across Asia, an earthquake in New Zealand, and, as the year ended, a tropical storm and mudslides in the Philippines.

With the reality of human mortality before us graphically and dramatically, one would think that people would come together for protection and support. And we mostly do when disasters occur. In the day-to-day world of civic discourse, however, 2011 seemed to hit a new low. Will the divisiveness in politics undermine the unity of spirit we need as a nation in times of trouble? Even absent trouble, how can we build communities that grow and improve when political differences polarize and political language demonizes?

Politically, the United States is roughly split in half between the right and the left, Republican and Democrat. While there is a cadre of extremists at both ends of the political continuum, multitudes of people cluster in the middle, sometimes tilting one way and then the other. There is no clear, unifying vision or direction among the electorate. Yet regardless of their personal ideologies, professional managers are expected to remain apolitical—to respect all legitimate political views and value the concerns of all citizens. Not surprisingly, as the external environment and elected bodies become more polarized, the pressures on the professional manager increase.

How will the political dynamics evolve over 2012? What are the implications for local government and professional managers? Can managers navigate political waters without being seen as partisan? Is there an app for this?

The Politics of an "Occupied" Economy

"The year 2011 will be remembered as the year when the idea of income inequality migrated from seminar rooms in colleges and think tanks to Zuccotti Park and main streets across America," according to Isabel V. Sawhill, senior fellow of economic studies at The Brookings Institution.[8] Ms. Sawhill reports that a CBS/*New York Times* poll, conducted at the end of 2011, "found that two thirds of Americans agreed the nation had too much inequality." She further reports on findings from a Congressional Budget Office study, which showed "that after-tax income for the top 1 percent had more than tripled since 1979 while that of the bottom 80 percent increased by only one-third." Findings from a Pew Research Center survey reveal that "about two-thirds of the public (66%) believes there are 'very strong' or 'strong' conflicts between the rich and the poor—an increase of 19 percentage points since 2009." The same survey reports that a 46% plurality "believes that most rich people 'are wealthy mainly because they know the right people or were born into wealthy families'"; however, "43% say wealthy people became rich 'mainly because of their own hard work, ambition or education.'" These results are largely unchanged from those reported in a 2008 Pew survey.[9] As stated above: people are divided almost equally, plus or minus the margin of error in most polling.

Income disparity and the economy will shape much of the 2012 political rhetoric. Early indications are that political parties will seek to distinguish themselves by pulling further apart rather than coming together, framing the debate as the politics of greed versus the politics of envy.

While some of the national economic issues will play out at the local level—witness the Occupy movement in about 90 cities—local governments will continue to face widely varying economic conditions within their own boundaries and regions. The impacts of the "Great Recession" have already been dramatic. According to PolitiFact.com, local government has been the sector hardest hit, sustaining a loss of 443,000 workers (3%) from January 2009 to June 2011, a loss of 204,800 local education workers (2.5%); and a loss of 238,400 noneducation workers (3.7%). This compares with an *increase* of more than 1 million workers in the private sector.[10]

Prospects for 2012 appear to be more of the same for many communities. At the end of 2011, Standard & Poor's reported declining housing values in 19 of 20 markets that they follow.[11] The National League of Cities reports that city finance officers expect local revenues, especially property taxes, to decline further;[12] this prediction is supported by Patrick Newport, an analyst with IHS Global Insight, who forecasts that housing prices could drop another 5%–10% in 2012 owing to the large number of foreclosures remaining.[13]

The best economic news of 2011 was the noncollapse of municipal bonds. Contrary to the wild prediction in December 2010 by Meredith Whitney, who said there would be "hundreds of billions of dollars" of defaults, Bloomberg reports that municipal defaults were about $1.1 billion, a quarter of the defaults in 2010 and "only 1% of all 2011 failures."[14]

Unfortunately, one of the defaults this year set a record: $4.1 billion in Jefferson County, Alabama.[15] This is a highly complex case that involves corruption, local politics, state politics, and arcane financing vehicles. So far Jefferson County has been seen as unique; accordingly, some financial analysts are strongly recommending municipal bonds for investors seeking tax-exempt income.[16] For local governments, interest rates on municipal bonds remain extremely low, making capital investments attractive, especially for essential infrastructure.

The looming economic issues for local governments on the cost side of government—even after shedding over 440,000 positions—remain pensions and benefits. Here we had a potentially important shift in 2011, led by conservatives in Wisconsin. For the first time since 2001, there are some elected officials who seem willing to tackle the unsustainable costs of some of the pension plans for state and local employees—with the emphasis on *some*. As Elizabeth Kellar discusses in "Public Pensions Face Record Pace of Change" (see pages 105–110 in this *Year Book*), many state and local governments have managed their pensions responsibly and have solid funding. Pensions have, however, become a maelstrom in some states, characterized by highly contentious political battles between fiscal conservatives and some unions. Wisconsin is a battleground. After experiencing major legislative losses in 2011, unions are fighting back with petition recall efforts. In August 2011, recall elections were held in six legislative districts, with incumbent Republicans retaining their seats in four of the six districts. In a recall election a week later, two Democrats held their seats against Republican challengers. As 2012 begins, a major effort is under way to recall the governor.[17]

How will fights like these affect local politics, and what impact will they have on local budget debates and the tone in council and board meetings?

Apps, Tweets, and Social Media in the Political Realm

One factor that is exerting a major influence on the intensity of the debate is the ubiquity of digital technologies. People are in contact with one another at a grassroots level as never before possible.

Apple now has over 230,000 smart phone apps, with 70,000 available for Google's Android platform. Last year reportedly saw 18 billion downloads from the Apple store and 10 billion Android downloads.[18] Android apps are growing at a rate of 1 billion downloads per month. In December 2011, both Android and Apple set new records for activation on Christmas: 6.8 million devices—a 140% increase over Christmas 2010.[19] Even more dramatic than the number of mobile devices in our community is what people are doing with them. Facebook reports 800 million users and Twitter reports over 100 million users tweeting 230 million times per day.[20]

It is easy to glaze over when reading such a list of numbers and miss how noteworthy they truly are. Society has fundamentally changed the way it communicates. The U.S. Postal Service and the landline telephone are on a path to obsolescence. Some people are even talking about e-mail as yesterday's technology. According to the BBC, the chief executive of a major international consulting and technology company headquartered in France announced a strategy to eliminate company e-mails by 2014. Theirry Brenton, Atos CEO, commissioned an internal study, which found that employees were spending 15 to 20 hours a week on internal e-mails, only about 15% of which were actually useful. His company is now in search of a better way to communicate.[21]

People have more ways to communicate with one another and with more speed than we can readily comprehend. In the United States, the capability was first seen in "flash mobs," which have largely been benign if not downright fun. For example, a flash mob singing the "Hallelujah Chorus" in a food court has had over 36 million views on YouTube since its posting in November 2010 and has elicited over 43,000 viewer comments.[22]

While there are many implications for the expansive adoption of digital technology, two are especially important for local government management: (1) the influence of digital technology over the political debate and (2) the risks for those excluded from such technology.

Digital Politics

The Arab Spring has been a wake-up call for all communities in that it demonstrated how the power of social media can be marshaled for social change. Similarly, the Occupy movement is making extensive use of social media to communicate among its constituency. There are Twitter accounts for Occupy movements in virtually every major U.S. city as well as in many smaller localities and cities across the world. The Occupy movement has a social network unlike anything conceived by the temperance movement, the suffrage movement, civil rights activists, or Viet Nam antiwar protestors. Professional managers need not personally tweet or post to Facebook; however, local governments that ignore what is happening on social media in their communities will be surprised and, at some point, caught off-guard.

As winter set in, many Occupy campsites became unoccupied, either voluntarily or involuntarily, but the movement was not over. It is unclear what will sprout in the spring of 2012, which will be ripe for protests, fueled by the rhetoric of the contentious presidential campaign. If lessons learned from the Arab Spring and from city managers who have already dealt with the Occupy movement are any indication,[23] local governments would be wise to make contingency plans, giving special consideration to the following:

- Maintaining situational awareness and knowing very quickly what is happening or what can happen
- Making direct contact with protestors and maintaining open, active channels of communication
- Negotiating ground rules with which everyone can live and determining how to enforce those rules
- Dealing with encampments from the beginning (will they be permitted and for how long?)
- Balancing the rights of the protestors with the rights of those affected by the protests.

The Digital 32%

Paradoxically, just as digital technologies are being used to promote social equity movements, the digital technologies themselves are actually creating a new form of social inequity: digital exclusion.

Online connectivity has increasingly become the norm for business and governmental transactions. Major employers now require online applications for even entry-level jobs. Applications and recommendations for many colleges are only accepted digitally. Every monthly bill that is sent through regular mail (a service that will decline in 2012) includes a plea to "go paperless."

What happens, however, to people who do not have digital connectivity in their homes—those who cannot afford connectivity or who simply are not aware of digital options and do not know how to access them? As of the end of 2011, 32% of households in the United States *did not* subscribe to broadband communications, compared with 10% in some Asian countries.[24] These households are at risk of becoming digitally excluded. Local librarians who assist people with public access computing will confirm that there are still people who do not know what a mouse is and how to use it.

Because of the speed and extent of societal adoption of digital technologies, two efforts have been advanced this past year to address the needs of people who may be left out and left behind. Both efforts focus on the uses of technology and on the importance of providing access to all populations, especially in the following areas:

- Economic development, including job searches and workforce development
- Education
- Health care
- Government interaction
- Social connectivity.

Beyond the need for digital inclusion is the larger question of how to make it actually happen. Toward this end, the Institute of Museum and Library Services (IMLS) is finalizing a framework for communities to use in assessing and planning for digital inclusion. This framework, which will be launched in 2012, will include a set of principles and goals in the above areas.[25] Future work could include case studies, a collection of leading practices, and the development of assessment and planning guidelines and/or tools. Simultaneously, the Bill and Melinda Gates Foundation is working with a coalition of nonprofit agencies (including ICMA) to create a set of benchmarks that will enable a public library to assess its capabilities, demonstrate its value to the community, and promote continued investment in public access to digital technologies. The project is branded as "Edge: Where People Connect, Communities Achieve."[26] A beta version of the benchmarks is expected in the first quarter of 2012.

Vibrant, successful communities have long had strategic and capital plans for water, sewer, and transportation infrastructure, but most communities have largely left communications infrastructure to the private sector. As for digital inclusion, efforts have largely been left to public libraries to provide public-access computers. Are these efforts adequate? Consider the following finding from the McKinsey Global Institute: "Internet access has a significant impact on growth, jobs and wealth creation across all sectors of the economy, contributing more to the national GDPs of developed countries than energy, agriculture and several other critical industries."[27] Do local comprehensive plans need a new element on digital technologies to ensure the competitiveness of the community and of its people? Are public-access resources sufficient in public libraries? How can we know, and to what standard should they be held?

Today's Effective Professional Manager: Politically Savvy and Politically Neutral

The dynamics that are described above have led to these compelling questions: To be effective today, does the professional manager have to be more "political" to be effective? *Can* a professional manager be "political"—that is, directly engaged with the community—and still be perceived as nonpartisan?

Historically, the role of the professional manager has been characterized by the myth of an administrative/political dichotomy, with the two functions separated by a bright line of demarcation. But the role of professional managers vis-à-vis elected officials has never actually functioned in this way; rather, it has always existed on a continuum. At opposite ends are unambiguous administrative and political functions, such as hiring personnel (administrative) and engaging in partisan politics (political). In between lies the vast, ambiguous area of policy along which the professional manager pushes and pulls and gets pushed and pulled.

There is a broad consensus among professional managers that they are most respected when they are seen as apolitical; however, being apolitical does not mean avoiding difficult policy issues. It is the manager's job to put a wider lens on issues and provide the long-term context and implications for decisions. It is obviously inappropriate for a professional manager to argue publicly against policies of the elected body; however, it is the manager's responsibility to help the elected officials avoid "bad policy"—especially policy made for short-term expediency but with long-term negative consequences.

In concrete terms, the question is to what extent professional managers should become more actively involved directly with the community—what is sometimes referred to as little-*p* politics. This is tricky. If managers interact with the community as advocates, they risk being seen as political and getting ahead of the council. Increasingly, however, members of the profession are talking about professional managers acting as conveners and facilitating genuine community conversations. In this context, managers are not advocating solutions but inviting the community to develop solutions together. As one manager observed, "If professional staff go into meetings and put up a lot of data in a PowerPoint, we will lose people. We instead need to tell stories. We need to better communicate the problems. We need to step back and listen."[28]

The biggest challenge for professional managers seeking to engage more directly with the public is getting support from the elected officials. In a discussion on this topic, a seasoned manager questioned why ICMA was pushing citizen engagement when the elected officials do not want it to happen. This is where the leadership skills of the professional manager face their most significant test: can the manager—often through extensive one-on-one conversations—help elected officials see the benefits of civic engagement and civil dialogue? And how can the manager do this if the elected officials are divided and divisive themselves? Can the manager coach them in leadership and statesmanship?

It was, of course, the politicization of local government that led to the creation of the profession of local government managers over 100 years ago. Professional local managers have been mostly successful at curbing patronage employment and biased contracting. Mitigating political conflict, however, is much more complicated, and some managers see this challenge as being outside their job description. Even more challenging is that some elected officials do not want the conflict mitigated, as can be seen on advocacy television and heard on advocacy radio every day.

In looking forward to the challenges facing managers in this decade, Robert O'Neill Jr. has been advocating eight approaches:

1. Focus on the positive rather than on the problems and the difficulties; create options that can lead to positive outcomes.
2. Have a vision of the future; describe concrete actions that build credibility and momentum to move forward.
3. Cross boundaries to connect the public, private, and nonprofit sectors.
4. Ask the right questions across the community and the local government organization, recognizing that in a complex world, it is hard to know what we do not know.
5. Take risks to encourage new ideas and approaches.
6. Connect the dots across what appear to be unrelated ideas.
7. Push performance, relentless in the pursuit of continuous improvement.
8. Create synergy, using "symphonic skills" to build a community where the whole is greater than the sum of its parts.[29]

These approaches resonate strongly today. The paradox may be that in becoming more little-*p* political, managers also have to increase their capital-*P* Professionalism. None of the suggestions above can be achieved without a manager being actively engaged in the policy arena and developing the capacity as noted in the eighth item: creating synergy.

In some political and community environments, the successful manager must lead without people being aware that he or she is doing so. This is not to suggest surreptitious actions. Transparency and honesty are core to a manager's credibility. Rather, managers are frequently called upon to be master artists of subtlety.

If the world ends on December 21, none of this will matter. The higher probability, however, is that most of us will be here—although, undoubtedly, a number of communities will experience devastating events. Will the communities that face calamity be prepared to respond—not just at a technical level but also in community spirit and resolve? For the vast majority of communities that avoid catastrophe, will the community and the lives of the people living in it be better than they are today? If the answer is yes to either of these questions, it will be because people of good intention and commitment used their collective skills to make it happen. It will be because people rose above political conflict and extreme rhetoric for a greater public good. There is no app for this.

Notes

1. FEMA, "Declared Disasters by State or Year," fema.gov/news/disaster_totals_annual.fema.
2. NOAA Satellite and Information Service, National Climatic Data Center, "Billion Dollar U.S. Weather/Climate Disasters" (June 2011), ncdc.noaa.gov/oa/reports/billionz.html#chron.
3. Ibid.
4. "Iraq," *New York Times*, December 27, 2011, topics.nytimes.com/top/news/international/countriesandterritories/iraq/index.html?scp = 2&sq = deaths%20in%20iraq&st = cse (accessed January 21, 2012).
5. iCasualties.org, "Operation Enduring Freedom" (2009), icasualties.org/OEF/index.aspx.
6. "Japan—Earthquake, Tsunami and Nuclear Crisis (2011)," *New York Times*, topics.nytimes.com/top/news/international/countriesandterritories/japan/index.html (accessed January 21, 2012).
7. World Food Programme, "Horn of Africa Crisis," wfp.org/crisis/horn-of-africa.
8. Isabel V. Sawhill, "2011: The Year That Income Inequality Captured the Public's Attention," December 19, 2011, brookings.edu/opinions/2011/1219_inequality_2011_sawhill.aspx.
9. Richard Morin, *Rising Share of Americans See Conflict between Rich and Poor* (Washington, D.C.: Pew Research Center, January 11, 2012), 1, 3, pewsocialtrends.org/files/2012/01/Rich-vs-Poor.pdf.
10. Louis Jacobson, "Paul Krugman Says Government Jobs Have Fallen by Half Million since January 2009," politifact.com/truth-o-meter/statements/2011/jul/11/paul-krugman/paul-krugman-says-government-jobs-have-fallen-half/.
11. S&P Indices, "The Fourth Quarter Starts with Broad-based Declines in Home Prices, According to the S&P/Case-Shiller Home Price," press release, December 27, 2011, standardandpoors.com/servlet/BlobServer?blobheadername3 = MDT-Type&blobcol = urldocumentfile&blobtable = SPComSecureDocument&blobheadervalue2 = inline%3B + filename%3Ddownload.pdf&blobheadername2 = Content-Disposition&blobheadervalue1 = application%2Fpdf&blobkey = id&blobheadername1 = content-type&blobwhere = 1245326665736&blobheadervalue3 = abinary%3B + charset%3DUTF-8&blobnocache = true.
12. Christopher W. Hoene and Michael A. Pagano, "City Fiscal Conditions in 2011" (Washington, D.C.: National League of Cities, September 2011), nlc.org/news-center/press-room/press-releases/2011/city-fiscal-conditions-2011.
13. Christine Hauser, "No Relief in Report on Housing," *New York Times*, September 27, 2011, nytimes.com/2011/12/28/business/daily-stock-market-activity.html (accessed January 21, 2012).
14. Michelle Kaske and Andrea Riquier, "Borrowing Costs Plummeting across U.S. for Local Governments: Muni Credit," *Bloomberg*, September 28, 2011, bloomberg.com/news/2011-09-28/borrowing-costs-plummeting-across-u-s-for-local-governments-muni-credit.html.
15. Mary Williams Walsh, "Bankruptcy Filing Raises Doubts about a Bond Repayment Pledge," *New York Times*, December 23, 2011, nytimes.com/2011/12/24/business/in-alabama-a-test-of-the-full-faith-and-credit-pledge-to-repay-bonds.html?sq = local%20government%20bonds&st = nyt&scp = 1&pagewanted = print (accessed January 21, 2012).
16. Jan M. Rosen, "Muni Bonds Are Stars, for Now," *New York Times*, October 8, 2011, nytimes.com/2011/10/09/business/mutfund/municipal-bonds-are-on-a-tear-but-for-how-long.html?scp = 5&sq = local + government + bonds&st = nyt (accessed January 21, 2012).
17. Associated Press, "2 Wis. Democrats Keep Their Senate Seats," *USA Today*, August 17, 2011, usatoday.com/news/politics/2011-08-16-wisconsin-recall-elections_n.htm (accessed January 22, 2012).
18. Wilson Rothman, "App Showdown: Android vs. iPhone," *MSNBC.com*, n.d., msnbc.msn.com/id/38382217/ns/technology_and_science-wireless/t/app-showdown-android-vs-iphone/#.TxGDbJjd6-I (accessed January 22, 2012); Manish Sahajwani, "Android vs iPhone: The Economy of Apps," *San Francisco Chronicle*, January 4, 2012, sfgate.com/cgi-bin/article.cgi?f = /g/a/2012/01/04/investopedia69024.DTL (accessed January 22, 2012).
19. Mark Kurlyandchik, "Nearly 7M Android and iOS Devices Activated on Christmas Day," *Daily Tech*, December 28, 2011, dailytech.com/Nearly + 7M + Android + and + iOS + Devices + Activated + on + Christmas + Day/article23617.htm.
20. "Facebook," *New York Times*, December 15, 2011, topics.nytimes.com/top/news/business/companies/facebook_inc/index.html (accessed January 22, 2012); Graeme McMillan, "Twitter Reveals Active User Number, How Many Actually Say Something," *Time*, September 9, 2011, techland.time.com/2011/09/09/twitter-reveals-active-user-number-how-many-actually-say-something/ (accessed January 22, 2012).
21. BBC News, "Atos Boss Thierry Breton Defends His Internal Email Ban," December 6, 2011, bbc.co.uk/news/technology-16055310.

22. YouTube, "Christmas Food Court Flash Mob, Hallelujah Chorus—Must See!" youtube.com/watch?v = SXh7JR9oKVE.
23. ICMA, "Most Jurisdictions Working Well with Occupy Protestors," November 10, 2011, icma.org/en/icma/newsroom/highlights/Article/101602/Most_Jurisdictions_Working_Well_with_Occupy_Protesters.
24. Timothy Karr, "Internet Regulation Matters to U.S. Economic Recovery," *Seattle Times,* January 13, 2012, seattletimes.nwsource.com/html/opinion/2017233861_guest15karr.html (accessed January 23, 2012).
25. Institute of Museum and Library Services, "Digitally Inclusive Communities," imls.gov/about/digitally_inclusive_communities.aspx?id = 9&pg = 1.
26. Edge, "Edge: Where People Connect, Communities Succeed," libraryedge.org.
27. Karr, "Internet Regulation," with reference to Matthieu Pélissié et al., *Internet Matters: The Net's Sweeping Impact on Growth, Jobs, and Prosperity* (McKinsey Global Institute, May 2011), mckinsey.com/Insights/MGI/Research/Technology_and_Innovation/Internet_matters.
28. Over the course of 2011, ICMA hosted a number of conversations on leadership in the context of the current drivers in communities. ICMA members participated in two large conversations at the annual conference in September. Earlier in the year, a group of 20 noted managers, assistants, and academics met in Chicago to begin to help frame today's leadership issues. These conversations centered on the changing role of local government, the changing roles of the professional manager, and the resulting impacts of both on the profession and ICMA. These conversations are the source for the leadership material discussed on this article.
29. Robert J. O'Neill Jr. and Ron Carlee, "Reflections on the First Decade of the 21st Century: Leadership Implications for Local Government," in *The Municipal Year Book 2011,* 3–11 (Washington, D.C.: ICMA Press, 2011), 10.

2

311/CRM Systems: A Potential Path to Service Improvement, Budget Savings, and Citizen Satisfaction

David Eichenthal
Public Financial Management, Inc.

Cory Fleming
ICMA

For most local governments, 311 and other centralized customer service systems that use constituent relationship management (CRM) technology represent a fundamentally different way of doing business.[1] With just a single phone call, text message, or e-mail, residents and businesses can request local government information or services. Now that 311/CRM systems are in place in more than 100 cities and counties, including most of the nation's largest cities, such systems have become a critical point of contact between citizens and local government.[2] In addition to improving customer service, 311/CRM systems can generate valuable business intelligence that local governments can use to reengineer their processes and procedures—and potentially increase efficiency, realize cost savings, and improve overall citizen satisfaction with local government services.

This article examines preliminary evidence on the extent to which 311/CRM systems are achieving their potential to transform local government. The first section considers the ways in which three local governments are using 311/CRM systems to increase efficiency and strive for continuous improvement. The second section explores how 311/CRM systems may affect overall citizen satisfaction.

SELECTED FINDINGS

Preliminary evidence indicates that 311/CRM systems can generate business intelligence that can be used to reengineer local government processes and procedures.

In the 15 years since the first 311 system was implemented, local governments have made significant progress in using 311/CRM data to drive performance management; when it comes to budgeting, however, the use of 311 data is less advanced.

While many citizen satisfaction surveys have confirmed the popularity of 311 service, there is little research to document a lasting relationship between 311 implementation and overall citizen satisfaction with government service delivery. For example, in Kansas City, Mo., in 2005, before 311 was implemented, 41% of survey respondents reported being satisfied or very satisfied with city services; by 2007, after the system was implemented, satisfaction had risen to 52%; by 2010, however, the percentage had declined to 43%—nearly the pre-311 level.

This project was funded by the Alfred P. Sloan Foundation.

Service Improvement and Budget Savings: Case Studies of Early Success

As revenues decline and costs increase, local governments face tough fiscal choices. For many jurisdictions, it is hard enough to maintain existing services, let alone add new ones. In the case of 311/CRM systems, the up-front capital costs—from software to hardware to contact center construction—often halt the discussion of 311/CRM implementation before it even begins.

Some local governments, however, have not only implemented 311/CRM systems but are also using them to catalyze government transformation. Baltimore, for example, which was the first city to implement a 311 system, also developed CitiStat, a comprehensive performance measurement initiative designed to drive management.[3] Under then-mayor Martin O'Malley, the two initiatives were closely linked: 311 data were an important source of information for CitiStat.[4] Using information collected through their 311/CRM systems, other cities are assessing performance, refining businesses processes, and improving both the efficiency and effectiveness of departmental operations.[5] For example, before the implementation of 311 in Chattanooga, the city lacked data on the volume of nonemergency service requests and response times. After implementing its 311 system, Chattanooga was able to make data-based decisions about filling vacant positions and to achieve budget savings without affecting service levels.[6]

When improved customer service is combined with better and more efficient service delivery, the case for implementing a 311/CRM system becomes compelling. The budgetary impact of such systems has not been well documented, however. Among cities that deploy 311/CRM systems but do not use them to help drive performance or budgeting, contact center consolidation may yield some savings, but most benefits are limited to improved customer service.[7] And even in cities where 311 has catalyzed performance improvement efforts, detailed analyses of the return on investment are hard to come by, often because the cities lack data on preimplementation costs against which to measure savings.[8]

Nevertheless, the fiscal and operational case for 311/CRM systems is growing. In Chicago, analysis of 311 data led to changes in the city's response to street and sewer defects—improving interdepartmental communication, reducing response time for complaints, and allowing work crews to handle more requests without an increase in costs or staff. Data collected through the 311 system also enabled the city to track the performance of individual tow truck drivers, provide performance-based incentives for drivers, and ultimately increase city revenues from towing.[9] In Kansas City, Missouri, analysis of 311 calls led to changes in the mowing schedule for city parks: because the frequency of mowing was adjusted to reflect actual need, the city achieved cost savings without reducing service levels.[10] And in Minneapolis, analysis of 311 service requests for graffiti removal enabled the city to cut response time by several days—first by shifting initial response from police to public works, then by providing public works crews with cameras to record the graffiti before they removed it. (Under the original system, a police officer had to first record the graffiti before a crew could be sent to remove it.)[11]

This section explores the use of 311 or CRM systems (and related performance measurement and management systems) in three different jurisdictions: Indianapolis–Marion County, Indiana; the city and county of San Francisco, California; and the city of Knoxville, Tennessee.[12] Although all three jurisdictions have assigned an expanded role to their 311 or CRM systems, they are at different stages in their use of 311 or CRM data to drive budgeting and performance management.

- Indianapolis (2010 pop. 820,445) is the nation's 12th-largest city. It is part of a consolidated city-county government (known as Unigov) that includes Indianapolis and Marion County. Although Indianapolis does not have a 311 number, the Mayor's Action Center (MAC), a centralized customer service system, has been in operation since 1992. In 2008, under Mayor Greg Ballard, the city launched IndyStat, a performance measurement initiative, which draws upon citizen contact data provided by the MAC.
- San Francisco (2010 pop. 805,235) is the nation's 13th-largest city. In 2007, when 311 was launched, then-mayor Gavin Newsom created the SFStat process, a performance measurement initiative. In addition, six times a year, the city controller publishes the *Government Barometer*, a charter-mandated report that tracks the city's performance on key indicators.
- Knoxville (2010 pop. 178,874) is Tennessee's third-largest city. In 2005, then-mayor Bill Haslam launched a 311 system. The city does not have a formal performance measurement process, but both staff and elected officials use 311 data to facilitate problem solving and decision making.

Indianapolis

The Mayor's Action Center, the city's principal resource for citizens with questions or service requests, implemented a CRM system in 2003 but has yet to institute a 311 phone number. The center operates Monday through Friday, from 7:30 a.m. to 5:30 p.m. There are three managers and 16.5 full-time-equivalent (FTE) service representatives. The MAC has an annual budget of $1.1 million, and funding comes from a chargeback system for city departments that use the service.

In 2010, the MAC handled 251,266 inbound calls, 19,000 online requests, and 21,244 outbound calls. (Indianapolis has one of the few local government call centers that provide systematic callbacks to report to citizens on the resolution of service requests.) With the June 2010 introduction of RequestIndy, an online portal, and the July 2011 launch of the RequestIndy iPhone application, citizens now have access to MAC services 24 hours a day, 365 days a year.

The MAC's role as a change agent for process improvement began in the summer of 2008, when Eli Lilly and Company, an Indianapolis-based pharmaceutical firm, lent Unigov an executive who had earned a Six Sigma black belt. (Six Sigma is a process improvement strategy that is designed to improve outcomes by identifying and eliminating potential problems early in the business process.) Before leading the first Six Sigma project for Unigov, the executive thoroughly familiarized himself with the inner workings of the government; doing so enabled him to demonstrate how process improvement could be incorporated into Unigov's operations. When Greg Ballard, the new mayor of Indianapolis, saw the potential of the Six Sigma approach to improve service delivery, he decided to institutionalize Six Sigma by linking it to the IndyStat program, which was already in place.

The incorporation of the Six Sigma process led to an emphasis on continuous improvement and ultimately fostered cultural change within Unigov. Since 2008, more than 40 projects have been implemented using the Six Sigma approach, and three to five such projects are generally under way at a time.

The MAC has played a pivotal role in the Six Sigma approach, providing critical data that allow officials to understand the scope of activities within a particular service: it generates daily reports for the directors and managers of service departments, as well as weekly and monthly reports for the mayor. In numerous instances, the MAC reports have proved invaluable. For example, one of the first Six Sigma projects involved a review of the processes used to fill potholes: aided by data supplied by the MAC reports, Unigov cut its 25-step process down to 12 steps.

The Mayor's Office of Constituent Services has trained all cabinet-level executives and department directors (and some of their managers) on how to interpret and use the data reports. Sarah Taylor, the director of constituent services and a member of the mayor's cabinet, attends all IndyStat review meetings to report on MAC call volume (including the number and types of information calls and service requests being received) and provide longitudinal trend analysis. Department directors view IndyStat meetings as an opportunity to meet with Indianapolis's "brain trust," and they rely on MAC data as a starting point for their continuous improvement efforts.

Even with the major process improvements already in place, MAC data must be carefully monitored. The winter of 2010–2011, for example, was particularly hard on streets; during the following spring, calls and online requests for pothole repair were off the charts (Figure 2–1). Ready access to trend analyses that compared the winter of 2010–2011 to past winters enabled Unigov to work with local union leaders to outsource a portion of the work and get the repairs done in a timely manner.

MAC data and the Six Sigma methodology also made it possible to address illegal dumping. When the Mayor's Neighborhood Liaisons—Unigov employees who work directly with neighborhood groups—began hearing about citizen dissatisfaction with response times to reports of illegal dumping, IndyStat convened stakeholder meetings to begin a Six Sigma project. (Figure 2–2 shows the patterns of illegal dumping reports from January 2009 through May 2011.) Using MAC data, Unigov was able to get a handle on the number and nature of the complaints, and the Six Sigma Team, which comprises agencies and departments from across the city and county, developed a plan to address the problem. In 2011, the pilot program (known as Clean Sweep) cleared 110 tons of trash from one neighborhood alone. The team is now focused on the outreach and prevention phases of the project.

In some instances, MAC data are used to monitor contractors' performance, a task that would otherwise be difficult. For example, if the MAC documents an unusually high number of complaints about trash pickup on certain routes, those data might be used to determine that a contractor is failing to comply with contractual standards and is therefore at risk of losing the contract. MAC data also proved useful for the Animal Care and Control Division of the Department of Public Safety, which reviewed historical data on incoming calls to determine whether resources could be better allocated—specifically, whether staffing levels could be matched to the volume of incoming calls.

Figure 2-1 Requests for Pothole Repair in Indianapolis

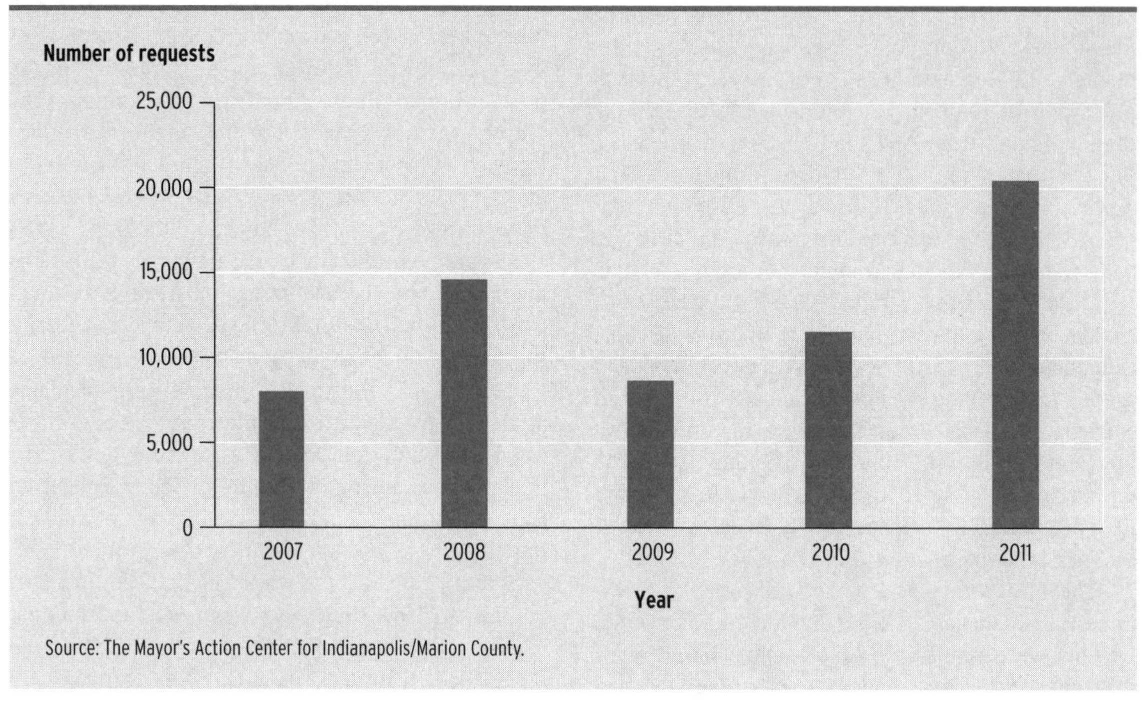

Number of requests
25,000
20,000
15,000
10,000
5,000
0
2007
2008
2009
2010
2011
Year

Source: The Mayor's Action Center for Indianapolis/Marion County.

Figure 2-2 Reports of Illegal Dumping in Indianapolis

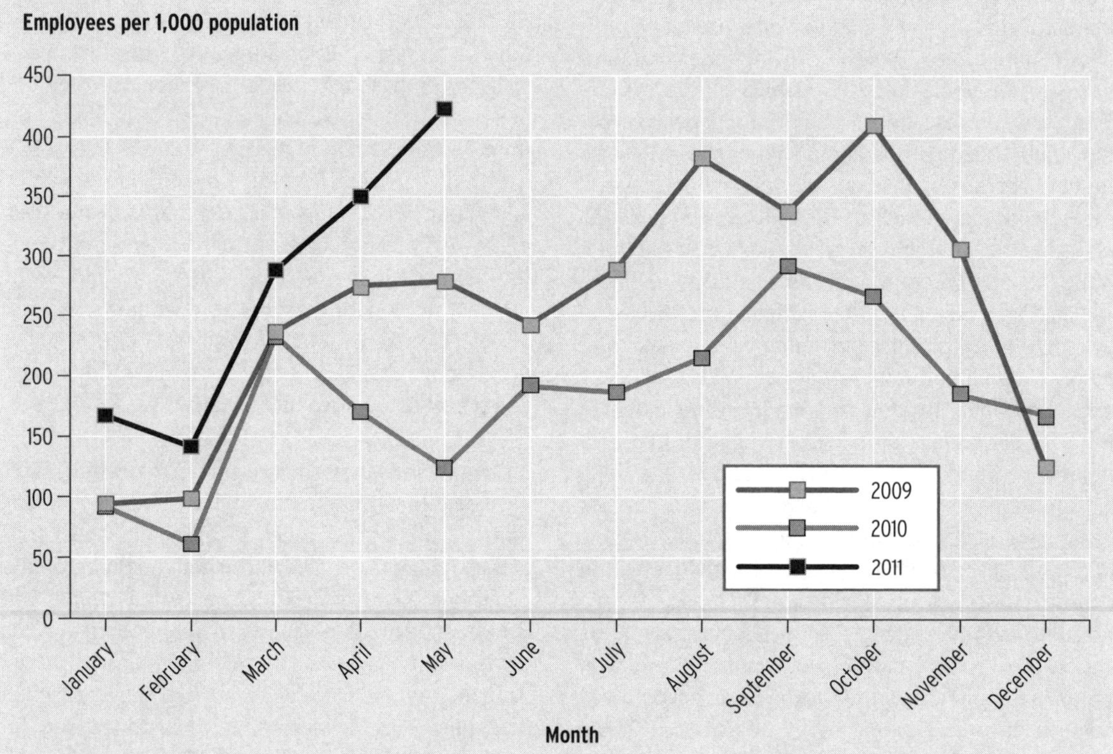

Employees per 1,000 population
450
400
350
300
250
200
150
100
50
0
January
February
March
April
May
June
July
August
September
October
November
December
Month
2009
2010
2011

Source: The Mayor's Action Center for Indianapolis/Marion County.

One of the most impressive uses of MAC data for process improvement came when Unigov decided to bring together quality-of-life programs—licensing, permitting, inspections, and nuisance abatement—within the newly created Department of Code Enforcement. Receiving no tax dollars, the department is funded entirely by license, permit, and inspection fees (and penalties). When it was first established, it lacked the resources to handle the volume of requests associated with two issues in particular: business licensing and high weeds and grass. An analysis of MAC data enabled the department to completely rebuild its fee structure, ensuring adequate staffing to address these issues in a timely manner.

Rick Powers, director of the code enforcement department, noted that he uses the daily MAC data reports to allocate staff; during the height of the season for high weeds and grasses, for example, he may divert a building inspector to conduct a high weeds and grass inspection in order to cope with the volume of calls coming into the MAC. "Without the MAC data, I might not make that decision," said Powers, who also said that inspectors routinely use the center to report problems they encounter in the field. According to Powers, "It's much easier to track complaints through MAC and its online portal."

The MAC is now fully integrated into the Six Sigma methodology. Sarah Taylor, the director of constituent services, notes that there have been "lots of internal discussions about who owns what data and which data reflect the customer's concerns. However, the mayor has made it clear that citizen contact begins with the MAC and ends with the MAC."

Although the MAC is generally deemed a success, there is room for improvement. For example, the MAC reports detail what types of service requests have been received and whether those requests are open or closed; but because the MAC does not maintain formal service-level agreements (SLAs) for service requests, and because the CRM system was implemented years before IndyStat, the MAC cannot provide data on how quickly service requests are being filled. Taylor notes that citizens who call the MAC are given informal estimates of service times for principal services, and that the adoption of SLAs is on the agenda for the future.

San Francisco

Five years ago, there were over 2,000 different telephone numbers for San Francisco government, and most departments had no means of tracking the most basic data on the number of service calls and their resolution. That changed with the March 2007 implementation of 311.

By 2010, San Francisco's 311 system had 67 call takers, 6 supervisors, and 15 support staff, and it was operating seven days a week, 24 hours a day. The call center's 2010 budget was $9.5 million, including $5.7 million from the San Francisco Municipal Transportation Agency. During fiscal year (FY) 2010, the center answered well over 2.7 million calls, including 48,172 requests for street and sidewalk cleaning (the most frequent request), 22,871 requests for graffiti removal, and 8,902 requests to remove abandoned vehicles (the second- and third-most-frequent requests). More than 75% of calls, however, were information requests, many of which concerned the city's transit agency, which is one of the nation's largest transit providers and is responsible for parking, traffic, and the operation of the Municipal Railway (MUNI) system. At least once each month, 311 staff meet with department representatives to identify and resolve issues, including data-related questions, specific requests, and recurring complaints. The 311 system also provides monthly reports to the mayor and the board of supervisors.

San Francisco has a robust performance measurement system. Under a 2003 charter amendment, the city controller is required to regularly monitor departmental performance. To this end, the charter amendment called for the creation of the City Service Auditor Division, to reside within the controller's office. The city service auditor has broad authority for

- Reporting on the level and effectiveness of the city's public services and benchmarking the city's performance in relation to that of other public agencies and jurisdictions
- Conducting financial and performance audits of city departments, contractors, and functions to assess the efficiency and effectiveness of processes and services
- Operating a whistleblower hotline and website and investigating reports of waste, fraud, and abuse of city resources
- Ensuring the financial integrity and improving the overall performance of city government.[13]

As part of the city's effort to measure agency performance, the controller (1) oversees a biennial citizen satisfaction survey and (2) maintains the Citywide Performance Measurement Program, a database of more than 1,100 measures that relies on data provided by the city's 48 departments.[14] Performance data are also reported in the city budget, and the controller has recently instituted a data validation process.[15]

Since 2009, the controller has published a bimonthly report—the *Government Barometer*—that provides data on 40 different performance indicators (including inputs, outputs, and outcomes) across city government.[16] The *Government Barometer* includes six indicators drawn from 311 data:

- Street-cleaning requests responded to within 48 hours
- Percentage of requests for graffiti removal from public property responded to within 48 hours
- Percentage of requests for pothole repair responded to within 72 hours
- Average daily number of MUNI customer complaints
- Average daily number of 311 contacts
- Percentage of 311 calls answered within 60 seconds.

Among city officials, there is no consensus on the role of the 311 system in performance improvement, as distinguished from performance measurement. Some see the 311 system as a catalyst for improvement, while others see it primarily as a customer service tool. Although departments have set SLAs as part of the implementation of 311, monitoring and enforcement of the agreements are minimal.

San Francisco's 311 system was implemented at the same time as SFStat, a performance management initiative that was led by the mayor and modeled after Baltimore's CitiStat. However, city officials noted that the focus of SFStat was primarily on overtime, workers' compensation, and sick leave rather than on operational efficiency or service delivery, and by 2010, SFStat meetings were no longer being convened as regularly as they had been in previous years. Nevertheless, data (311 data, in particular) have been used to drive performance in the Department of Public Works (DPW) and the Recreation and Park Department.

In 2010, DPW launched DPWStat, "a new . . . performance management tool [that] allows managers and staff to monitor the performance of key departmental activities and works to improve the quality of services delivered."[17] According to Edward Reiskin, who was then the department director, the monthly DPWStat meetings focused on "how we are doing and what we need to get better."

DPWStat's guiding principles are closely aligned with those of other similar performance measurement initiatives:

- Engage staff from all levels of the department.
- Ensure that senior managers and other decision makers are present.
- Develop and use timely and accurate performance data to set targets and inform decisions.
- Reward candor in identifying and diagnosing performance barriers—and reward creativity and commitment in overcoming them.
- When the data indicate that action is needed, quickly and clearly specify what needs to be done, who will do it, and when it will be done.
- Be persistent in following up, and be clear in maintaining accountability.
- Encourage a respectful learning environment.

DPWStat focused on volume and response-time data, derived largely from the 311 system, on street cleaning; graffiti removal; roadway and pothole repair; and tree management and landscaping. Data are presented geographically (by zone) and temporally (in relation to previous quarters and years).

DPWStat appears to be having an impact. According to the February 2011 *Government Barometer*,

> The Department of Public Works . . . has significantly increased how promptly it responds to pothole service requests over the past year. As of February 2011, the department was addressing nearly 90% of requests to fill potholes within 72 hours. The department attributes its success to a number of factors. It has been more carefully analyzing the pattern of requests to better understand the need. It has reviewed the process through which it fills potholes and made scheduling and other operational improvements to increase efficiency. In cases where there have been process bottlenecks, the department has engaged in team problem solving to identify solutions.[18]

Before DPWStat was implemented, less than 60% of requests were addressed in 72 hours. According to the controller, "As the department's staffing levels have been shrinking over the past three years, efficiency projects such as DPWStat have been key to lessening the impact of budget cuts on the public."

DPW has also used the 311 system to make process improvements that have led to budget savings. For example, by mapping the volume of service requests, DPW was able to reduce the frequency of street cleaning in residential areas by nearly one-half. Initial reductions led to savings of approximately $1 million annually in labor, fuel, and equipment.

The Recreation and Park Department has partnered with the San Francisco Neighborhood Parks Council (NPC) to use the 311 system as a means of addressing citizen complaints about conditions in city parks. Before the 311 system was implemented, the NPC had launched the ParkScan project, under which neighborhood residents and other volunteers regularly recorded maintenance and other issues in city parks and reported those problems to the city.[19] With the advent of 311, ParkScan was integrated into the system so that complaints would be immediately translated into service requests. In 2006, one year before the 311 system was implemented, only 65% of ParkScan complaints were resolved in the year in which they were reported. By 2010, the city had increased that percentage to 85%.[20]

Although 311 data are widely reported in both the *Government Barometer* and the annual budget, budget analysts make only limited use of the data when considering budget requests. Some officials have indicated that because the city lacks a single set of budget priorities, the budget process does not lend itself to being driven by metrics that would be aligned with such priorities. Instead, budgeting appears to be based on a more incremental approach. According to the officials interviewed for this study, budget analysts have expressed interest in using the performance measures that are tracked by the controller's office to help drive the budget process, but the analysts' attention tends to be focused on more immediate issues, such as budget deficits.

Knoxville

Knoxville launched its 311 system in May 2005. In FY 2010, the system had a budget of just under $400,000; was staffed by six full-time employees, one part-time employee, and a director; operated from 7 a.m. to 5 p.m., Monday through Friday; and received 253,262 calls (roughly one-and-one-half times the number of city residents). Most of the calls were information requests; only 37,000 were service requests. During the first five years of operation (May 2005 through March 2010), five categories of complaint accounted for just over half of the 127,718 service requests:

- Complaints about trash-strewn lots (41,855)
- Complaints about overgrown lots (7,666)
- Requests to have dead animals picked up (6,043)
- Requests for brush pickups (5,277)
- Complaints about abandoned cars (5,004).

The 311 system automatically monitors the efficiency of call center operations (e.g., how long it takes to answer a call, how long the calls last); the system also provides quarterly reports to the mayor and key management officials on (1) the volume of calls and (2) the timeliness of responses to service requests by department, request, council district, and service area.

Implementation of the 311 system coincided with a drop in 911 calls. According to information provided by the Knoxville government, between 2005 and 2009, 911 calls declined by nearly 11%—from 317,626 to 283,780—even as the number of reported crimes and the population both increased.[21] During the same period, the number of 311 calls increased from 100,173 to 259,636, or 159%. In addition to having very likely diverted calls from 911, the implementation of the 311 system made it possible to consolidate call-taking functions for nonemergency services. Before the 311 system was created, city government supported 21 FTE positions whose primary responsibility was call taking; after the system was implemented, 10 of the original positions were eliminated through attrition, and a number of other staff members were reassigned within the city government.

Since its inception, the 311 system has also handled calls to the city court. By relieving court staff of primary responsibility for telephone service, the 311 system allowed the court to shift 1.5 FTE staff members to revenue collection. Knoxville has not conducted a detailed study of the impact of this shift (as opposed to other potential influences), but court revenues steadily increased after the 311 system was implemented (by nearly 38% between FY 2005 and FY 2009), before declining in FY 2010.[22]

While Knoxville has not implemented a program like Baltimore's CitiStat, operations staff have used 311 data to inform problem solving, and city officials cited a number of specific examples in which intelligence garnered from 311 data has allowed them to make better decisions about the allocation of staffing and equipment. Like other local governments, Knoxville has often based service delivery on a model that calls for public works staff, such as those who undertake street paving and brush pickup, to be deployed evenly throughout the city. Using 311 data, however, officials determined that the demand for such services was uneven. In response, the city began to shift resources—for example, reducing brush pickup in some areas to allow more repaving to be undertaken in others.

The city has also used 311 data to address seasonal and geographic differences in the demand for leaf pickup—changing the type of equipment being used, reducing the size of crews, and directing more resources to the western parts of the city, where tree coverage was greatest. By sending fully staffed crews to the western parts of Knoxville, the city has reduced its reliance on overtime—cutting annual costs from approximately $1 million to $300,000 and improving service quality.

The Public Works Department also used 311 data to transform its response to zoning complaints.

Before the 311 system was implemented, citizens who wished to register such complaints had to call a dedicated line that was staffed by three different people. Now, all calls go to the 311 system, and front-yard and zoning complaints are forwarded to a single staff person, who then assigns complaints to inspectors. There was also no way, before the system was implemented, to track how quickly service requests were resolved. Now, the 311 system automatically informs managers of outstanding and overdue requests. And when vacancies developed for inspectors, data from the 311 system played an important role in the decision not to hire new staff but instead to meet the need by cross-training existing staff.

Data from the 311 system are used at both the senior management and department levels. Sam Anderson, who served as senior director of operations and efficiency until his retirement in 2010, said that until the advent of the 311 system, senior managers "were paper shufflers. . . . If you don't use the data generated by 311, don't bother." At the department level, the Department of Public Service routinely uses data based on responses to 311 service requests to drive performance: the city is divided into zones, and zone managers compete to achieve the most timely responses to service requests. Similarly, before the 311 system was implemented, it took as many as 10 days to repair a pothole after a service request; today, Knoxville has a 48-hour pothole guarantee. Finally, in a move that was driven by analysis of 311 data, Knoxville reduced the response time for mowing overgrown lots from 50 to 33 days.

Knoxville does not formally integrate 311 data (or other performance data) into its budgeting process. Nevertheless, city council members regularly review performance data generated by the 311 system on service requests for their own districts to obtain a data-based, rather than anecdotal, perspective on how well service delivery is meeting demand.

Summary

The role of 311/CRM systems in government reform can best be thought of as a work in progress. It has been only 15 years since Baltimore became the first city to implement a 311 system. By comparison, the period between the first implementation of a 911 system in the United States and the New York City Police Department's implementation of CompStat was more than 30 years. By that standard, the extent to which 311/CRM systems are now being used to drive performance improvement is somewhat remarkable. Although Indianapolis, San Francisco, and Knoxville differ in the extent to which 311 or CRM data have catalyzed government transformation, the implementation of a 311 or CRM system has led, in all three cases, to improvements in processes and service, budget savings, and greater operational efficiency.

One way to represent the role of 311/CRM systems in transformative initiatives is along a continuum, as shown in Figure 2-3.

For most cities, the likely immediate benefit of a 311/CRM system will be an improvement in customer service, on two fronts: (1) easing citizen access to government in general and (2) professionalizing front-line customer service through centralization—sparing citizens the task of dealing with hundreds, if not thousands, of different telephone numbers. In most cases, local governments should realize some savings

Figure 2-3 The Role of 311/CRM Systems in Transformative Initiatives

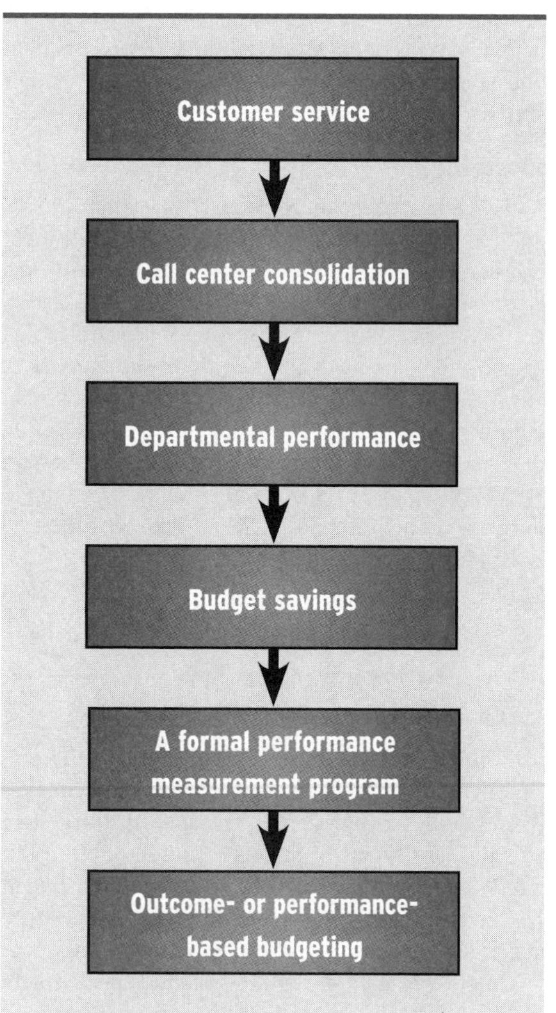

by consolidating call center functions. The extent of the savings, however, will depend on how the consolidated functions are restructured and staffed. Savings may not be immediate; instead, they may occur only through attrition as department-level call-taking positions are eliminated.

Improved customer service and consolidated call centers, however, are unlikely to cover the up-front investment in 311/CRM systems. Far greater opportunities for savings arise when department heads and senior management begin to use 311/CRM data to obtain business intelligence. At that point, real transformation can begin—both because senior officials will realize the importance of data in decision making and because government staff will be able to identify specific opportunities for budget savings and improved service delivery.

Knoxville and San Francisco have made it to this point in the continuum—which, again, is remarkable, given the relatively short time since they implemented their 311 systems. Both cities offer examples, from leaf pickup to pothole repair, of 311 data driving performance. Much as it did in Chicago, Kansas City, and Minneapolis, close analysis of performance data has permitted Knoxville and San Francisco to reengineer processes and increase efficiency.

Neither Knoxville nor San Francisco, however, has reached the next point on the continuum: the integration of data, including but not limited to 311 data, into a formal performance measurement process. In Knoxville, an informal performance measurement process took hold: senior officials were clearly looking at 311 data on a regular basis. This was less true in San Francisco, despite then-mayor Newsom's interest in a formal performance measurement process and the extraordinary level of public reporting of citywide performance in the *Government Barometer*.

Indianapolis seems to have come closest to using CRM data to transform local government. IndyStat, a critical component in the daily management of city government, has led not only to program improvements similar to those undertaken in Knoxville and San Francisco, but also to a more enterprise-wide approach to measuring and managing performance. Nevertheless, even in Indianapolis, CRM data (and performance data in general) are used only sparingly in the budget process. Indianapolis has implemented an outcomes-based budgeting process that is designed to align spending with outcome priorities, but the budget provides little or no data on the extent to which outcomes assigned priority have actually been achieved.

311/CRM Systems and Citizen Satisfaction: A Preliminary Review

To the extent that 311/CRM systems can improve customer service and the quality of service delivery, implementation should also drive increases in citizen satisfaction with local government. A preliminary review suggests the need for additional research on this point.[23] None of the cities with 311/CRM systems has undertaken pre- and post-implementation research to specifically test the impact of its system on citizen satisfaction. Many cities, however, have surveyed general citizen satisfaction both before and after implementing 311/ CRM systems. These survey findings, while not definitive, offer at least a preliminary approach to understanding the impact of such systems on the customer service experience and on citizen satisfaction.

After discussing the transition to 311/CRM as a point of contact between citizens and local government, as well as the popularity of 311 systems, this article uses data from citizen satisfaction surveys in seven cities—Denver, Houston, Kansas City, Minneapolis, New York, Philadelphia, and San Antonio—to explore the impact of 311/CRM systems by comparing (1) satisfaction among citizens before and after system implementation, (2) perceptions of service quality in cities with 311/CRM systems and cities without them, and (3) satisfaction among 311/CRM users and nonusers (see sidebar on the next page for survey methodologies).

The Transition to 311/CRM as a Point of Contact with Local Government

In some jurisdictions, 311/CRM systems may have become the principal point of contact between citizens and local government; for example, 311/CRM systems are now being used by more members of the public than is the more ubiquitous 911 emergency system.[24] Nevertheless, it is difficult to track usage levels of 311/ CRM systems. Although most local governments with such systems track the total number of calls to the system in a given year, there is no way to distinguish between unique and repeated calls (a total of 10,000 calls may have been made by 5,000 unique users, each of whom called twice in the course of a year).[25]

Another way to track the use of a 311/CRM system is to survey residents and determine the percentage of those who report having used the system. For example, a 2008 citizen survey conducted in New York found that 68% of respondents had used the city's 311 system at least once in the previous year; by comparison, only 32% had called 911 for an emergency service.[26] Similarly, a 2009 citizen survey conducted in Houston found that 58% of respondents had called 311 in the

Survey Methodologies

Denver
Mail-out, mail-back surveys sent to a random sample of 3,000 households citywide. (All city residents were free to respond to the survey, however.) Total number of responses: 919; margin of error: +/-3%.[1]

Houston
Telephone survey of 1,246 randomly selected and participating households; an additional 4,339 self-selected residents completed a web-based version of the survey. Margin of error: +/-1.31%.

Kansas City
Mail-out, mail-back surveys sent to a random sample of 2,000 households every quarter throughout the year. Telephone follow-up with nonrespondents. Total number of responses: 4,637 (approximately half by mail and half by telephone). Margin of error: +/-1.43%

Minneapolis
Telephone survey of 1,172 randomly selected and participating households. Margin of error: +/-3%.

New York
Mail-out, mail-back surveys sent to a random sample of 136,642 households citywide. Total number of responses: 24,339 (91% by mail and 9% on the web). Margin of error: +/-1%.

Philadelphia
Telephone survey of a random sample of 1,300 landline users and 302 cell phone users. Margin of error: +/-2.5%.

San Antonio
Telephone survey of 1,013 randomly selected and participating households. Margin of error: +/-3%.

1 Margin of error is based on the entire sample; data drawn from subsamples will have higher margins of error.

previous year versus 23% who had called 911 for an emergency service.[27] And in Kansas City, a 2010 citizen survey found that 46% of respondents had called 311 in the previous year versus 33% who had called the police.[28] Moreover, this survey revealed that the percentage of respondents who reported using the 311 system had nearly doubled since the inception of the service: in 2007, when 311 was first implemented in Kansas City, only 25% of respondents reported having used the service during the previous year.[29]

The Popularity of 311/CRM

While building awareness of a 311/CRM system takes time, survey data suggest that once citizens discover it, the service becomes popular and is viewed as one that works.

- In a 2010 survey conducted in San Antonio, 78% of respondents were satisfied or very satisfied with 311, and 90% indicated that it was easy to use.[30]
- In Houston, 76% of respondents surveyed in 2009 were satisfied or very satisfied with the performance of 311 call agents.[31]
- In New York City, 29% of respondents surveyed in 2008 rated 311 service as excellent, and another 42% rated it as good.[32]
- In Philadelphia, among respondents to a 2009 survey who had called 311, 77% were satisfied with the 311/CRM staff; 68% were satisfied with responses to requests for information; and 60% were satisfied with responses to service requests.[33]

Citizen Satisfaction with 311/CRM Service and Overall Service Quality: Three Evaluative Methodologies

In a 311/CRM system, call agents provide information and process service requests, but they do not actually fulfill the requests: that responsibility resides with local government service departments. Thus, residents who are satisfied with the 311/CRM system are not necessarily satisfied with overall service quality. Theoretically, however, a combination of improved frontline customer service and better tracking of citizen service requests—both of which are made possible by a 311/CRM system—should improve service delivery. In the absence of surveys specifically designed to explore the effect of 311/CRM systems on service delivery, available citizen survey data can be analyzed using three different methodologies.

Examination of Citizen Satisfaction before and after Implementation of 311/CRM Systems To put the before-and-after analysis into context, it is important to note its limitations. Numerous factors other than the presence or absence of a 311/CRM system may affect both the quality and citizens' perceptions of service delivery. For example, a 311/CRM system could have been implemented at a time of massive budget cuts or significant funding increases. In addition, not all services are driven by calls to a 311/CRM system. In particular, citizens' perceptions of overall service quality may be dramatically affected by their views of public safety services—even though residents may be more likely to use a 311/CRM system than to call 911. Despite these limitations, citizen survey data from Kansas City and Denver are instructive.

Kansas City's 311 system was phased in during 2006 and 2007. The start-up period coincided with an increase in citizen satisfaction with overall service delivery. In 2005, 41% of survey respondents indicated that they were satisfied or very satisfied with city services; by 2007, satisfaction had increased to 52%; by 2010, however, the percentage of residents who were satisfied or very satisfied had declined to 43%—nearly the pre-311 level.[34] One possible explanation for the drop: even if the 311 system had led to an initial increase in satisfaction, once the system ceased to be a novelty, residents may have regarded city government from a "What have you done for me lately?" perspective.

In 2005, even before the 2006 launch of Denver's 311 system, 63% of survey respondents were satisfied or very satisfied with service delivery; by 2009, overall satisfaction had increased to 68%, only to decline to 66% in 2010.[35] In addition to asking respondents about their satisfaction with service delivery, the Denver survey also asked citizens whether they were satisfied with the value of the services they received in relation to the taxes they paid. In 2006, 54% of respondents were satisfied with the value of services received; by 2007, after the implementation of the 311 system, 62% were satisfied. But by 2010, only 53% of respondents were satisfied—even fewer than before the introduction of the 311 system.[36]

In both Kansas City and Denver, the implementation of a 311 system may have led to a small, short-term gain in citizen satisfaction with overall service quality; but over time, such gains appear to drop off.

Assessment of Perceptions of Service Quality in Communities with and without 311/CRM Systems Like the first approach, the assessment of citizen satisfaction in communities with and without 311/CRM systems has serious limitations. Local government organizational structures vary tremendously, as do citizen expectations and the levels of service provided. As a result, numerous factors other than the presence or absence of a 311/CRM system can affect perceptions of service quality in different jurisdictions.

That said, it is worth examining the 2010 Kansas City citizen survey, which includes detailed data from 13 other cities, all in the central United States and all with comparable populations: Arlington, Texas; Dallas, Texas; Denver, Colorado; Des Moines, Iowa; Fort Worth, Texas; Houston, Texas; Indianapolis, Indiana; Minneapolis, Minnesota; Oklahoma City, Oklahoma; San Antonio, Texas; St. Louis, Missouri; Tulsa, Oklahoma; and Wichita, Kansas. Five of these cities (in addition to Kansas City) have 311 centers that use CRM systems; three have action centers that centralize service requests but do not use a 311 number; and the remaining five jurisdictions do not have a 311 or a CRM system.[37]

In each city, survey respondents were asked to rate satisfaction with service quality in various areas, using a five-point scale in which a 5 was the highest possible rating. Table 2–1 shows the percentage of respondents in each city that assigned a rating of 4 or 5 to each of five areas.

Of the five areas surveyed—maintenance, parks, public safety, code enforcement, and communications—311 or CRM systems would be expected to have the greatest impact on maintenance, code enforcement, and communications, and the least impact on parks and public safety. The results, however, were unexpectedly complex:

- With respect to maintenance, an average of 35% of respondents in cities with 311 or CRM systems assigned a rating of 4 or 5 to the service; in cities without either system, the percentage was close to 35%.
- With respect to code enforcement, cities that had only CRM systems outperformed both those with 311 systems and those that had neither 311 nor CRM: 51% of respondents in only-CRM cities assigned a rating of 4 or 5, compared with 47% of respondents in cities with 311 or CRM and 46% of respondents in cities with neither.
- With respect to communications, respondents in cities with 311 or CRM systems were less likely to assign a rating of 4 or 5 than were those in cities with neither system. On average, 47% of respondents in cities with 311 or CRM systems assigned ratings of 4 or 5 to communications, versus 51% in cities with neither 311 nor CRM systems.

Table 2-1 Citizen Satisfaction in Cities with 311 Systems, CRM Systems, or Neither

	Percentage of respondents who assigned a rating of 4 or 5 to the service				
City	Maintenance	Parks	Public safety	Code enforcement	Communications
Cities with 311 systems					
Dallas	33	50	56	40	56
Denver	42	69	68	46	50
Houston	39	52	59	40	41
Kansas City	22	56	74	32	33
Minneapolis	53	72	74	60	53
San Antonio	42	71	70	56	44
Average	38.5	61.7	66.8	45.7	46.2
Cities with CRM systems					
Indianapolis	35	60	57	52	36
Oklahoma City	23	62	81	52	58
Tulsa	27	68	82	49	51
Average	28.3	63.3	73.3	51.0	48.3
Average for cities with 311 or CRM systems	35.1	62.2	69.0	47.4	46.9
Non-311/CRM cities					
Arlington	49	72	67	55	49
Des Moines	31	74	70	55	60
Fort Worth	36	63	77	46	55
St. Louis	22	67	64	31	39
Wichita	36	63	79	41	51
Average	34.8	67.8	71.4	45.6	50.8

Source: Office of the City Auditor, *Performance Audit: Kansas City Citizen Survey Report, Fiscal Year 2010* (Kansas City: Office of the City Auditor, August 2010), 15, 20, 24, 28, 31.

Comparison of Satisfaction Ratings of 311/CRM System Users and Nonusers Given that one of the aims of 311/CRM technology is to improve customer service, 311/CRM users might be expected to have a higher level of satisfaction with local government than nonusers. This hypothesis was confirmed in Minneapolis, where, among respondents to a 2011 survey, 39% of 311 users reported that it was easy to get in touch with city government, versus 24% of nonusers.[38] But in Kansas City—the one jurisdiction that publicly reported disaggregated data on overall service quality—39% of 311 users were satisfied or very satisfied with the quality of city services, versus 46% of nonusers. And in response to a question about citizen satisfaction with the value received for taxes paid, 23% of 311 callers were satisfied or very satisfied, versus 30% of all survey respondents.[39]

Summary

In cities that have implemented 311/CRM systems, survey data reveal that a high percentage of city residents are familiar with the system and make use of it. In most cities for which survey data are available, residents are more likely to call the 311/CRM system than its emergency counterpart, 911. Finally, in cities that have implemented them and for which survey data are available, 311/CRM systems appear to be relatively popular.

More far-reaching impacts are harder to assess. In both Denver and Kansas City, implementation of 311 systems coincided with an increase in citizen satisfaction with overall service quality, but there did not appear to be any lasting impact. And when citizen satisfaction ratings from cities with and without 311/CRM systems are assessed, the picture is fuzzy at best. Finally, in Kansas

City, users of the 311 system were less satisfied with city services than were nonusers. Of course, it is impossible to generalize from this one result.

Taken together, the findings point to the need for greater research and analysis. The best way to explore the link between 311/CRM systems and perceptions of service quality would be through pre- and post-implementation surveys that would focus specifically on how the 311/CRM system influenced respondents' satisfaction with overall service delivery. Moreover, the research design would have to control for other factors that could influence the perception of service quality.

Conclusion

311/CRM systems are a work in progress. It is hard to dispute the customer service benefits of creating a contact center that makes it easier for citizens to request nonemergency services and obtain information from local government. Survey data suggest that 311/CRM systems provide a popular service that quickly becomes the principal point of contact between residents and their government. Case studies from Indianapolis, San Francisco, and Knoxville demonstrate that 311/CRM systems can also become a critical source of business intelligence, but the full potential of 311/CRM systems as tools to increase efficiency, improve performance, and yield cost savings has yet to be realized.

The effect of 311/CRM systems on overall citizen satisfaction is less clear; the limited data that are available suggest that the impact is either temporary or limited. As more governments implement 311/CRM systems, this should be a priority area for future research.

Notes

1. CRM is the technology used to process requests for information and services; 311 is a standardized, three-digit telephone number that is used specifically to access nonemergency local government services. Although 311 call centers generally use CRM technology, a call center that uses CRM does not necessarily have a 311 telephone number.
2. Evelina Moulder, *ICMA's Local Government Customer Service Systems Survey* (Washington, D.C.: ICMA Results Network, 2007).
3. CitiStat was based on the New York City Police Department's COMPSTAT program, which relied on timely and accurate data to deploy police officers and to develop strategies that successfully reduced crime.
4. Lenneal Henderson, *The Baltimore CitiStat Program: Performance and Accountability* (Arlington, Va.: IBM Endowment for the Business of Government, May 2003), businessofgovernment.org/sites/default/files/CitiStat.pdf.
5. See Robert D. Behn, "Designing PerformanceStat: Or What Are the Key Strategic Choices That a Jurisdiction or Agency Must Make When Adapting the CompStat/CitiStat Class of Performance Strategies?" *Public Performance and Management Review* 32, no. 2 (December 2008): 206–235.
6. David Eichenthal, "Using 311 Data to Measure Performance and Manage City Finances," *Government Finance Review* 24 (August 2008): 47–50.
7. Local governments that implement a 311/CRM system often consolidate existing call centers, which may reduce the number of total call center staff, increase productivity, or both.
8. See Shayne Kavanagh and Spencer Stern, "Investing in CRM: Building the Business Case and Cost-Benefit Model," in *Call 311: Connecting Citizens to Local Government; Final Report*, ed. Cory Fleming (Washington, D.C.: ICMA, 2008), bookstore.icma.org/freedocs/43547.pdf.
9. Kavanagh and Stern, "Investing in CRM."
10. David Eichenthal, Cory Fleming, and Nish Keshav, *Kansas City 311 Action Center* (Washington, D.C.: Ochs Center for Metropolitan Studies and ICMA, 2009).
11. Cory Fleming, *Minneapolis 311 System* (Washington, D.C.: ICMA, 2008).
12. The authors obtained information on the implementation and use of 311/CRM systems through staff interviews. In Indianapolis, interviewees were Manuel Mendez, director, Office of Audit and Performance; Rick Powers, director, Department of Code Enforcement; Jeff Seidenstein, budget manager, Office of Finance and Management; and Sarah M. Taylor, director, Mayor's Office of Constituent Services. In San Francisco, interviewees were Nancy Alfaro, director, 311 Customer Service Center; Manish Goyal, fiscal and policy analyst, Office of the Mayor; Andrew Murray, deputy director, City Services Auditor Division; and Edward Reiskin, director, Department of Public Works. In Knoxville, interviewees were Sam Anderson, senior director, Operations and Efficiency; David Brace, deputy director, Public Service; Russ Jensen, director, 311 Customer Service Center; Steve King, director, Public Works; Chevelle Lewis, code administrator; and Blake Young, financial analyst, Office of Management and Budget.
13. City and County of San Francisco, Office of the Controller, "About the City Services Auditor," sfcontroller.org/index.aspx?page=73.
14. City and County of San Francisco, Office of the Controller, "City Survey," sfcontroller.org/index.aspx?page=406.
15. City and County of San Francisco, Office of the Controller, "Performance Measurement," sfcontroller .org/index.aspx?page=43.
16. City and County of San Francisco, Office of the Controller, "City Survey."
17. Graffiti Advisory Board, "Minutes for November 18, 2010" (draft), City and County of San Francisco, 38.106.4.205/Modules/ShowDocument.aspx?documentid=1173. Information on DPWStat was obtained during an interview with DPW director Edward Reiskin; the director's office also provided the authors with an internal program plan

that indicated that GMAP, the Government Management Accountability and Performance initiative that has been put in place by the State of Washington, was a model for DPWStat.

18. City and County of San Francisco, Office of the Controller, City Services Auditor, *Government Barometer* (February 2011): 3, sfcontroller.org/Modules/ShowDocument.aspx?documentid=1945.
19. For more information on ParkScan, see parkscan.org.
20. Neighborhood Parks Council, *ParkScan San Francisco: 2010 Annual Report*, 3, parkscan.org/sites/default/files/ParkScan%20Annual%202010.pdf.
21. U.S. Census Bureau, "Population Estimates; All Incorporated Places: 2000 to 2009," census.gov/popest/data/cities/totals/2009/tables/SUB-EST2009-04-47 .csv; and U.S. Department of Justice, Federal Bureau of Investigation, "Uniform Crime Reporting Statistics," ucrdatatool.gov/.
22. Knoxville's comprehensive annual financial reports are available online at ci.knoxville.tn.us/cafr/default.asp.
23. Research undertaken by the Fund for the City of New York suggests that improved customer service can affect citizens' overall perceptions of local government. Specifically, a series of focus groups revealed that direct experience with frontline personnel in local government significantly influences citizens' views of local government efficiency or effectiveness. See Barbara J. Cohn Berman, *Listening to the Public: Adding the Voices of the People to Government Performance Measurement and Reporting* (New York: Fund for the City of New York, 2005).
24. Comparisons with 911 service are particularly relevant because 311 was established in the mid-1990s by the Federal Communications Commission expressly to alleviate the burden of nonemergency phone calls being made to 911.
25. Unless all citizens are willing to provide their name and address when calling 311—and many choose to call anonymously—there is currently no way to determine the number of unique users.
26. City of New York, Mayor's Office of Operations, "NYC Feedback: Citywide Customer Survey Results" (December 2008), 26, 34, nyc.gov/html/ops/html/data/feedback.shtml.
27. Jefferson Wells, "2009 City-Wide Citizens Survey," Report No. 2010-02, C-6–C-7, houstontx.gov/controller/audit/2010-02.pdf.
28. In this survey, calls to the police department were used as a substitute measure for calls made to 911.
29. Office of the City Auditor, *Performance Audit: Kansas City Citizen Survey Report, Fiscal Year 2010* (Kansas City: Office of the City Auditor, August 2010), 54.
30. ETC Institute, "2010 City of San Antonio Community Survey: Final Report" (July 2010), viii, sanantonio .gov/news/commsurvey/2010CommunitySurveyFinalReport .pdf.
31. Wells, "Citizens Survey," C-7.
32. City of New York, "NYC Feedback," 24.
33. Philadelphia Research Initiative, *A Work in Progress: Philadelphia's 311 System after One Year* (March 2010), 1, pewtrusts.org/uploadedFiles/wwwpewtrustsorg/Reports/Philadelphia_Research_Initiative/FINAL%20311%20Report%20030210.pdf?n=3297.
34. Office of the City Auditor, *Performance Audit*, 47.
35. National Research Center and ICMA, *National Citizen Survey: City of Denver* (2011), 35, denvergov.org/Portals/9/documents/Citizen%20Survey/2010%20Citizen%20Survey.pdf.
36. Ibid., 34.
37. Wichita introduced a centralized customer service system in January 2011.
38. National Research Center, *Minneapolis, MN Resident Survey* (April 2011), 31, minneapolismn.gov/www/groups/public/@council/documents/webcontent/convert_285361.pdf.
39. Office of the City Auditor, *Performance Audit*, 31.

3

Local Government Use of Development Impact Fees: More Fallout from a Poor Economy?

Larry L. Lawhon
Kansas State University

SELECTED FINDINGS

Local government use of impact fees has been steadily increasing since 2002. City imposition of impact fees increased from 26% in 2002 to 40% in 2011, while county imposition increased from 7% in 2002 to 17% in 2011. But since 2006, that increase among cities has slowed considerably.

Imposition of impact fees in 2011 was most prolific in cities and counties above 50,000 in population, in cities in the Mountain and Pacific Coast divisions, and in counties in the Mountain division.

Development impact fees are one-time fees assessed against new development to generate funds for the new or expanded infrastructure and services that such development will require.[1] Development impact fees were solidly recognized as a common local government revenue device by 1988, the year in which the American Planning Association published *Development Impact Fees: Policy Rationale, Practice, Theory, and Issues,*[2] a seminal book compiled from several impact fee symposia. In the book, contributors James E. Frank and Paul B. Downing investigated the patterns of impact fee use, drawing on the history of local government's role in land use regulation and provision of public facilities.[3] Local government authority in both areas had been broadened by the Standard State Zoning Enabling Act (1924) and Standard City Planning Enabling Act (1928). At that time, according to Thomas Snyder and Michael Stegman, it was fairly common for local governments to use police power to require "on-site" public improvements as a condition of new development approval.[4] "What is new about impact fees," wrote Frank and Downing in 1988, "is the idea that growth should pay for facilities located *outside the development site,* the need for which results from numerous developments."[5]

Prior to the spread of development impact fees, outside or "off-site" needs were typically paid for by general revenue sources and/or general obligation bonds that required resident approval and often resulted in higher property taxes. In the 1960s, the public began to resist this approach to paying for new development, thus providing "a powerful stimulus to the expanding use of impact fees"[6] as a new revenue device.

From their research, Frank and Downing concluded that more local governments were using impact fees, that the dollar magnitude of the fees was increasing, and that the fees were being used for a wider range of facilities than in the past.[7] The authors found that impact fees were often used for water, sewer, roads, schools, parks, solid waste, libraries, emergency service facilities, fire stations, and police stations; they further found that local governments in Colorado, Florida, Oregon, Texas, and Washington were the most frequent users.[8]

Several other studies have also investigated local government use of development impact fees. In 1984, Gus Bauman and William Ethier surveyed 1,000 U.S. communities and found that 36% of the 220 respondent communities imposed impact fees; from their findings they concluded that adoption of impact fee policies was increasing and more likely to occur in western and Pacific states.[9] A 1985 survey by ICMA determined that communities in 36 states were using either impact fees or exactions to pay for community infrastructure.[10] A second ICMA study, in 1991, verified that states in the Pacific Coast, Mountain, and South Atlantic geographic divisions were the most prolific users of impact fees, and that suburban cities were more likely to use them than were central or independent cities.[11]

Impact fee use has gained credibility as a viable local government finance method for off-site infrastructure for several reasons, including taxpayer refusal to approve general obligation bonds and be saddled with higher taxes, state and federal fund reductions earmarked for local infrastructure, and environmental concerns related to sprawl. Because these trends have left local governments with reduced revenues to make public facility improvements and provide services related to growth and development, impact fees have moved to the forefront as a revenue device to defray the cost of new development. The primary motivations for community-level imposition of impact fees are (1) to shift the burden from existing taxpayers to new development, (2) to better synchronize capital projects with new growth, (3) to cause developers to consider the true costs associated with new development, (4) to enhance a community's preferred image by excluding some types of uses and social groups, and (5) to engage decision makers in "symbolic politics" as they respond to public demands that growth pay its own way.[12]

The use of development impact fees to shift the cost of construction for new community growth from existing residents to new development is an option that Frank and Downing describe as "politically beguiling."[13] Fees may also be used to provide services that address community quality-of-life issues.[14] For example, several authorities have suggested that development impact fees provide a solid foundation for both economic and physical growth.[15] In particular, Arthur Nelson and Mitch Moody identify impact fees as the "grease" for economic development.[16] Others, however, believe them to be a damper on local economic development activities, especially in regions where some communities charge impact fees and others do not.

Background and Definitions

Mandatory exactions and dedications, or fees in lieu of dedication, have historically been used as the preferred method to ensure that new development provides, funds, and installs all on-site infrastructure and improvements necessary to support itself. These tools require developers to install streets, water and sewer lines, and parks on-site, or to pay fees in lieu, for the primary benefit of those using or residing in the newly developed area. Upon subdivision approval and acceptance by the local government, these improvements become public responsibility, which implies that the facilities have been constructed to community standards and that future maintenance is guaranteed by local government.

Mandatory dedication requirements are typically established by a local government's subdivision regulations. The actual on-site improvements, a condition of subdivision approval, may be specified and constructed to local government standards or, in some cases, negotiated between the developer and the local government, which is generally represented by the city engineer, public works director, city planner, or all three. However, on-site exactions and improvements do not address the off-site impacts of the development. Impact fees fill this gap.

Impact fees are considered a type of exaction—that is, "a governmental requirement that a developer dedicate or reserve land for public use or improvements, or pay a fee in lieu of dedication, which is used to purchase land or construct public improvements."[17] However, impact fees are often used to mitigate the impact of a single new development on a broader range of facilities and services external to the project. Such off-site improvements may include arterial roads needed to accommodate additional traffic; interceptor sewer lines, and water and sewer facilities and treatment plants; schools, libraries, and civic buildings; trails and regional parks; and fire/police/emergency services, structures, and staff.[18] Some local governments also require impact fees for off-site storm-water systems, purchase of open space, and purchase of future water rights.

These practices acknowledge that the impact of new development occurs outside the boundaries of the development as well as inside, and that this impact should be mitigated to protect and preserve the health, safety, and general welfare of the jurisdiction. They also suggest that a local government has latitude in deciding its menu of impact fee charges unless it is specifically limited by state impact fee enabling legislation.

Assessment and Payment of Fees

An impact fee may be assessed on commercial, industrial, and residential development. The fee itself is not typically negotiated. Rather, the amount is established by ordinance and applicable to all similarly situated development.[19] Because different types of development create different infrastructure needs, the fee structure established to mitigate the impact of residential development on the community, for example, may differ from that established for commercial or industrial development. It is through this fee structure that impact fees offer the business and development community a mechanism by which to appease any local opposition to growth and development that arises in response to an inadequate level of infrastructure or services, whether imagined or real. In other words, if local residents believe that new growth is paying its way, they may be less likely to oppose a new development project.

Although impact fees are generally assessed at the time of development approval, local policy determines whether payment may be deferred until the permit is taken out or until a certificate of occupancy is issued (indicating that the building is ready and safe to inhabit). Impact fees are typically placed in an earmarked account for required improvements, may be expended only for those earmarked improvements, and must bear a reasonable relationship to the impact created by the proposed development.

Authority to Impose Fees

The right of local governments to impose impact fees is based in two types of authority: local police powers and state enabling legislation.

Local Police Powers

Impact fees became widely used even in those states where enabling legislation was not adopted. This is because local governments, through local police power, are authorized to pursue regulations that protect—or benefit—the health, safety, and general welfare of the community and its residents. For example, inadequate fire protection in a growing area of the community may place residents and structures at risk; therefore, requiring an impact fee to build and equip a new fire station in that area might be successfully defended on the grounds that the community acted to adequately protect its citizens. "In most states, with or without impact fee enabling acts, local governments have the authority to require payment of a fee at the time of meter purchase or connection to the public utility system."[20]

Additionally, local police power serves as authority for impact fees before state enabling legislation can be adopted. Loveland, Colorado, for example, opted for a local impact fee regulation about two decades before state enabling legislation was approved in 2001. Loveland already had in place water and sewer capital expansion fees when it approved additional impact fees of $1,548 for low-density development in 1984.[21] The Loveland impact fees initially included fees for general government, parks and recreation, law enforcement, fire protection, libraries, museums, and streets. A trails impact fee was then added in 1993, and a fully equipped provision was added in 1997 for fire protection facilities; finally, an open space category was added in 2002. The utility, nonutility, and storm-water fees in Loveland combined are currently about $23,800 for a typical single-family home.

Duncan Associates in Austin, Texas, frequently surveys cities that charge impact fees.[22] While these surveys are not random, they nevertheless provide valuable information about average impact fee charges by land use category in the United States. For example, its 2010 survey found that the national average (among those cities charging an impact fee) is $11,796, while nonutility fees average $8,509 for a typical single-family home (Table 3-1).

State Enabling Legislation

States may enable impact fees through legislation that authorizes local governments to impose these fees for specific and potentially limited purposes. In 1987 Texas became the first state to approve state enabling legislation for impact fees.[23] Such legislation specifies the items for which impact fees can be imposed, sets standards for their imposition, and limits amounts that can be charged. With such stipulations in place, enabling legislation

- Reduces court challenges of local impact fee ordinances—at least in theory
- Reduces the potential for overzealous local governments to establish a wide menu of impact fee charges
- Reduces some of the uncertainty that developers and the business community experience when encountering local opposition to new development.

Table 3-1 Average Fees, in Dollars, by Type and Land Use, 2010

Facility type	Single-family (unit)	Multifamily (unit)	Retail (1,000 square feet)	Office (1,000 square feet)	Industrial (1,000 square feet)
Roads	3,227	2,179	5,946	3,360	2,060
Water	3,693	1,420	653	602	627
Wastewater	3,521	1,685	772	718	786
Drainage	1,734	829	1,089	904	1,073
Parks	2,955	2,254	—[a]	—[a]	—[a]
Library	412	307	—[a]	—[a]	—[a]
Fire	512	381	419	375	262
Police	385	303	430	261	181
General government	1,470	1,132	614	619	400
Schools	4,835	2,684	—[a]	—[a]	—[a]
Total nonutility[b]	8,509	5,617	6,294	4,036	2,690
Total[b]	11,796	6,985	6,524	4,394	3,137

Source: Survey of 275 jurisdictions reported by Clancy Mullen, *National Impact Fee Survey: 2010* (Austin, Tex.: Duncan Associates, November 2, 2010), 5, impactfees.com/publications%20pdf/2010_survey.pdf. Used with permission of Duncan Associates, September 2011.

a Rarely charged to nonresidential land uses, with the exception of school fees in California.

b Totals do not represent sum of average fees since not all jurisdictions charge all types of fees.

Currently, 28 states have adopted state enabling legislation authorizing impact fees[24] (Table 3-2). Some states do not have a general impact fee enabling act but allow impact fees for "individual jurisdictions through special acts of the legislature."[25] For example, in Maryland (except for code home rule counties), North Carolina, and Tennessee, the state legislatures may grant impact fee authority to governmental bodies.

Duncan Associates reports that state enabling legislation predominantly contains language such that impact fees can be used only to "charge new developments for the capital costs that they actually impose on the community."[26] Specific to this topic, both local ordinances and state enabling acts identify a new development's share as being "proportional" or "reasonably related" to the impact of the development upon the local government area. An impact fee regulation that does not meet this criterion might be open to legal challenge.

Case law indicates that impact fees will likely be upheld by the courts if there is (1) "an *essential nexus* [between] some legitimate governmental purpose" and the impact fee imposed, and (2) "a *'rough proportionality'* between the . . . impact fee and the impact of, or need created by, the proposed development."[27] Some jurisdictions have been unsuccessful in defending their impact fee ordinances and have subsequently repealed them. Ultimately, however, given that the goal of any impact fee policy is to ensure an adequate level of community infrastructure and services so as to protect the health, safety, and general welfare of residents, impact fees make good public sense and are often defensible when challenged in court.

Local governments that are considering the imposition of impact fees should first consult the state's impact fee enabling legislation, if it exists. The most burdensome part of impact fee consideration is determining the "proportional share" of the fee structure, and it may take several months to determine the cost of a "unit of service/infrastructure" for several different facilities and land use types. Some local governments develop the fee structure in-house while others hire impact fee consultants to prepare the fee structure. Communities without state enabling legislation should seek legal advice to establish an impact fee ordinance. Planning and land use control law textbooks provide a good overview of legal issues surrounding the imposition of impact fees.[28] In addition, the U.S. Department of Housing and Urban Development's *Impact Fees and Housing Affordability: A Guide for Practitioners* is an excellent source of useful information about how a local government might structure its fees.[29]

Table 3-2 State Impact Fee Enabling Acts

State	Year adopted
Texas	1987
Illinois	1987
Maine	1988
Arizona	1988
California	1989
Vermont	1989
Nevada	1989
New Jersey	1989
Virginia	1990
West Virginia	1990
Georgia	1990
Pennsylvania	1990
Oregon	1991
Washington	1991
New Hampshire	1991
Indiana	1991
Maryland	1992
Hawaii	1992
Idaho	1992
Wisconsin	1993
New Mexico	1993
Utah	1995
South Carolina	1999
Rhode Island	2000
Colorado	2001
Arkansas	2003
Montana	2005
Florida	2006

Source: Clancy Mullen, "State Impact Fee Enabling Acts" (Austin, Tex.: Duncan Associates, September 2011), 1, impactfees.com/publications%20pdf/state_enabling_acts.pdf. Used with permission of Duncan Associates.

Policy Considerations

Local governments turn to development impact fees as a "revenue device" for a variety of reasons. In many cases, the move is "politically beguiling" since those who will be paying the fees are usually not present to oppose them. Nelson identifies this as an issue of "representational equity" in that "impact fees are assessed on new homes bought by new residents of the community . . . [who] had no say in the adoption of the policy."[30] This makes it easier for decision makers to approve impact fee ordinances than to increase property taxes of established residents.

Local governments often justify imposing impact fees on the basis that the fees make new growth pay its own way. However, impact fees are often criticized for their exclusionary effects; impact fees, many sources charge, increase the price of development and make housing and other development more expensive, excluding lower-income residents who find it difficult to afford housing. Gregory Burge and Keith Ihlanfeldt cite "three frequently mentioned motivations . . . [for] exclusionary land-use regulations—the externality rationale, the fiscal rationale, and pure prejudice."[31] The externality rationale asserts that multifamily uses may lower surrounding property values and/or create other negative externalities, and a community may be encouraged to withhold development approval that creates such externalities. The fiscal rationale asserts that less affluent households do not pay their fair share of public services and infrastructure, and if these households occupy less costly housing, they pay less property tax. Finally, some communities develop exclusionary regulations simply to keep out those unlike themselves, and such regulations are predicated on prejudice; as a result, apartments and smaller dwelling units may not be approved. With respect to impact fees, the literature often suggests that exclusionary effects result from increased housing prices that accompany impact fees. These effects may adversely affect lower-income households and the lower-wage workforce.[32]

A chief concern about the incidence of impact fees relates to housing affordability. Again, early literature suggested that impact fees adversely affect housing affordability and result in exclusionary effects; however, Keith Ihlanfeldt and Timothy Shaughnessy dispute this.[33] They note that "not much is known regarding the economic incidence of impact fees—i.e., who is it that actually bears the burden of the fees—developers, new homebuyers, or owners of undeveloped land?"[34] They emphasize that *how this burden is distributed* is important for policy reasons—namely, "the availability of affordable housing for lower-income households in job-rich suburban communities and the negative externalities that allegedly result from suburban sprawl."[35]

Ihlanfeldt and Shaughnessy review and criticize past research on the incidence of impact fees for not being consistent with expectations derived from economic theory. Specifically, they present two theoretical views contained in the literature on the incidence of impact fees: the "old view" and the "new view." Early research on impact fees and affordability subscribed to what Ihlanfeldt and Shaughnessy suggest is an outmoded view. This view

- Treats impact fees as an exciselike tax on developers and ignores the new capital facilities and services that impact fees finance.

- Encourages "the supply of new housing . . . [to increase with] the amount of the fee, resulting in a higher price paid by new homebuyers, a lower net price received by developers, and a lower quantity of new homes built."
- Means that "both the new homebuyer and the developer [in the short run] share the burden of the fee—the new homebuyer in the form of a higher price and the developer in the form of economic losses."
- Suggests that "because new and existing housing are close but imperfect substitutes, . . . impact fees will cause some homebuyers who otherwise would have purchased a new home to instead buy an existing home." This increases the price of existing homes to somewhere below the price of new homes.
- Acknowledges that since the market is depressed, land prices decline.[36]

The new view of the economic effects of impact fees, however,

- "Incorporates the public capital services that are financed by the fees" into the price of housing.
- "Recognizes the impact of property tax capitalization on the incidence of the fees."
- "Assumes that the housing demand curve facing construction firms in a single jurisdiction is horizontal" (i.e., buyers are mobile).
- Means that "the benefits that accrue to new homebuyers from the infrastructure financed from the fees are capitalized into new home prices. If the increase in price that results from the capitalization of benefits equals the fee, then neither the developer nor the landowner bear[s] any burden of the fee since developers' profits remain at the normal level. The fee is borne by the homebuyer in the form of a higher housing price, but net of the benefits received from the fee-financed infrastructure there is no burden."
- Signifies that "if these benefits are less valued by the new homebuyer and therefore result in a house price increase that is less than the fee, restoration of developers' profits to a normal level requires that the price of land declines."[37]

To corroborate this new view, Ihlanfeldt and Shaughnessy show that the price of both new and existing housing in Dade County, Florida, increased at the same rate, and the resulting price increase was commensurate with the value of the capital facilities constructed with the impact fees. They conclude that in Dade County, the capital facilities paid for by impact fees are capitalized into the price of housing and thus "provide no support for the argument that impact fees reduce homeownership affordability."[38]

By way of further illustration, Ihlanfeldt and Shaughnessy refer to an empirical study of the Loveland, Colorado, impact fees program conducted by Larry Singell and Jane Lillydahl in 1990.[39] Singell and Lillydahl found that the price of both new and existing housing increased with the imposition of impact fees. Specifically, their quantitative research suggested that the average price of new homes in Loveland increased by approximately 7% between 1983 and 1986 and that about two-thirds of that amount was attributed to the capital expansion fees (CEFs), or impact fees. The authors concluded that CEFs negatively affected housing affordability. However, in analyzing Singell and Lillydahl's research, Ihlanfeldt and Shaughnessy calculated that the initial fee in Loveland, which they report as being about $1,200, increased the price of new homes by $3,800 and the price of an existing home by $7,000—different amounts which they contend are inconsistent with impact fee theory.[40] John Yinger, in reviewing the Singell and Lillydahl results, also found "the magnitude of the effects implausibly large."[41] To Ihlanfeldt and Shaughnessy, economic theory suggests that price increases for both new and existing housing should be similar, and from their findings in Dade County, Florida, they determined that both new and existing housing increased about $1.60 for each $1 of impact fees, which was capitalized into the price of the home.[42]

Many researchers have also raised concerns about the effect of impact fees on multifamily housing construction. Burge and Ihlanfeldt contend that empirical evidence on "the effect of impact fees on low-income housing construction in the suburbs is ambiguous."[43] In a study of the effects of impact fees on multifamily housing construction in 33 sample Florida metropolitan counties, the authors found that water and sewer impact fees in central cities, inner suburbs, and outer suburbs reduce the amount of multifamily housing constructed there.[44] Yet they also found that the effects of nonwater/sewer impact fees (e.g., fees for schools, roads, libraries, and parks) in the same communities "contrast[ed] sharply...[with those seen] for water/sewer impact fees. For central city and outer suburban areas, estimated effects are insignificant. . . . However, for inner suburban areas, nonwater/sewer impact fees have positive, statistically significant effects on multifamily housing construction."[45] The authors suggest that while water and sewer impact fees can reduce the amount of multifamily housing constructed, nonwater/sewer fees, which provide amenity facilities, seem to encourage it in certain settings.

Recent research seems to contradict the conventional old view that impact fees increase the price of housing dramatically and make it unaffordable. Both Burge and Ihlanfeldt and Ihlanfeldt and Shaughnessy suggest that the price of housing would be about the same whether impact fees are imposed or not. This is partly because where impact fees are not imposed, mill levies/property taxes are likely to increase to fund the infrastructure necessary to accommodate growth. Meanwhile, where impact fees are imposed, the value of the funded improvements is capitalized into the price of new housing. Ultimately, these two sets of authors posit that no burden is imposed by the impact fee, a rather dramatic divergence from old-view studies.

Survey Sample and Methodology

In 2002, 2006, and 2011, random surveys were sent to approximately 2,000 local governments to investigate their use of development impact fees. The survey questions were identical in each of the three survey periods so that results could be compared. The research findings presented below, which summarize results from the third survey, indicate that local government use of development impact fees has been on the increase over the past decade, although the increase since 2006 has been slight.

The sample used in the third, or current, survey was drawn from 10,404 U.S. cities and counties with populations greater than 2,500 throughout the nine geographic divisions identified by the U.S. Census Bureau. The term *city,* as used in this research, includes city, town, village, borough, and township. The term *county* includes county governments and parishes. In all, 18 separate survey pools were selected, representing the nine geographic divisions for both cities and counties. Thus, 1,440 communities and 561 counties/parishes—about 19% of both U.S. city and county governments—were surveyed. To ensure a representative sample nationwide regardless of density in the different divisions, the random sample maintained the same proportion of cities and counties in each division as is found across the country. Surveys were mailed in June 2011 and addressed to either the governing body's financial officer or its administrator. Table 3–3 shows the response rate by population group and geographic division.

Table 3–3 Survey Response

	Cities[a]			Counties[a]		
		Respondents			Respondents	
	No. surveyed (A)	No.	% of (A)	No. surveyed (B)	No.	% of (B)
Total	1,440	308[b]	21	561	102[b]	18
Population group						
50,000 or more	93	30	32	167	37	22
25,000–49,999	135	34	25	122	16	13
10,000–24,999	304	62	20	156	21	14
Less than 10,000	908	176	19	116	25	22
Geographic division						
New England	143	19	13	9	2	22
Mid-Atlantic	244	28	12	28	3	11
East North-Central	279	62	22	84	9	11
West North-Central	139	53	38	109	24	22
South Atlantic	180	34	19	104	29	28
East South-Central	90	15	17	69	11	16
West South-Central	150	36	24	85	8	9
Mountain	79	28	35	47	12	26
Pacific Coast	136	33	24	26	4	15

a For a definition of terms, please see "Inside the *Year Book*," xii–xiv.

b Six cities and three counties did not specify their population size on the response card, so the numbers in the population breakdowns do not add up to the total number of respondents.

In a cover letter describing the purpose of the survey, jurisdictions were advised that the survey was a follow-up to ones that were conducted in 2002 and 2006. Included with the letter was a postage-paid postal survey card containing the following definition of a development impact fee:

> A development impact fee is a monetary payment, predetermined by a formula adopted by the governmental unit, levied to fund large-scale, *off-site improvements, public facilities and services* that are necessary to serve new development adequately.[46]

That statement was followed by three questions. The first asked the respondent to indicate, based on the definition provided on the card, whether the jurisdiction imposes a development impact fee. Table 3–4 provides a summary of the responses to this survey question as well as to the same question on the two earlier surveys. If the jurisdiction imposes an impact fee, the respondent was asked to select from among eight intervals, beginning with "Prior to 1950" and ending with "2010 to Present," to identify when the impact fee was first imposed. As shown in Figure 3–1, only four cities and counties have adopted impact fees since 2010, while the majority of impact fee users adopted impact regulations between 1980 and 2009. The third question asked the respondent to indicate the jurisdiction's population on the basis of four defined population groups; responses to this question also appear in Table 3–3.

Findings

The results of the 2011 survey confirm that local government use of development impact fees is increasing. However, the proportions currently reporting that they impose such fees—40% of cities and 17% of counties—are only slightly higher than those reported in 2006 (39% and 10%, respectively). Thus, while these results indicate an upward trend, they also suggest some constraint. As noted earlier, only four respondent local governments have adopted impact fees since 2010.

One explanation for the very moderate expansion of impact fee use over the past five years could be the current economic climate. Some historically strong impact fee states now have large numbers of homes in foreclosure. This situation, especially in high-growth states, has led to a reduction in, if not complete cessation of, the construction of new homes as well as of commercial and industrial development. To the extent that impact fee policies are considered a disincentive to development, local governments in such a climate tend to forgo them in order to provide a more development-friendly environment.

In Florida (a strong impact fee state), for example, eight counties that had impact fee policies in 2009 had suspended them by 2010, possibly as a result of the economy.[47] This is in keeping with the trend that began to emerge in late 2000 as local governments adjusted to declining economic conditions. Some Florida legislators sought a moratorium on new or increased impact fees in 2009 but were unsuccessful in that attempt. Legislators in Arizona, on the other hand, succeeded in enacting a moratorium on both new and increased impact fees in 2010.[48] Arizona subsequently revised its statutes to narrow the legal applicability of impact fees to only "necessary public services," causing some cities to reevaluate existing impact fee ordinances.[49] As an alternative to waiving impact fees during the economic downturn, other local governments are deferring the imposition of impact fees until a certificate of occupancy is issued, thereby reducing the developer's carrying cost.

Given the current economic environment, one source suggests that future legislative battles involving impact fees will likely revolve around preserving impact fee authority rather than expanding it.[50] Conservative legislators may seize this opportunity to impose moratoria on, if not completely repeal, impact fee policies, as they sought to do in Florida and Arizona. Should such efforts succeed, the question will then be a matter of who will bear the burden of growth. Continued strain on their general funds may cause local governments to look elsewhere for revenue sources to fill the gap. One possible outcome might be that the cost of new and expanded infrastructure and services related to growth is once again shouldered by local residents. Another might be that such infrastructure improvements and services are simply not provided at all.

A second explanation for the slowed expansion of impact fee use is that cities facing build-out may have eliminated impact fees because they fear such fees make them less economically competitive with cities that do not impose impact fees. Plano, Texas, in 2009 "ended its practice of charging developers impact fees, a tool that growing cities use to pay for new infrastructure."[51] Plano had initiated impact fees for water and sewer in 1990 when the growth rate of the city began to explode; however, as Plano reaches build-out, impact fees have become less attractive. Plano decision makers hope that the absence of impact fees will improve the homebuilding and

Table 3-4 Local Government Impact Fee Use, by Geographic Division, 2011, 2006, and 2002

	Cities									Counties								
	2011 survey respondents			2006 survey respondents			2002 survey respondents			2011 survey respondents			2006 survey respondents			2002 survey respondents		
		Impose impact fees			Impose impact fees			Impose impact fees			Impose impact fees			Impose impact fees			Impose impact fees	
Classification	Total (A)	No.	% of (A)	Total (B)	No.	% of (B)	Total (C)	No.	% of (C)	Total (A)	No.	% of (A)	Total (B)	No.	% of (B)	Total (C)	No.	% of (C)
Total	308[a]	124	40	292[a]	114	39	388	101	26	102[a]	17	17	124[a]	12	10	143[a]	10	7
Population																		
50,000 or more	30	20	67	26	15	58	34	15	44	37	13	35	35	7	20	45	7	16
25,000–49,999	34	13	38	38	20	53	30	9	30	16	2	13	23	2	9	29	0	0
10,000–24,999	62	28	45	45	35	48	92	27	29	21	1	5	35	3	9	41	3	7
Less than 10,000	176	62	35	35	44	31	232	50	22	25	1	4	24	0	0	27	0	0
Geographic division																		
New England	19	6	32	24	2	8	48	9	19[b]	2	0	0	1	0	0	2	0	0
Mid-Atlantic	28	10	36	45	15	33	13	0	0	3	0	0	4	0	0	3	0	0
East North-Central	62	20	32	55	17	31	87	20	23	9	0	0	18	1	6	20	1	5
West North-Central	53	14	26	40	8	20	56	11	20	24	0	0	40	3	8	39	1	3
South Atlantic	34	16	47	40	19	48	41	11	27	29	8	28	26	4	15	26	4	15
East South-Central	15	2	13	13	3	23	24	2	8	11	3	27	11	1	9	12	0	0
West South-Central	36	15	42	27	8	30	57	12	21	8	0	0	12	0	0	16	0	0
Mountain	28	15	54	18	15	83	33	18	55	12	5	42	8	2	25	15	1	7
Pacific Coast	33	26	79	30	27	90	29	18	62	4	1	25	4	1	25	10	3	30

a Six cities and 3 counties in 2011, 13 cities and 7 counties in 2006, and 1 county in 2002 did not specify their population size on the response card, so the numbers in the population breakdowns do not add up to the total number of respondents.

b Incorrectly reported as 18% in *The Municipal Year Book 2002* because of a rounding error.

Figure 3-1 Year Impact Fee Was Adopted

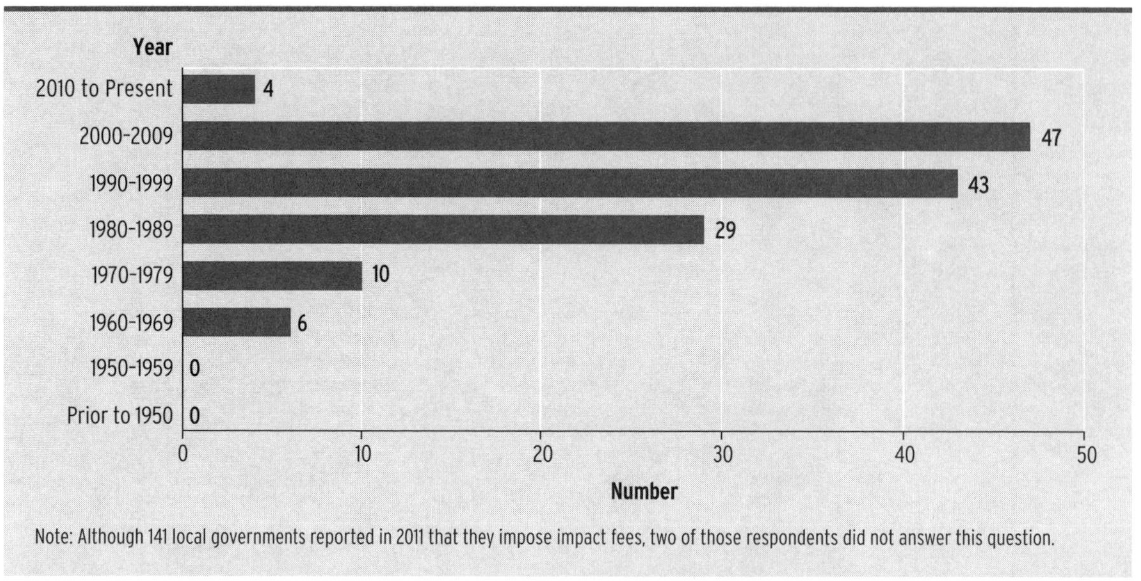

Note: Although 141 local governments reported in 2011 that they impose impact fees, two of those respondents did not answer this question.

development climate in the community. Other cities have also raised the build-out issue and are debating how impact fees should be handled when build-out is imminent.

Conclusion

The results of the recent survey suggest that impact fee use continues to be a viable revenue source for local governments that seek funds to provide infrastructure and services necessary to accommodate community growth. That the results indicate only a slight expansion of impact fee use since the 2006 survey might be explained by the current economic climate, which has been marked by large numbers of foreclosed homes and a decline in homebuilding and development activity. Future or expanded use of impact fees will likely be closely tied to an improved economy and a rebound in homebuilding. Until that happens, however, the current economic climate appears to favor those who oppose impact fee policies and seek their repeal. As noted above, Clancy Mullen of Duncan Associates suggests that the new Arizona act cited above, which restricts impact fee use for only "'necessary public service,'" will no longer allow impact fees to be used "for general government facilities, solid waste facilities, library buildings larger than 10,000 square feet and library books or equipment, fire and police administrative and training buildings and aircraft, parks larger than 30 acres and community centers larger than 3,000 square feet."[52] Unfortunately, such legislation, which may be enacted to grant relief to the development community, may ironically end up adversely affecting the adequacy of local government infrastructure and services and thus discouraging future growth and development.

Notes

1. See, e.g., Robinson & Cole LLP, *Growth Management Fact Book*, 2nd ed. (Washington, D.C.: Robinson & Cole LLP and National Association of Realtors, 2008), 21, realtor.org/smart_growth.nsf/docfiles/growth_management_book.pdf/$FILE/growth_management_book.pdf; Arthur C. Nelson, ed., *Development Impact Fees: Policy Rationale, Practice, Theory, and Issues* (Washington, D.C.: Planners Press, 1988); and Gregory Burge and Keith Ihlanfeldt, "The Effects of Impact Fees on Multifamily Housing Construction," *Journal of Regional Science* 46, no. 1 (2006): 5–23, localgov.fsu.edu/publication_files/Burge_Ihlanfeldt_multi.pdf.
2. Nelson, *Development Impact Fees* (see note 1).
3. James E. Frank and Paul B. Downing, "Patterns of Impact Fee Use," in Nelson, *Development Impact Fees*, 3–21.
4. Thomas Snyder and Michael Stegman, with contributions by David H. Moreau, *Paying for Growth: Using Development Fees to Finance Infrastructure* (Washington, D.C.: Urban Land Institute, 1986).
5. Frank and Downing, "Patterns of Impact Fee Use," 3.
6. Ibid.
7. Ibid., 5.
8. Ibid., 5, 10.
9. Gus Bauman and William H. Ethier, "Development Exactions and Impact Fees: A Survey of American Practices," *Law and Contemporary Problems* 50 (Winter 1987): 51–68, esp. 57, 59–60.
10. ICMA, "Capital Finance—1985," survey (Spring 1985), as cited in Maureen G. Valente and Clayton Carlisle,

"Developer Financing: Impact Fees and Negotiated Exactions," *MIS Report* (ICMA) 20, no. 4 (1988): 3.

11. Dan Hoxworth and Charles Spindler, "Impact Fees: Issues and Case Studies," *MIS Report* (ICMA) 23, no. 12 (1991): 3.
12. Frank and Downing, "Patterns of Impact Fee Use," 17.
13. Ibid.
14. Robinson & Cole LLP, *Growth Management Fact Book*, 21.
15. See, e.g., Benjamin Chintz, "Communities Turn to Impact Fees to Pay for Growth," *National Association of Counties—County News* 21 (June 1989): 11; and Snyder and Stegman, *Paying for Growth*.
16. Arthur C. Nelson and Mitch Moody, "Paying for Prosperity: Impact Fees and Job Growth," discussion paper (Washington, D.C.: Brookings Institution Center on Urban and Metropolitan Policy, 2003), vii, brookings .edu/reports/2003/06metropolitanpolicy_nelson.aspx.
17. Bauman and Ethier, "Development Exactions and Impact Fees," 56.
18. According to Julian Conrad Juergensmeyer and Thomas E. Roberts in their book *Land Use Planning and Control Law* (St. Paul, Minn.: West Group, 1998), states may allow impact fees to be used within the development as well, but this is not at all the prevailing practice; consequently, for the purposes of this research, we have not expanded the accepted definition of impact fees to include intradevelopment.
19. Robinson & Cole LLP, *Growth Management Fact Book*, 21.
20. Clancy Mullen, "State Impact Fee Enabling Acts" (Austin, Tex.: Duncan Associates, September 2011), impactfees .com/publications%20pdf/state_enabling_acts.pdf.
21. City of Loveland, Colo., Ordinance No. 3045, approved January 3, 1984.
22. Duncan Associates offers an excellent source of information on development impact fees, state enabling acts, and comparison of fee structures of communities that impose impact fees. This information can be found at impactfees.com and impactfees.com/publications%20 pdf/2010_survey.pdf.
23. Mullen, "State Impact Fee Enabling Acts," 1.
24. Ibid.
25. Ibid., 2.
26. Ibid.
27. Robinson & Cole LLP, *Growth Management Fact Book*, 22.
28. Juergensmeyer and Roberts, *Land Use Planning and Control Law*.
29. U.S. Department of Housing and Urban Development (HUD), Office of Policy Development and Research, *Impact Fees and Housing Affordability: A Guidebook for Practitioners* (Washington, D.C.: HUD, June 2008), huduser.org/portal/publications/impactfees.pdf.
30. Ibid., "Appendix D: Proportionate Share Impact Fees and Housing Affordability," 104.
31. Burge and Ihlanfeldt, "Effects of Impact Fees on Multifamily Housing Construction," 6.
32. Benjamin F. Bobo, *Locked In and Locked Out: The Impact of Urban Land Use Policy and Market Forces on African Americans* (Westport, Conn.: Praeger, 2001).
33. Keith Ihlanfeldt and Timothy Shaughnessy, "An Empirical Investigation of the Effects of Impact Fees on Housing and Land Markets," *Regional Science and Urban Economics* 34, no. 6 (2004): 639–661, impactfees.com/ publications%20pdf/Ihlanfeldt_Shaughnessy.pdf.
34. Ibid., 640.
35. Ibid.
36. Ibid., 641.
37. Ibid., 642.
38. Ibid., 659.
39. Larry D. Singell and Jane H. Lillydahl, "An Empirical Examination of the Effect of Impact Fees on the Housing Market," *Land Economics* 66, no. 1 (1990): 82–92.
40. Ihlanfeldt and Shaughnessy, "Empirical Investigation of the Effects of Impact Fees," 645.
41. John Yinger, "The Incidence of Development Fees and Special Assessments," *National Tax Journal* 51 (1998): 23–41, as cited in Ihlanfeldt and Shaughnessy, "Empirical Investigation of the Effects of Impact Fees," 645.
42. Ihlanfeldt and Shaughnessy, "Empirical Investigation of the Effects of Impact Fees," 656.
43. Burge and Ihlanfeldt, "Effects of Impact Fees on Multifamily Housing Construction," 6.
44. Ibid.
45. Ibid., 17–18.
46. Brian W. Blaesser and Christine M. Kentopp, "Impact Fees: The 'Second Generation,'" *Journal of Urban and Contemporary Law* 38 (Fall 1990): 55–113; and Robinson & Cole LLP, *Growth Management Fact Book*, 21.
47. Clancy Mullen, *National Impact Fee Survey: 2010* (Austin, Tex.: Duncan Associates, November 2, 2010), 4, impactfees.com/publications%20pdf/2010_survey.pdf.
48. Mullen, "State Impact Fee Enabling Acts."
49. Parker Leavitt. "Study of Impact Fee Legal Effects May Cost Gilbert up to $150K," *Arizona Republic*, September 2, 2011, azcentral.com/community/gilbert/articles/2011 /09/02/20110902gilbert-impact-legal-fee-costs.html.
50. Mullen, *National Impact Fee Survey: 2010.*
51. Theodore Kim, "Plano Ends Impact Fees on Developers in Hopes of Attracting Projects," *Dallas Morning News*, August 28, 2009, impactfees.com/pdfs_all/plano%20 ends%20impact%20fees.pdf.
52. Mullen, "State Impact Fee Enabling Acts," 10.

4

Local Government Employee Health Insurance Programs, 2011

Evelina R. Moulder
ICMA

Jeffrey Amell
CIGNA HealthCare

Providing health care coverage to support a healthy workforce makes sense for all local governments, just as it does for all employers. To assess the range of options of health care coverage as well as of health and wellness programs, ICMA partnered with CIGNA HealthCare to conduct a national survey.

Survey Methodology and Response

The survey instrument was developed by ICMA and CIGNA, with CIGNA providing the content expertise. CIGNA's participation reflects its commitment as an ICMA Strategic Partner to helping local governments meet the challenges of providing effective, efficient health care to employees. Preliminary results of the survey were presented in a session at the 2011 ICMA Annual Conference in Milwaukee, Wisconsin, and CIGNA prepared a summary report. Subsequently, close to 350 additional local governments responded to the survey. The survey results described in this article include those additional surveys.

The overall survey response rate was 26% (Table 4–1). The city response rate was 30%, and the county response rate was 20% (not shown). The percentages responding in each population group show some fluctuation but to a lesser extent than is seen among the geographic divisions. Noticeably higher percentages of respondents are from council-manager cities and council-administrator counties than from localities with other forms of government.

SELECTED FINDINGS

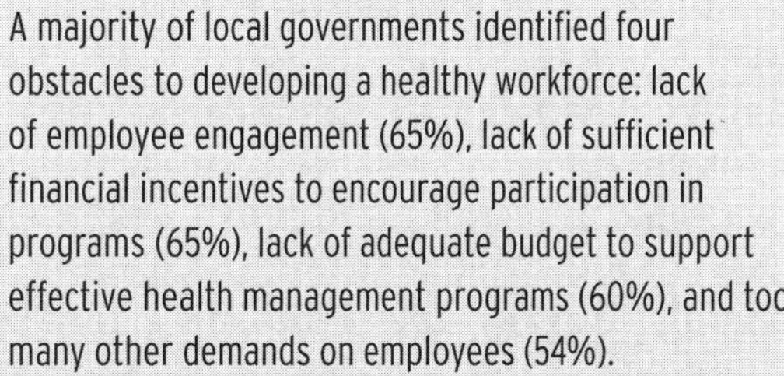

A majority of local governments identified four obstacles to developing a healthy workforce: lack of employee engagement (65%), lack of sufficient financial incentives to encourage participation in programs (65%), lack of adequate budget to support effective health management programs (60%), and too many other demands on employees (54%).

Cost of employee health care benefits is one of the top concerns reported by local governments, and survey results show that many local governments would benefit from putting programs in place to address workforce health care concerns.

Local examples provided by survey respondents indicate that local governments of all sizes can develop creative approaches to wellness and health improvement programs for their city/county employees and dependents.

Of the 1,472 local governments responding to the survey, all but 5 reported that they offer health insurance to employees. The five that do not are counties: two in Missouri, one in Vermont, one in Kentucky, and one in Tennessee. These are all relatively small counties—under 50,000 in population. Respondents that do not offer health insurance were told that they did not need to continue and complete the rest of the survey.

Table 4-1 Survey Response

Classification	No. of municipalities/ counties[a] surveyed (A)	Respondents	
		No.	% of (A)
Total	5,664	1,472	26
Population group			
Over 1,000,000	37	16	43
500,000-1,000,000	86	21	24
250,000-499,999	146	42	29
100,000-249,999	454	139	31
50,000-99,999	802	206	26
25,000-49,999	1,424	356	25
10,000-24,999	2,715	692	26
Geographic division			
New England	395	72	18
Mid-Atlantic	685	109	16
East North-Central	1,085	286	26
West North-Central	588	184	31
South Atlantic	869	304	35
East South-Central	492	83	17
West South-Central	637	124	20
Mountain	322	119	37
Pacific Coast	591	191	32
Metro status			
Central	996	361	36
Suburban	2,471	589	24
Independent	2,197	380	17
Form of government			
Mayor-council	1,195	228	19
Council-manager	1,883	714	38
Commission	70	20	29
Town meeting	106	20	19
Representative town meeting	46	9	20
County commission	1,214	173	14
Council-administrator (manager)	735	232	32
Council-elected executive	415	76	18

a For a definition of terms, please see "Inside the *Year Book*," xii-xiv.

Top Three General Operating Concerns

Overall budgets and employee health care costs are the top two concerns identified by the highest percentages of respondents (Figure 4–1). However, there is variation among population groups and geographic divisions. (Throughout the rest of this article, breakdowns by population group and geographic division are not shown except in the case of Table 4–3.)

Among local governments with a population over 1,000,000, all respondents (100%) identified the budget as one of their top three concerns. After the budget, service delivery was identified by 71%, funding employee/retiree pensions by 43%, and both employee health care costs and unfunded mandates by 36%. Among the rest of the population groups, the budget was again identified by the highest percentage (at least 92%) as one of their top three concerns, followed by employee health care costs. Service delivery was reported to be the next biggest concern for all population groups except the smallest (10,000–24,999), which instead identified unfunded mandates.

As the population decreases, the percentages reporting the budget as one of the top three concerns generally *decrease* while the percentages reporting health care as one of the top three concerns generally *increase*. This suggests that smaller localities are struggling more with health care costs than larger ones are.

The percentages identifying the budget as one of the top three concerns range from 92% to 100% (8 percentage points) among population groups and from 83% to 98% among the geographic divisions (15 percentage points). Health care costs, on the other hand, were identified as one of the top three concerns by 36% to 76% among the population groups, but by 47% to 88% among the geographic divisions and by local governments in all nine of those divisions.

Among the "other" concerns that respondents identified are economic development, infrastructure, reduced revenues from states, and capital improvements.

Workforce Health Concerns and Programs

Respondents reported that their top three workplace health concerns are obesity (66%), stress management (36%), and fitness (35%) (Figure 4–2). Although there are interesting variations among population groups and geographic divisions, for each of these concerns the percentage of local governments reporting that they have a program in place is also among the highest (see Table 4–2). Heart disease and smoking are the concerns reported by the fourth highest percentage of respondents (31% and 30%, respectively).

In contrast to the overall findings, localities with a population of 500,000 or above reported their top three concerns to be obesity, diabetes, and heart

Figure 4-1 Top Three Operating Concerns

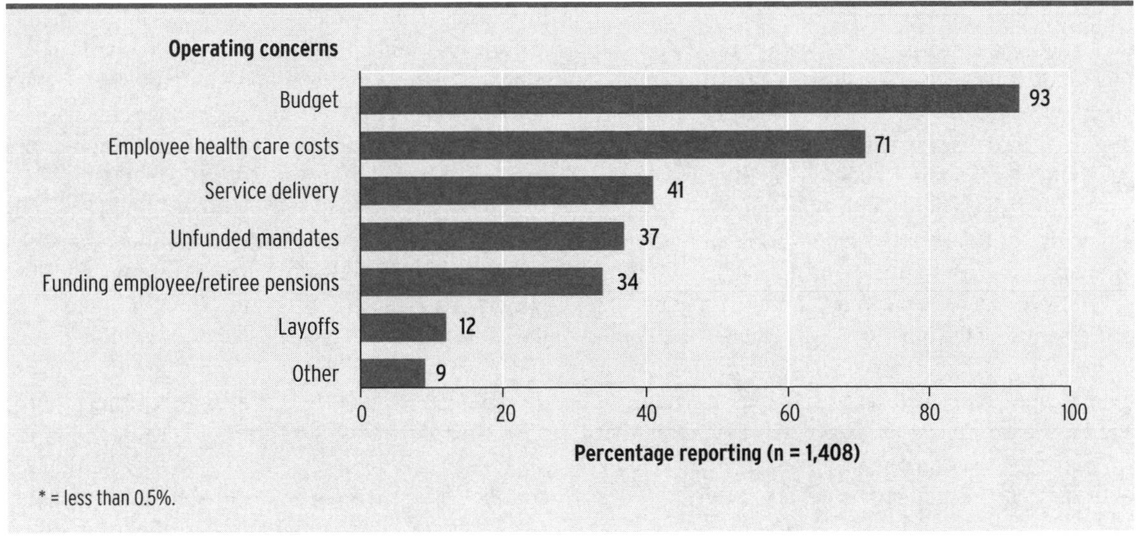

Figure 4-2 Top Three Workplace Health Concerns

Workplace health concerns

Obesity/weight management 66

Stress management 36

Fitness 35

Heart disease 31

Smoking 30

Disease prevention 27

Diabetes 25

Cancer 17

Nutrition 15

Depression 8

Low back pain 7

Asthma 1

At-risk pregnancy *

Other 1

0 10 20 30 40 50 60 70

Percentage reporting (n = 960)

* = Less than 0.5%.

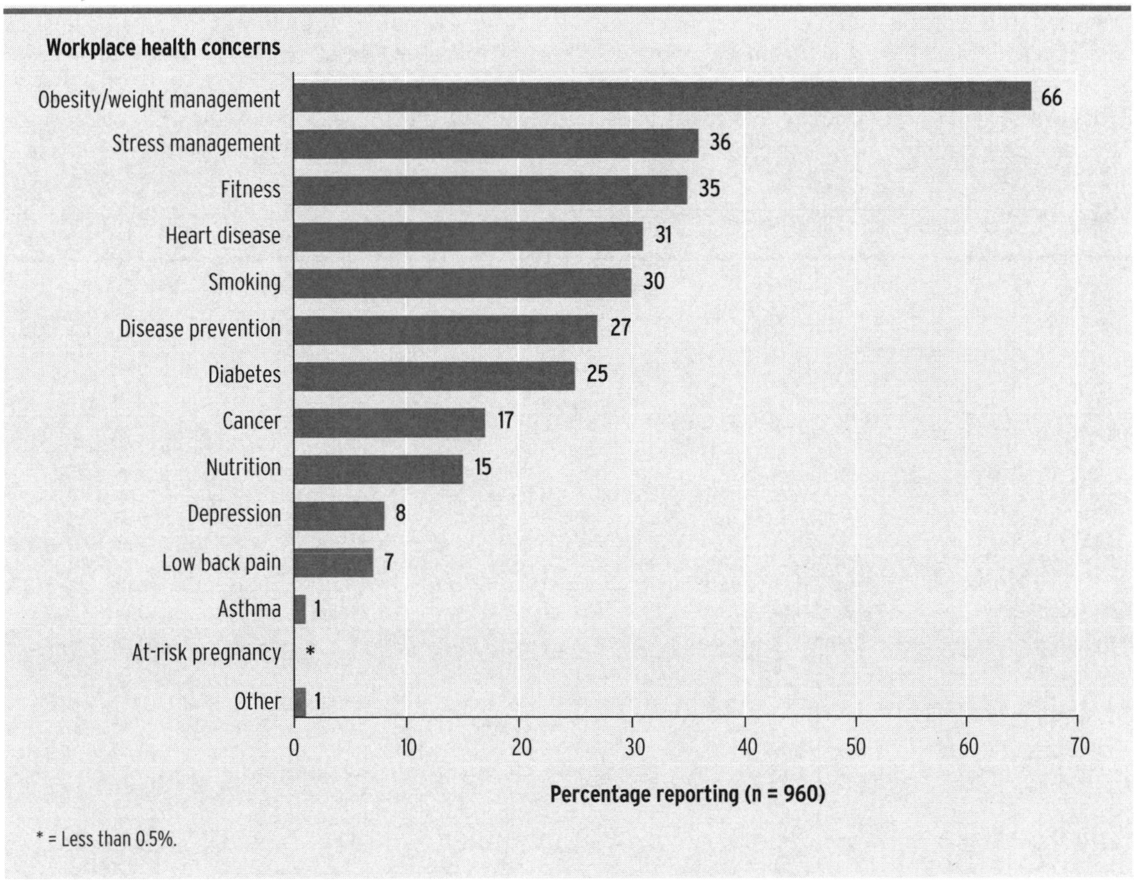

disease. Localities with populations of 250,000–499,999 identified obesity, diabetes, and smoking, followed closely by heart disease and stress management. For the smallest population group covered in the survey (10,000–24,999), the top three concerns are obesity, stress management, and fitness.

Local governments are making efforts to address their concerns. Programs to mitigate obesity, increase fitness, or manage stress may have a positive impact on other health concerns, such as diabetes and heart disease. The survey collected information on local government programs to address specific workforce health concerns. Although the only concern for which a majority of local governments (51%) are currently offering a program is fitness, the data show that local governments are considering offering programs to address most of the other concerns (Table 4–2). Population and geography appear to be factors in determining whether local governments offer programs to address health concerns; in general, it is clear that smaller local governments are less likely to offer some of these programs than are larger ones.

Obesity/Weight Management

With obesity linked to some of the most serious and costly health concerns, such as heart disease and diabetes, and with approximately one-third of the nation's adult population and 17% of its children obese,[1] helping local government employees address weight management problems provides multiple benefits. Overall, 43% of local governments have a program in place to address obesity/weight management and 21% are considering such a program, but 36% reported that they neither have nor are considering implementing an obesity/weight management program.

The highest percentages of local governments reporting an obesity/weight management program are in the larger populations groups—notably, a majority of those with populations of 50,000 and above. Among the 36% that reported not having a program and not considering one, the percentages increase as population size decreases, reaching 45% among the smallest local governments (10,000–24,999).

Local governments in the Mountain, South Atlantic, and New England divisions show the highest percentages (52%–56%) reporting an obesity/weight management program. However, those in the Mid-Atlantic, Pacific Coast, West North-Central, and East South-Central divisions show the highest percentages (46%–49%) reporting that they do *not* have such a program and are not considering offering one. According to the Centers for Disease Control and Prevention (CDC), states in some of these divisions have among the highest rates of obesity in the country.[2]

Stress Management

With stress linked to physical problems as well as to absenteeism,[3] stress management can offer broad benefits. However, almost identical percentages of local governments reported either having a stress management program (41%) or not having one and

Table 4–2 Workforce Health Concerns

		Local government		
Concern	No. reporting (A)	Offers a program now (% of A)	Does not have a program but is considering one (% of A)	Does not have a program and is not considering one (% of A)
Obesity/weight management	1,288	43	21	36
Stress management	1,243	41	19	40
Smoking	1,277	44	20	37
Nutrition	1,236	38	20	42
Disease prevention	1,218	37	18	45
At-risk pregnancy	1,116	18	9	74
Asthma	1,179	21	12	68
Diabetes	1,230	34	17	50
Depression	1,190	34	15	51
Heart disease	1,215	32	19	48
Low back pain	1,179	23	16	61
Cancer	1,168	22	15	63
Fitness	1,295	51	21	28

not planning to introduce one (40%), while close to 20% reported that they are considering offering one.

A majority of all local governments with a population of 50,000 or over reported that they offer stress management programs, and the percentages generally increase among the larger localities. Conversely, the smaller the population group, the larger the percentage of localities reporting that they do not offer such a program and are not considering doing so.

Local governments in the Mountain (57%), South Atlantic (48%), and Pacific Coast (46%) divisions show the highest percentages reporting that they offer a stress management program. Local governments in the East South-Central division show the lowest percentage (28%) reporting that they offer such a program and the highest percentage (58%) reporting that they are not considering offering one.

Smoking

Forty-four percent of local governments reported that they offer a smoking cessation program now and 20% are considering offering one. These programs have proven to be rewarding for a number of the local governments that participated in this survey. In addition, several local governments reported offering financial incentives for employees to stop smoking as well as imposing a surcharge on those who continue to smoke.

As with other programs covered in this report, smoking programs are in place in a majority of local governments with a population of 50,000 or over. However, slightly over 40% of those with a population under 50,000 have no smoking cessation program in place and are not considering instituting one.

Among the geographic divisions, the Mid-Atlantic and Pacific Coast local governments show the highest percentages reporting that they do not offer a smoking program and are not considering doing so (53% and 51%, respectively). Statistics from the CDC show that the states in the East South-Central division—Alabama, Kentucky, Mississippi, and Tennessee—have among the highest rates of smoking in the nation,[4] yet 41% of the local governments in that division also reported that they do not have a smoking cessation program and are not planning to implement one. By contrast, the South Atlantic states, which also have high rates of smoking, especially West Virginia and North and South Carolina, have next to the highest percentage (54%) of local governments that reported offering a smoking cessation program; the highest percentage (55%) to do so is in the Mountain division, in which two states—Utah and Arizona—have among the lowest rates of smoking in the nation.

Nutrition

Closely related to controlling obesity, healthy nutrition programs generally follow the pattern of obesity programs among local governments. Overall, only 38% of local governments reported offering a nutrition program, a percentage lower than the overall percentage of those reporting an obesity/weight management program.

Among local governments with populations of 100,000 and over, a majority reported that they offer a nutrition program; among local governments in the smallest population group (10,000–24,999), that percentage drops to 30% while 50% reported that they are not considering such a program. Geographically, the highest percentage of local governments offering a nutrition program is in the Mountain division (49%), followed closely by the South Atlantic division (48%); the lowest percentage is in the East South-Central division (28%), followed by the East North-Central division (29%). Local governments in the East South-Central division also show the highest percentage indicating that they are not considering offering a nutrition program (53%).

Disease Prevention

Disease prevention programs are offered by 37% of local governments overall, whereas 45% reported that they are not considering offering such a program. An open-ended question later in the survey asked about successful practices that have been undertaken, and many local governments reported implementing wellness programs, which may have a disease prevention component not reflected in the answers to the specific question about a disease prevention program.

A majority of those local governments with a population of 250,000 or above reported offering a disease prevention program; among localities with a population of 10,000–24,999, the percentage drops to 29%. Local governments in the Pacific Coast (28%), New England (27%), and Mid-Atlantic (26%) divisions show the lowest percentages reporting a disease prevention program; those in the Mountain (53%), West South-Central (48%), and South Atlantic (47%) divisions show the highest percentages.

At-Risk Pregnancy

Overall, at-risk pregnancy programs are offered by the smallest percentage (18%) of local governments. It is unclear whether this is because the programs are offered through other resources once a doctor has determined that a woman is at risk, but at-risk pregnancy is another program area that could have a significant impact on the health and well-being of local government employees as well as on their health care costs.

Approximately 42% of the local governments with a population of 250,000 or above reported that they offer a program for at-risk pregnancy, but the other population groups show much smaller percentages reporting such a program—from 28% down to only 11% for the smallest population group (10,000–24,999). The highest percentage of local governments in any of the geographic divisions offering an at-risk pregnancy program is in the Mountain division at 31%. A majority in each geographic division reported no such program and no plans to offer one.

Asthma

With the rate of asthma increasing in both adults and children,[5] prevention and management are of utmost importance. However, survey results show that only 21% of local governments have a program to address asthma concerns whereas 68% reported that they neither have such a program nor are considering one.

A majority of local governments (62%) with a population over 1,000,000 have an asthma program in place. The percentages reporting an asthma program decrease as population decreases, while the percentages reporting not offering such a program increase as population increases. The local governments in the Mountain division show the highest percentage reporting an asthma program (31%), followed by those in the South Atlantic (25%) and West South-Central (24%) divisions. Although states in the New England, Mid-Atlantic, and Pacific Coast divisions show high rates of asthma (see Figure 4-3), they also show the highest percentages of local governments reporting that they do not have an asthma program and are not considering one.

Diabetes

Diabetes patients—especially those with Type 1 diabetes—often experience related health concerns, such as peripheral neuropathy and vision problems. Approximately one-third of local governments reported offering a diabetes program, compared with 50% that do not and are not considering offering one.

Figure 4-3 Adults with Asthma in the United States, by State, 2009

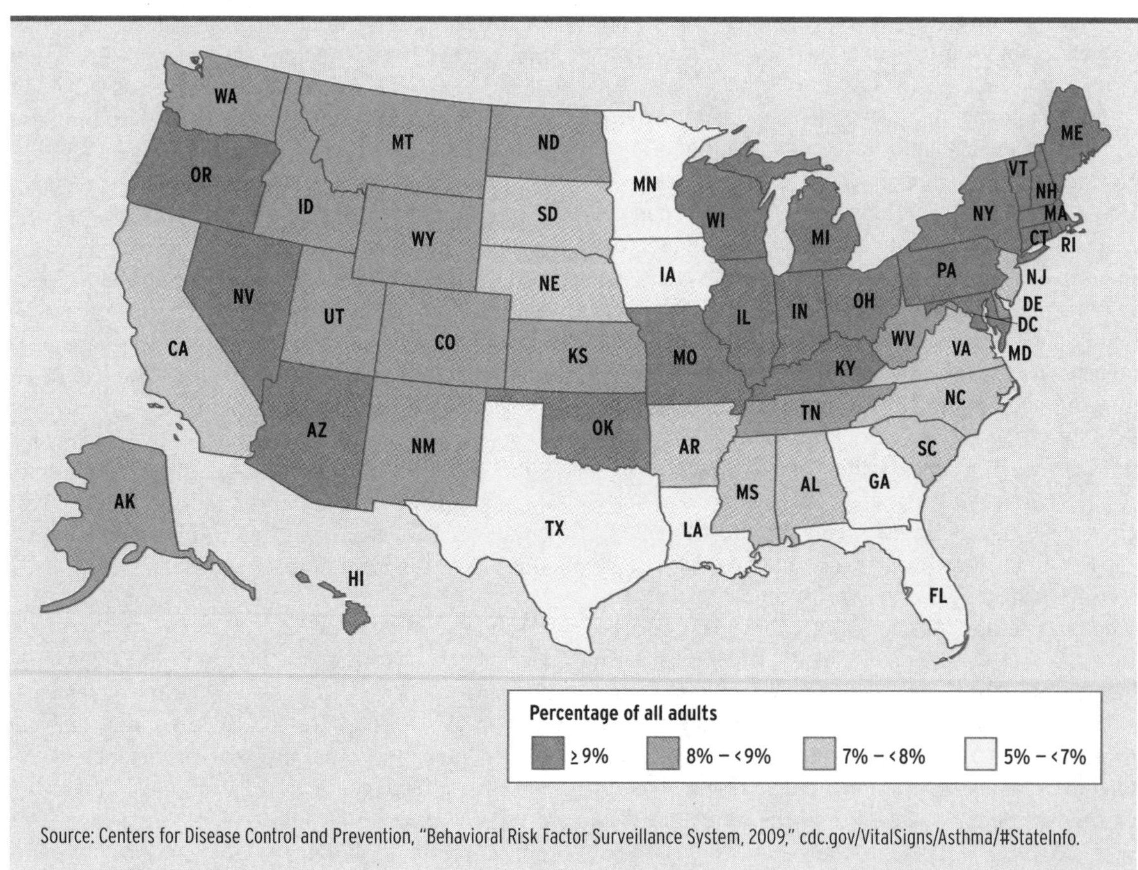

Source: Centers for Disease Control and Prevention, "Behavioral Risk Factor Surveillance System, 2009," cdc.gov/VitalSigns/Asthma/#StateInfo.

Close to 80% of the largest local governments (over 1,000,000) offer a diabetes program, as do approximately 70% of those with a population of 500,000–1,000,000. The percentages then drop consistently. Among the smallest localities (10,000–24,999), 61% reported that they do not offer and are not considering offering such a program. Geographically, the highest percentages of local governments offering a diabetes program are in the South Atlantic (45%), Mountain (44%), and West South-Central (40%) divisions. The South Atlantic division shows high rates of diabetes according to the CDC,[6] so it is promising that its local governments have implemented diabetes programs.

Depression

Overall, approximately one-third of local governments reported offering a program to address depression. This includes 67% of local governments in the population group 500,000–1,000,000, the highest percentage reporting such a program. But the majority of local governments do not offer any programs to address depression, nor do they plan to do so.

Of the local governments that reported offering a program for depression, 48% are in the Mountain division, followed by 38% in the South Atlantic and 37% in the Pacific Coast divisions; the lowest percentage (23%) is in the New England division.

Heart Disease

Although the CDC reports that heart disease is the number one cause of death in the United States, 48% of local governments reported that they do not offer a program to address heart disease and are not considering one. However, the survey had asked about a number of programs that, if in place, would address heart disease, so it may be that even though 48% do not have a program specific to heart disease, they have weight management, stress management, fitness, and other programs that can help reduce the risk factors for heart disease.

Among the population groups, a majority of local governments with a population of 250,000 or above offer a heart disease program, whereas a majority of those under 50,000 do not and are not considering doing so. Three geographic divisions—Mountain (44%), West South-Central (40%), and South Atlantic (40%)—show the highest percentages reporting a heart disease program; the rest show between 22% and 32% offering a program.

Low Back Pain

Overall, 23% of local governments reported offering a program to address low back pain while 61% indicated they do not offer and are not considering offering such a program.

Cancer

Twenty-two percent of local governments overall reported offering a program to address cancer as a health concern, and 15% are considering offering such a plan. As with some of the other programs listed, even though local governments might not self-identify as having a specific program to address cancer, they may offer mammograms in a wellness program, have a smoking cessation program, or promote other initiatives that can help to reduce the risk of cancer.

Generally, the percentages of local governments offering a cancer program decrease with population. Localities in the 500,000–1,000,000 and 250,000–499,999 population groups show 45% and 42%, respectively; the percentages then drop to a low of 18% in the 10,000–24,999 population group. Among the geographic divisions, the highest percentage offering a program to address cancer is for localities in the Mountain division (33%).

Fitness

A slight majority (51%) of local governments overall reported that they offer a fitness program, while 21% reported that they are considering one.

A majority in all population groups except those under 50,000 offer a fitness program. Among the geographic divisions, however, the percentages tell a somewhat different story. In six of the nine divisions, a majority of local governments offer a fitness program, but in the Mid-Atlantic (37%), East North-Central (45%), and East South-Central (42%) divisions, the majority of localities do not.

Geographic Differences in Program Offerings

If the availability of programs to address workforce health concerns is examined by geographic division, it becomes apparent that the Mountain division shows the highest percentages of local governments reporting each type of program except diabetes. The highest percentage of local governments that reported offering a diabetes program is the South Atlantic division, which reported the second highest percentages of programs offered in 10 other health concern areas. On the other hand, local governments in the Mid-Atlantic and Pacific Coast divisions show the highest overall percentages of local governments that do not offer and do not plan to offer programs that could have a significant impact on improving the health of their workforce (Table 4–3).

Table 4-3 Local Governments That Neither Have nor Plan to Have a Specific Type of Health Care Program, by Geographic Division

	Type of program						
Geographic division	Obesity/weight management (%)	Stress management (%)	Smoking (%)	Fitness (%)	Asthma (%)	Diabetes (%)	Heart disease (%)
New England	23	35	31	20	74	51	46
Mid-Atlantic	49	48	53	40	79	67	59
East North-Central	37	43	37	31	68	55	54
West North-Central	46	48	45	35	71	58	58
South Atlantic	23	31	21	18	57	32	33
East South-Central	46	58	41	38	69	52	49
West South-Central	31	44	37	27	67	39	37
Mountain	24	27	26	18	58	36	34
Pacific Coast	48	38	51	32	76	65	64

Note: Bases for percentages are not shown because not every respondent reported on each of the various types of programs.

Health Insurance Benefits

With employee health care costs identified by respondents as one of their top three general operating concerns, it is interesting to learn about the benefits provided and to whom.

Current Employee Plans

All local governments with a population of 100,000 or above reported offering medical insurance, and some also reported offering high-deductible plans with a health reimbursement account (HRA) or a health savings account (HSA). A few communities offer high-deductible plans with an HRA or an HSA instead of traditional medical insurance. Plans with a high deductible are reported by the smallest percentage of respondents (Table 4-4); the highest percentages offering such plans are localities in the 500,000–1,000,000 population group (43%) and those in the Mountain division (40%).

Table 4-4 Current Employee Plans

Current employee plans	Percentage of local governments with plan (n = 1,467)
Medical insurance	99
High-deductible plan with a health reimbursement account (HRA) or health savings account (HSA)	25
Pharmacy	92
Dental	92
Employee assistance plan (EAP)	75
Disability insurance	74
Other	26

Among the rest of the options, there are no discernable patterns to the percentages reported except with employee assistance plans (EAPs) and disability insurance programs, in which the percentages offering these plans clearly decrease as population size decreases. Noticeably higher percentages of local governments in the Pacific Coast division reported offering both EAPs and disability insurance (96% and 92%, respectively) than are seen in the other geographic divisions, while localities in the East South-Central division show the lowest percentages reporting these plans (44% and 59%, respectively).

Under "other," the highest proportions of respondents providing information wrote in eye care and life insurance. Other responses included AFLAC, cancer policies, flexible spending accounts, and gym memberships.

Early Retiree (Pre-65) Plans

Overall, 74% of local governments offer medical insurance for early retirees (Table 4-5). Among localities with a population below 250,000, the percentages reporting these plans decrease with population size. Geographically, the highest percentage offering medical insurance for early retirees is in New England (90%) and the lowest is in the Mountain division (54%).

Under "other," vision plans were listed by the highest proportion of those responding.

Table 4-5 Early (Pre-65) Retiree Plans

Early retiree plans	Percentage of local governments with plan (n = 1,467)
Medical insurance	74
Stand-alone health reimbursement account (HRA)	4
Pharmacy	54
Dental	42
Other	13

Retiree (65 and Older) Plans

Fifty-six percent of local governments reported that they offer retirees the same plan as they offer current employees (Table 4–6). Although the percentages generally decrease from 81% in local governments with a population over 1,000,000 to 51% in localities of 10,000–24,999, this appears to be the case in a majority of local governments in each population group.

Table 4-6 Retiree Plans

Retiree plans	Percentage of local governments with plan (n = 1,467)
Same medical insurance as active employees	56
Medicare Advantage	9
Medicare Supplement	25
Stand-alone health reimbursement account (HRA) (without medical plan)	2
Medicare Part D Pharmacy	12
Other pharmacy plan	12
Dental	24
Other (specify)	10

For all the other plans, the percentages again generally decrease with population size, with the most noticeable drops between localities of 500,000–1,000,000 and 250,000–499,999 and between localities of 250,000–499,999 and 100,000–249,999. Among the geographic divisions, the New England localities generally show the highest percentages offering each plan.

Paying for Health Insurance

Local governments often pay a sizeable portion of the health insurance premium, not only for current employees but also for retirees. Sometimes these arrangements are contractual and difficult to renegotiate.

Current Employees

Because the percentages reading across Table 4–7 add up to more than 100%, it appears that some local governments have more than one payment method in place. It may be that some local governments pay the full premium for a few employees, while in the majority of cases, employees contribute to the cost of the premium. Only three local governments (0.2%) reported that the employee pays the full premium cost.

It is interesting to note that the percentages of local governments reporting that they pay the full cost of the premium *increase* as population size decreases, with 33% of local governments with a population under 50,000 paying the full premium compared with none of the 16 local governments with a population over 1,000,000 and only 2 of those with a population of 500,000–1,000,000. (Because 2 of the 21 local governments in the 500,000–1,000,000 population group also reported that they share the cost of the premium with employees, there are probably legacy arrangements that explain what seems to be a contradiction.)

Table 4-7 Paying for Health Insurance

Employee/retiree groups	No. reporting (A)	Premium is fully paid by local government (% of A)	Employer and employee share cost of premium (% of A)	Premium is available at cost paid solely by employee or retiree (% of A)	Local government does not offer health insurance (% of A)
Current employees	1,424	29	75	*	0
Early retirees	1,309	12	33	37	21
Retirees	1,332	10	22	35	36

Note: Local governments that do not offer health insurance were identified at the beginning of the survey and instructed not to complete the rest of the survey. Among those that did complete the survey, some local governments appear to have more than one payment method in place as the percentages exceed 100%.

* = Less than 0.5%.

When the responses are arrayed by geographic division, there is more variation. The highest percentage of local governments that reported cost sharing with employees (97%) is in the New England division, whereas the highest percentage reporting that they pay the entire premium cost (55%) is in the West South-Central division.

Early (Pre-65 Retirees)

A plurality of local governments (37%) reported that the early retiree is solely responsible for the cost of health insurance, followed by 33% reporting that the cost of the premium is shared (Table 4-7). Although only 12% overall reported that the local government pays the full cost of premiums for early retirees, the percentages are higher in the smaller population groups than in the larger groups.

Among the geographic divisions, 33% of local governments in the Mid-Atlantic division indicated that premiums for early retirees are paid in full by the local government. One could hypothesize that it is because 98% of the Mid-Atlantic localities also reported that some of their employees are union members; however, 100% of New England localities reported union employees while only 6% of them reported that they pay the full cost of premiums for early retirees (not shown). Contractual agreements and date of negotiation could explain these differences.

The cost of premiums is paid solely by early retirees in 60% of local governments in the West North-Central division; this is the highest percentage reporting that arrangement.

Retirees 65 and Older

Thirty-six percent of local governments reported that they do not offer health insurance for retirees 65 and older, 35% reported that it is available at cost for retirees, 22% share the cost with retirees, and only 10% indicated that retiree health insurance premiums are fully paid by the local government (Table 4-7). Among those 10%, the percentages are somewhat higher in the smaller local governments (25,000–99,999). The percentage is also noticeably higher in the Mid-Atlantic division (30%) than in the Pacific Coast division, which registered the next highest percentage (13%).

The percentage reporting that the premium is shared between employer and employee is higher among the larger localities and in the New England division (57%). Forty-three percent of local governments with a population over 1,000,000 reported that the premium is shared while 57% reported that health insurance is available at full cost to the retiree. Between 26% and 42% of local governments under 500,000 in population do not offer retiree health insurance. On a geographic basis, the highest percentages reporting that they do not offer retiree health insurance are in the Mountain (56%), East South-Central (54%), and West North-Central (51%) divisions, compared with only 10% of New England local governments.

Planning for the Future

Respondents who do not currently offer an HSA were asked whether their local governments might consider offering selected health plans in the near future. In general, the results show that none of the plans listed in Table 4-8 is likely to be considered by more than a few local governments in the next one to two years.

Respondents were also asked about the current availability or future likelihood of other product offerings (see Table 4-9). Notable distinctions in their responses by population group and geographic division are not shown but are described below.

- *On-site clinics, health coaches, and online options.* Five of the sixteen (31%) local governments with a population over 1,000,000 show that they currently have an on-site clinic. This option may be more cost-effective for larger localities than for smaller ones unless a few could share a clinic. The next highest percentage reporting an on-site clinic is in the 250,000–499,999 population group (23%). The percentages reporting that they are considering an on-site clinic are higher among larger local governments, reported by 55% in the 500,000–1,000,000 population group. Local governments in the South Atlantic division show the highest percentage (18%) reporting an on-site clinic and also the highest percentage reporting that one is being considered (25%).
- *Health adviser/coach.* A majority of local governments with a population of 500,000 and greater reported offering health advisers/coaches. Smaller local governments are less likely to offer health coaches and are generally less likely to consider offering them.

Table 4-8 Health Plan Offerings under Consideration

Plan offerings	Percentage considering offering in the next 1-2 years (n = 1,467)
High-deductible medical plan with a health savings account (HSA)	17
Health reimbursement account (HRA) with an underlying medical plan	12
Stand-alone HRA without a medical plan	2

Table 4-9 Other Product Offerings

Product offerings	No. reporting (A)	Offer now (% of A)	Are considering (% of A)	Do not offer/are not considering (% of A)
On-site clinic	1,327	9	12	79
Health adviser/coach	1,341	27	12	61
Online health plan enrollment for employees	1,359	29	26	46
Online tools to help employees select a plan and allow them to enroll online	1,344	27	26	47
Online tools to allow employees to customize their benefits	1,334	11	18	72

- *Online health plan enrollment for employees.* A slight majority of local governments are now offering or considering online health plan enrollment. A majority of those with a population of 250,000 or above currently offer online enrollment; the percentages then drop among the smaller population groups, which were most likely to report not considering this option. Local governments in the South Atlantic division show the highest percentage (37%) offering online enrollment, followed by those in the Mountain division (35%) and the Pacific Coast (34%). The geographic divisions that show the highest percentages offering online enrollment also show the highest percentages that are considering offering it, surpassed only by the West South-Central division at 32%.
- *Online tools to help employees select a plan and allow them to enroll online.* Not surprisingly, the responses to this question are similar to those regarding online enrollment. A majority of local governments with a population of 500,000 and over offer such tools now; smaller local governments are less likely to be considering them. Approximately one-third of local governments in the South Atlantic (33%), Mountain (35%), and Pacific Coast (39%) offer these options now.
- *Online tools to allow employees to customize their benefits.* It seems as though it may be the "customization" feature that has resulted in lower percentages offering this option than offering the other online tools. In general, a sizeable majority of local governments do not offer this option now and are not considering it.

Obstacles to Developing a Healthy Workforce

Respondents were asked to identify the top five obstacles that limit their local government's success in developing a healthy workforce. To be included in the analysis, respondents had to identify exactly five obstacles. In general, regardless of population size or geographic division, results show that local governments in each population group and geographic division identified the same five obstacles (Table 4–10):

1. Lack of employee engagement
2. Lack of sufficient financial incentives to encourage participation in programs
3. Lack of adequate budget to support effective health management programs
4. Too many other demands on employees/not enough time
5. Lack of organizational structure/staffing to support it.

Table 4-10 Obstacles to Developing a Healthy Workforce

Obstacle	Percentage reporting (n = 1,295)
Lack of employee engagement	65
Lack of sufficient financial incentives to encourage participation in programs	65
Lack of adequate budget to support effective health management programs	60
Too many other demands on employees/not enough time	54
Lack of organization structure/staffing to support it	41
Lack of adequate internal staff	36
Lack of evidence about which practices work best	23
Lack of appropriate tools to be successful	22
Lack of senior management support	11
Lack of actionable data/information from insurance administrator	10
Poor or inadequate communication of health management programs	10
Poor coordination with partners (e.g., other benefit carriers/providers)	8
None of the above	7
Other	5

There are, however, a few exceptions among the population groups. The local governments in the over-1,000,000 population group identified "lack of evidence about which practices work best" and "lack of adequate internal staff" to the same extent that they did "lack of organization structure/staffing to support it" (31% each).

Although 95 local governments checked "none of the above," not one of them described any obstacles under "other." Among those that did provide information under "other," there do not seem to be strong patterns in the responses. Some localities wrote in lack of employee motivation, understanding, etc., which could be subsumed under "lack of employee engagement." A few identified a lack of political support, and one wrote in "the food industry." One commented that employees distrust the "health police."

Approaches to Reducing Health Care Expenses/Claims Costs

Presented with a list of 22 approaches, respondents were asked which approaches their local governments are taking to reduce health care expenses and claims costs. Highlights of the findings are presented below and shown by total respondents in Table 4–11.

In all but one category, the majority of local governments reported that they have taken no action to reduce health care expenses/claims costs, and in some instances, that may not be a bad thing. For example, 77% have not *delayed or canceled new health care and productivity program offerings* and do not intend to do so. Similarly, 72% have not *delayed or canceled plan design enhancements* and do not intend to do so. If the enhancements include a coach or a disease management program, that would be a positive outcome. Also positive is that 89% have not *reduced or eliminated health promotion programs* and do not plan to do so.

In other areas, local governments have been more active than inactive. Forty-two percent of local governments have *significantly increased pharmacy copays, deductibles, or coinsurance,* and 23% have not yet done so but plan to in the next two years. A majority in each population group has already taken or will be taking action in this regard; among the geographic divisions, however, a majority in the Pacific Coast and East South-Central divisions have neither taken nor plan to take action.

Nearly three-quarters of local governments reported taking no action to *replace ineffective medical plan administrators* and not planning to do so, but that may be because their plan administrators are—or are perceived to be—effective.

A majority of local governments (61%) have taken or plan to take action to have employees *complete a health risk appraisal,* although the percentages decrease among the smaller population groups. In the Mid-Atlantic, Pacific Coast, and East South-Central divisions, a majority indicated that they have taken no action in this area and plan no action.

Seventy-six percent reported that they have taken no action to *consolidate or integrate health and disability/absence management programs under a single vendor* and have no plans to do so.

A slight majority of local governments have *increased the share of health costs paid by employees,* and of those that have not yet acted, 29% plan to do so in the next two years. The East South-Central division localities show the highest percentage that have neither taken action nor plan to act in this regard.

Less than a majority of local governments (47%) have instituted *biometric screening to determine risk for certain diseases* or expect to do so in the near future. Where it has been taken, this approach seems more prevalent in larger local governments (populations of 250,000 and over) and in the South Atlantic, West North-Central, West-South Central, and Mountain divisions.

Close to a majority (48%) have taken or plan to take action to *create incentives to encourage employees to use high-quality/low-cost hospitals and physicians.* The exceptions are the smallest local governments (10,000–24,999) and localities in the Mid-Atlantic, East South-Central, West North-Central, and Pacific Coast divisions, in which a majority have taken no action and plan no action.

Results show that a majority do not plan to *reduce plan options* or have participants *complete an adult health exam.* Neither have they already taken action on these measures.

Maintaining blood pressure, maintaining BMI within target levels, and *maintaining cholesterol levels* all show a surprising majority of local governments taking no action and planning no action despite the health risks that high blood pressure, high body mass index, and high cholesterol present. Seventeen percent that have not yet acted in these areas reported that they plan to do so in the next two years, and while this is a higher percentage than those that have already taken action, it is still low. But there does appear to be movement among some of the larger local governments, as localities with a population of 50,000 or above show above-average percentages reporting plans to implement these approaches in the next two years. Among the geographic divisions, only in the South Atlantic and Mountain divisions are the percentages (23% each) well above the 17% average planning to take action in the next two years.

Table 4-11 Other Approaches to Reducing Health Care Costs

Concern	No. reporting (A)	Already taken action: Expect to take further action (% of A)	Already taken action: No further action expected (% of A)	No action taken: Expect to take action in the next two years (% of A)	No action taken: No action expected (% of A)
Reward/penalize based on smoker, tobacco-use status	1,352	7	6	23	64
Significantly increase pharmacy co-pays, deductibles, or coinsurance	1,373	22	20	23	36
Replace ineffective medical plan administrators	1,340	6	11	9	74
Completion of a health risk appraisal	1,356	25	14	22	40
Consolidate/Integrate health and disability/ absence management programs with single vendor or health plan	1,349	6	8	11	76
Increase the share of total health care costs paid by employees (e.g., co-pays, premiums, deductibles, etc.)	1,397	36	15	29	20
Delay/cancel adding new health and productivity program offerings	1,356	7	6	10	77
Delay/cancel benefit plan design enhancements	1,342	8	7	13	72
Completion of a biometric screening (determines risk for certain diseases including diabetes, heart disease, asthma and other medical conditions)	1,364	21	9	17	53
Reduce/eliminate health promotion programs	1,357	3	4	4	89
Create incentives to encourage employees to use high-quality/low-cost hospitals and physicians	1,363	14	11	23	52
Reduce plan options	1,368	11	11	18	60
Completion of an adult health exam	1,357	17	11	15	58
Maintaining BMI (body mass index) within target levels	1,351	10	7	17	67
Maintenance of blood pressure within target levels	1,362	11	8	17	64
Maintenance of cholesterol level within target levels	1,358	11	8	17	64
Actively managing vendor-prepared communication/education on health care costs and living a healthier lifestyle	1,365	28	15	19	39
Participation in disease management program for those with chronic condition	1,367	25	13	15	47
Audit or review eligibility or enrollment in your health plan	1,365	31	15	15	39
Integrate employee participation in wellness programs with health plan data	1,362	27	10	27	36
Compliance with evidence-based course of treatment	1,334	10	6	16	68
Provide different disability benefit levels based on health management program participation	1,348	2	2	11	86

Note: Percentages may exceed 10% because of rounding.

Survey results show that 62% of respondents either already *actively manage vendor-prepared communication/education on health care costs and a healthier lifestyle* or plan to do so.

As for having employees *participate in disease management programs,* a slight majority (53%) of respondents reported that they have already taken action, expect to take further action, or plan to take action in the next two years. Especially encouraging is the fact that above-average percentages of smaller localities reported that they plan to implement this approach in the next two years.

Over 60% have *audited or reviewed eligibility or enrollment in the health plan* or plan to do so in the next two years.

In all population groups, as in the overall results, a majority of respondents (64%) have already *integrated employee participation in wellness programs with health plan data* or are planning to do so in the next two years. This same level of consistency is not seen in the geographic divisions, however: a majority in the Pacific Coast and Mid-Atlantic divisions reported that they have taken no action in this regard and do not plan to do so.

Compliance with an evidence-based course of treatment is an approach that has been taken or is planned by a majority of respondents in the three largest population groups. Among each of the smaller population groups, the percentages of those reporting such action drop. Overall, however, more than two-thirds of local governments neither have taken action nor plan to. None of the geographic divisions shows a majority reporting compliance with evidence-based treatment.

Providing different disability benefit levels based on health management program participation is shown to have next to the highest overall percentage (86%) of respondents reporting that they have neither taken nor plan to take action.

Impact of Federal Health Care Reform Legislation

Respondents were asked about their understanding of federal health care reform legislation. While 30% reported that they understand the legislation (not shown) regardless of whether they have assessed its impact, results show that population size is clearly influential in this regard. A majority of those responding from localities with a population of 250,000 or above reported that they completely understand the legislation. Some of the smaller local governments reported that they have heard about it but do not understand it, and a majority of local governments under 250,000 in population reported partially understanding.

The percentages differ among the geographic divisions, with a majority in each division showing that they partially understand the legislation but need to learn more. Unlike the population groups in which a majority of the larger jurisdictions reported that they completely understand the legislation, none of the geographic divisions shows a majority of local governments reporting complete understanding, regardless of whether they have assessed its impact.

Changes to Health Care Benefits

As for making changes to health care benefits, virtually all local governments (98%) reported that they either will wait and see how the health reform legislation unfolds before making changes or are not currently planning to make any changes (not shown). Only 4% have conducted an analysis to quantify the costs and benefits of moving their employees to a state health insurance exchange, which will be offered in 2014. Among those local governments that have not conducted such an analysis, only 14% reported that they planned to do so in 2011.

Sources of Assistance for Understanding Health Care Reform

A majority of survey respondents indicated that webinars, e-newsletters, and publications would help them gain a better understanding of the health care reform legislation. Among smaller local governments, slightly smaller percentages reported an interest in webinars, but the distributions among population groups were otherwise relatively even.

Thirty percent of respondents selected presentations at the ICMA annual conference. This response probably reflects, in part, the role of the person completing the survey. Typically, for example, human resource directors and benefit administrators do not attend ICMA conferences, but the chief administrative officers (CAOs) and assistant CAOs do, so the percentage may be underreported simply because someone else completed the survey.

Decision Making

With health care costs making up a significant percentage of the budget for employee benefits, it is important to have a rigorous process in place for selecting a health insurance provider.

Development of a Proposal for Health Insurance

When asked how they develop a request for proposal for health insurance, 61% of local governments overall reported using a broker or consultant for guidance (not shown), as did a majority of all local governments with a population under 1,000,000 and 50% or more of localities in each geographic division.

Another option—committee involvement in preparing the specifications—was reported by 13% overall, with the highest percentage (21%) reported by local governments in the West North-Central division. And a third option—use of a general procurement form/process—was reported by 16% of local governments overall, with the highest percentage (25%) reported in the East South-Central division.

Regarding the comments written in as "other," many do not relate directly to an "other" option.

Rather, local governments mentioned that they are self-insured, are part of a consortium, or belong to a state plan. The other options reported are a combination of committee and broker, human resources, etc.

Final Decision in Selecting Health Plans

Fifty-nine percent of local governments reported that the elected official/governing body is responsible for making the final decision on health plans (not shown). Presumably that decision is based on recommendations presented by the CAO and staff, who have thoroughly evaluated the available options. The next highest percentage (21%) reported that the city or county manager makes the final decision, and the results show that this is the case more often in smaller local governments; only 3 out of 78 local governments with a population of 250,000 or above reported that the city or county manager makes the final decision.

It is interesting to note that the highest percentage by far reporting that the elected official makes the final decision—82%—is in the East South-Central division, which is also one of the divisions that has generally shown the least use of innovative wellness programs, disease management, or employee incentives for lowering health care costs.

Thirteen local governments—all under 100,000 in population—reported that the union makes the final decision. Of these respondents, eight provided the percentage of employees who are union members, and six of those eight reported that percentage to be 90–95%.

Purchasing

Although 62% of local governments reported purchasing health insurance plans independently (not shown), there are interesting variations among the population groups and geographic divisions. Approximately 80% of those with a population of 500,000 or over purchase plans independently, as do 73% of those with a population of 250,000–499,999—both well above the average. The local governments reporting in the Mid-Atlantic and Pacific Coast divisions are least likely to purchase plans independently.

The two groups under 50,000 in population show the highest percentages (20% and 25%) reporting that they purchase insurance through an association/coalition. This is also the case for local governments in the New England and Mid-Atlantic divisions (nearly 40%), while the Pacific Coast local governments show fairly even percentages reporting purchasing through a coalition or the state plan (26% and 21%, respectively). Twenty-one percent of respondents in the Mid-Atlantic division also reported purchasing through a state plan; among them are 16 local governments in New Jersey and 6 in New York, but none in Pennsylvania.

Funding

A slight majority of local governments reported that they are fully insured (not shown), with the employer paying a premium to an insurance company, which pays employee claims. Among larger local governments, a higher percentage is self-funded (55% of those with a population of 500,000–1,000,000 and 53% of those with a population of over 1,000,000 or of 100,000–249,999). Forty percent of those with a population of 500,000–1,000,000 reported that they are funded by a combination of self-insurance and full insurance, compared with an overall 18% reporting this funding mechanism.

Geographically, a majority in all but three divisions reported being fully insured (including 73% of Pacific Coast divisions), and even among the other three, a plurality reported full insurance.

Considerations in Selecting a Carrier

By far the top three considerations in selecting a carrier are price/co-payments and other charges (88%), network access and discounts (77%), and ability to improve employee health through wellness programs (43%) (Figure 4-4). For the latter two considerations, the distribution of responses varies by population group and geographic division.

Best Practices

Local governments were asked to share what they consider to be the most successful or most promising programs they have implemented in the last three years. Numerous local governments cited their wellness programs and some on-site clinics. A few of the other highlights are described below:

- **Boulder, Colorado:** The city added employer-paid blood/health screening as part of its wellness plan.
- **Larimer County, Colorado:** The county opened an employee health clinic in 2010 and anticipates saving $2 million over the first three years.
- **Palm Beach Gardens, Florida:** The city reported that by changing from fully insured to self-funded, it has saved $1.5 million. It is also ensuring the same level of benefits for all employees and gradually increasing the employee share for dependent coverage.
- **Plantation, Florida:** The city established an on-site health and wellness care center for employees,

Figure 4-4 Top Three Considerations in Selecting a Carrier

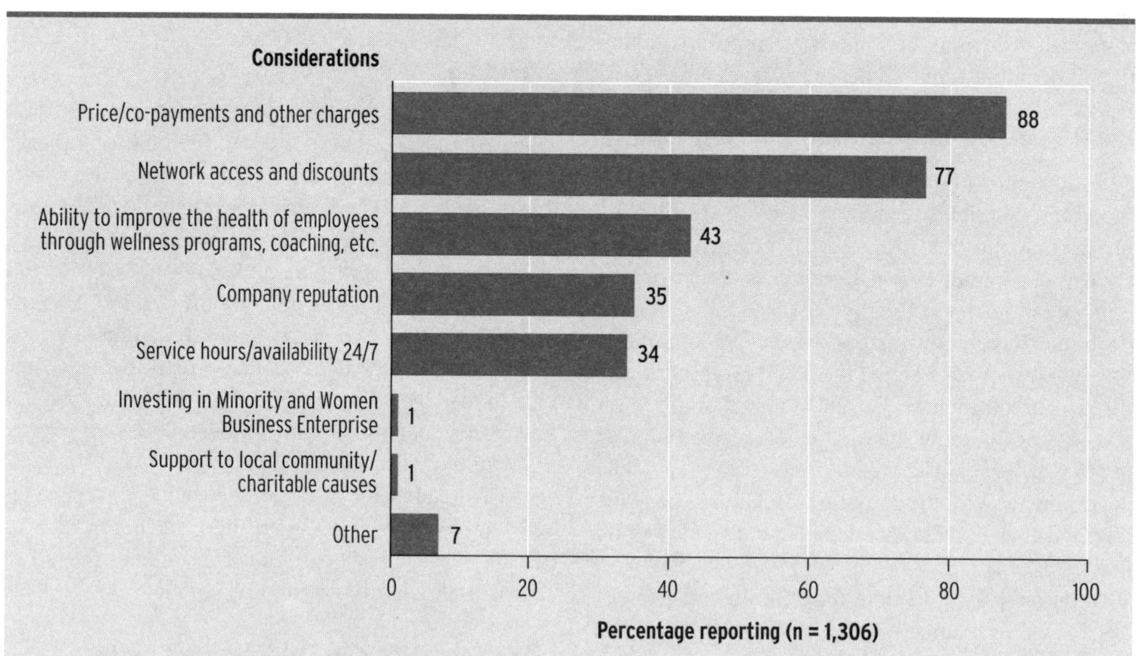

spouses, and dependents age 15 years and older. In the first nine months, the city saved over $100,000 and absenteeism was reduced by 10%.

- **LaGrange, Georgia:** The city offers financial incentives to employees for managing blood pressure, diabetes, smoking, and cholesterol.
- **Chesterfield, Missouri:** The city held a "biggest loser" contest, which has been a huge success. Employees lost weight, some are off medications, and overall health risks have been reduced.
- **Bozeman, Montana:** The Montana League of Cities and Towns participates in a self-insured health insurance pool for league members through the Montana Municipal Interlocal Authority.
- **McMinnville, Tennessee:** Employees receive discounts on their premiums if they are nonsmokers and have an annual physical. Because most employees have not had a physical in years, this benefit encourages them to be proactive.
- **Mesquite, Texas:** An on-site clinic and pharmacy has resulted in savings of $3 million over four years.

Summary

Local governments of all sizes have taken steps to improve employee health and reduce the cost of health care benefits. At the same time, the results show that there is more that local governments can do to meet the challenges. Some of the programs that are most advantageous to local governments in the long run may require some initial costs; however, the long-term benefits are significant.

Notes

1. Centers for Disease Control and Prevention (CDC), "Overweight and Obesity: U.S. Obesity Trends" (July 21, 2011), cdc.gov/obesity/data/trends.html.
2. Ibid.
3. Buck Consultants, "Toll of Stress Impacting Health Care Costs, Absenteeism and Workplace Safety, According to Survey," Wolters Kluwer, employmentlawdaily.com/index.php/news/toll-of-stress-impacting-health-care-costs-absenteeism-and-workplace-safety-according-to-survey (accessed November 19, 2011).
4. CDC, Behavioral Risk Factor Surveillance System, apps.nccd.cdc.gov/StateSystem/ComparisonReport/ComparisonReports.aspx#ReportDetail.
5. CDC, "Vital Signs: Asthma in the US," cdc.gov/VitalSigns/Asthma/?utm_source = AdWords&utm_medium = CPC&utm_campaign = VitalSigns.
6. CDC, "Diabetes Data and Trends: County Level Estimates of Diagnosed Diabetes—U.S. Maps," apps.nccd.cdc.gov/DDT_STRS2/NationalDiabetesPrevalenceEstimates.aspx?mode = DBT.

5

Off the Beaten Path: Sustainability Activities in Small Towns and Rural Municipalities

George C. Homsy
Cornell University

Mildred Warner
Cornell University

Judging by the amount of attention they receive in the media,[1] sustainability policies should be spreading like wildfire throughout cities and towns across the country. But the reality is otherwise. Despite the hype, the adoption of environmental sustainability policies by municipalities has been growing—but slowly.[2]

One reason for the misperception could be the publicity generated by such initiatives as green roofs in Chicago, PlaNYC in New York City, and Boston's greenhouse gas reduction plan. But these big-city achievements paint an incomplete picture of sustainability policy making. Although most people in the United States live in metropolitan regions that surround big cities, in 2010 just over half resided in separate, smaller jurisdictions with fewer than 25,000 people. Only 23 cities have populations of 500,000 or more, and another 215 have populations between 100,000 and 499,999.[3] And because small cities and rural towns face capacity challenges, both fiscal and technical, that are not faced by larger places with higher levels of civic activism[4] and more progressive political environments,[5] they have been slower to adopt sustainability policies.

SELECTED FINDINGS

The most common sustainability policies among small municipalities are recycling, building energy audits, and walkability. The most sustainable small communities also upgrade or retrofit buildings for higher energy efficiency as well as purchase hybrid vehicles for municipal fleets.

The average adoption rating for small communities (under 25,000 in population) is about one-quarter that for large municipalities (populations of 1,000,000 and above) (14% vs. 55%). Local technical and fiscal capacities are limiting factors.

Small municipalities that form citizen advisory commissions adopt sustainability policies at a higher rate than those that do not (19% vs. 13%). It may be one way for smaller municipalities to overcome capacity constraints.

This project was funded, in part, through the Cornell University Population Program and a Lowell Harriss Dissertation Fellowship from the Lincoln Institute of Land Policy.

In 2010, in conjunction with Arizona State University, ICMA conducted a national survey of municipalities to gauge their adoption of sustainability policy actions. The survey was described in detail by James Svara in "The Early Stage of Local Government Action to Promote Sustainability," published in ICMA's *Municipal Year Book 2011*.[6] Almost 2,200 municipalities and counties responded to that survey, and the resultant data yielded important findings about overall trends in the sustainability movement as well as insights into the use of policy priorities, component strategies, and specific activities.

But again, national trends do not necessarily reflect trends that prevail among distinct demographic categories. This article provides further analysis of the data from the 2010 sustainability survey but focuses primarily on smaller communities, which we define as cities, villages, and towns with fewer than 25,000 residents.

Context and Methodology

The ICMA sustainability survey provided respondents with a list of 109 specific sustainability activities organized into 12 issue areas, and it asked them to identify which activities their communities have undertaken. The issue areas are presented below, followed by the number of activities listed in each area:

- Greenhouse gas and air quality, 8
- Water quality, 5
- Recycling and solid waste, 12
- Energy use in transportation and exterior lighting, 9
- Energy use in buildings, 15
- Alternative energy generation, 5
- Transportation alternatives, 8
- Transportation improvements, 12
- Building and land use regulations, 14
- Land conservation and development rights, 5
- Social inclusion, 8
- Local production and green purchasing, 8.

In this article, we examine two aspects of local sustainability: the municipality and the particular sustainability policy or activity that might be adopted. For each community Svara used in his analysis, we assigned a sustainability adoption rating, which is the average percentage of activities enacted by that municipality in each of the 12 issue areas. By capturing both the amount and the breadth of activity,[7] this methodology ensures that a local government that focuses on only one issue area does not get a deceptively high score, which could result if all the individual policies undertaken were simply averaged. When we talk about the prevalence of particular activities among municipalities, we simply average the percentage of governments using that specific activity.

For our analysis, we examined the responses of 1,844 municipalities (i.e., the original respondent base excluding counties), including 1,355 localities that fit our definition of a small municipality. Table 5-1 shows the population and metro status distribution of respondents.

For the discussions that relate to income, homeownership, educational attainment, and proportion of college students, we used averages from the *American Community Survey 2005–2009*, grouped communities into quintiles from low to high, and then averaged the sustainability policy adoption ratings for each group.

Table 5-1 Survey Response by Population Size and Metro Status

Classification	No. respondents
Total	1,844
Population	
Large municipalities (≥25,000)	
Over 100,000	101
50,000-99,999	153
25,000-49,999	236
Total	490
Small municipalities (<25,000)	
10,000-24,999	507
5,000-9,999	446
2,500-4,999	402
Total	1,355
Metro status	
Large municipalities (≥25,000)	
Core city[a]	162
Suburban[b]	279
Independent (rural)	48
Total	489
Small municipalities (<25,000)	
Core city[a]	12
Suburban[b]	810
Independent (rural)	533
Total	1,355

Source: 2010 Census Summary File 1 prepared by the U.S. Census Bureau, 2011.

a Core cities contain at least 10,000 people.

b Municipalities within a metropolitan or micropolitan statistical area, but not the core city.

Small Communities and Sustainability

To gain a more rigorous and comprehensive understanding of sustainability policy making in smaller communities, we can start by asking the following questions:

- How does the adoption of sustainability policies in large cities differ from that in small ones?
- What effect do local fiscal and technical capacities have on the adoption of sustainability policies in smaller communities?
- What role do growth pressures play in the instigation of policy adoption in smaller communities?
- What socioeconomic factors correlate with increased policy adoption by smaller communities?

Population

As shown in Figure 5-1, small communities are less likely to adopt sustainability policies than are large ones: the average adoption rating for municipalities with populations under 25,000 is 14.2%, whereas the average rating for municipalities with populations of 1,000,000 and above is 55.2%. In the smallest localities (those with fewer than 5,000 residents), the policy adoption rating is about one-third that of municipalities with populations between 100,000 and 999,999.

The top 20 activities undertaken by small municipalities are listed in Table 5-2. The top four activities are typical among both large and small communities. The two most common are residential and municipal recycling: three-quarters of survey respondents from small municipalities have residential recycling programs, and two-thirds of them collect recyclable material in their municipal offices. The adoption rates for recycling may actually be even higher, however: the survey asked specifically if *all three* recyclable items (i.e., paper, plastics, *and* glass) were collected, so communities that collect only one or two of these items would not have been counted.

One noteworthy difference between large and small communities is the greater support among the latter for recycling programs for commercial properties. For communities under 25,000 in population, this strategy ranks tenth; for those with populations of 25,000–99,999, it drops to 19th place, and for communities with populations of 100,000–999,999, it is the 33rd most prevalent strategy. One possible explanation for this difference is that smaller communities may be less attractive to private service providers, so they may need to meet the needs of local businesses by providing their own recycling services.

Figure 5-1 Average Sustainability Adoption Ratings, by Population

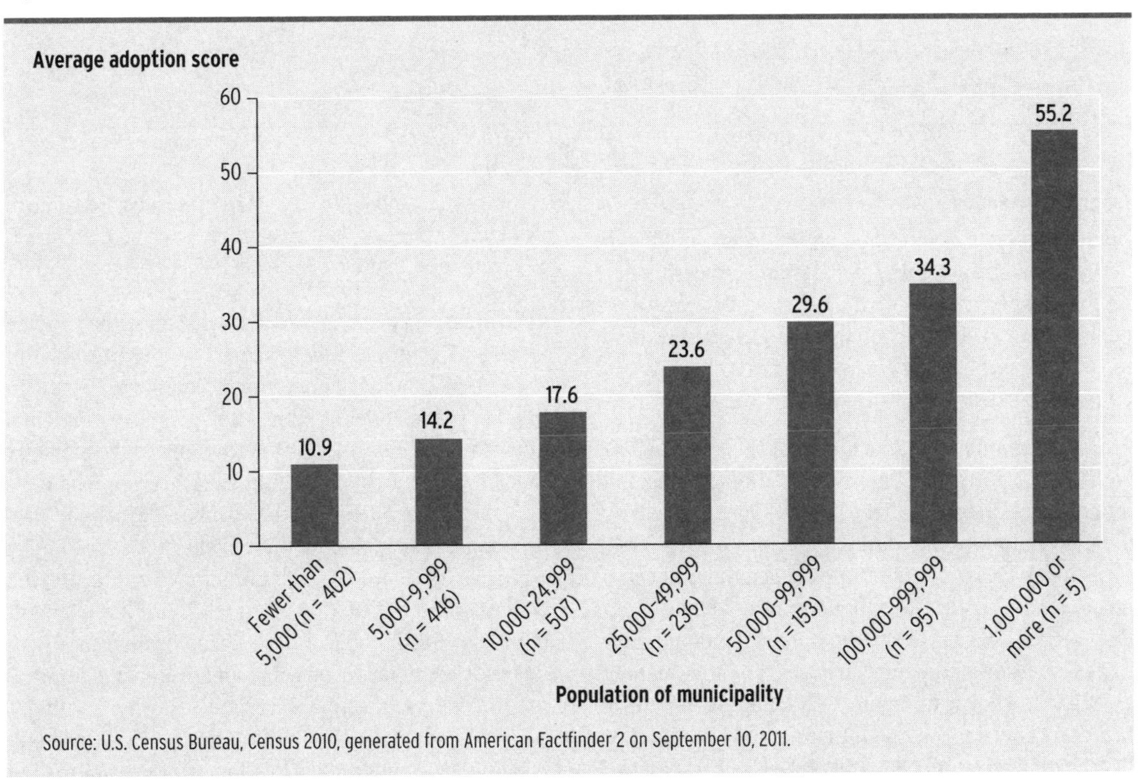

Source: U.S. Census Bureau, Census 2010, generated from American Factfinder 2 on September 10, 2011.

Table 5-2 Top 20 Sustainability Actions, by Population of Community

	Percentage of municipalities adopting action		
Sustainability action	Population <25,000 (n = 1,355) % (rank)	Population 25,000-99,999 (n = 389) % (rank)	Population 100,000 or higher (n = 100) % (rank)
Community-wide recycling collection program for paper *and* plastic *and* glass for residential properties	75 (1)	87 (1)	91 (2)
Internal program that recycles paper *and* plastic *and* glass in your local government	67 (2)	86 (2)	88 (3)
Added biking and walking trails	57 (3)	78 (4)	88 (4)
Conducted energy audits of government buildings	55 (4)	80 (3)	93 (1)
Require sidewalks in new development	52 (5)	76 (5)	71 (16)
Support a local farmer's market	51 (6)	68 (9)	65 (19)
Recycling of household hazardous waste	48 (7)	69 (8)	80 (8)
Upgraded or retrofitted facilities to higher energy-efficiency office lighting	47 (8)	74 (6)	87 (5)
Recycling of household electronic equipment (e-waste)	45 (9)	66 (11)	73 (13)
Community-wide recycling collection program for paper *and* plastic *and* glass for commercial properties	44 (10)	51 (19)	50 (33)
Plan for tree preservation and planting	42 (11)	64 (13)	77 (11)
Installed energy management systems to control heating and cooling in buildings	38 (12)	62 (14)	79 (10)
Use water price structure to encourage conservation	38 (13)	44 (26)	52 (30)
Increased the purchase of fuel-efficient vehicles	33 (14)	70 (7)	84 (7)
Community-wide collection of organic material for composting	33 (15)	41 (31)	44 (42)
Zoning codes to encourage more mixed-use development	32 (16)	49 (20)	51 (32)
Actions to conserve the quantity of water from aquifers	32 (17)	42 (27)	52 (29)
Upgraded or retrofitted traffic signals to improve efficiency	30 (18)	67 (10)	85 (6)
Set limits on impervious surfaces on private property	30 (19)	41 (30)	36 (57)
Locate recycling containers close to refuse containers in public spaces such as streets and parks	30 (20)	48 (22)	50 (34)

Local Capacity

In many smaller places, the limiting factor in terms of adoption of sustainability policies and programs may be local capacity, which can be assessed from three perspectives: fiscal resources of local government, technical expertise available in the community, and civic engagement.

Fiscal Resources Fiscally healthy governments would be expected to more readily adopt sustainability policies—an expectation that was borne out by the data. When per capita local tax revenue is used as the measure of fiscal capacity, the higher the per capita revenue, the higher the adoption rating (Figure 5–2). Fiscal capacity also affects the ability of communities to dedicate staff to the implementation of sustainability policies. As shown in Figure 5–2, communities in the higher revenue-raising quintiles are more likely to have dedicated staff who can provide technical expertise regarding sustainability and make the best use out of available resources. The presence of such staff increases the likelihood that adopted policies will be carried out.

Technical Expertise Technical capacity can be evaluated from another perspective: the presence of a professional local government manager. Such an official brings greater professionalism to municipal operations; for example, a professional city manager tends to push for policies that have been proven elsewhere and have been vetted, in many cases, by professional management organizations.[8] Accordingly, entities such as ICMA, U.S. Conference of Mayors, the National League of Cities, and ICLEI-Local Governments for Sustainability have become important conduits for technical knowledge and political legitimacy for innovative sustainability policies. And as might be expected, municipalities with the city manager form of government tend to adopt more sustainability

Figure 5-2 Per Capita Local Revenue and Adoption Ratings for Small Communities

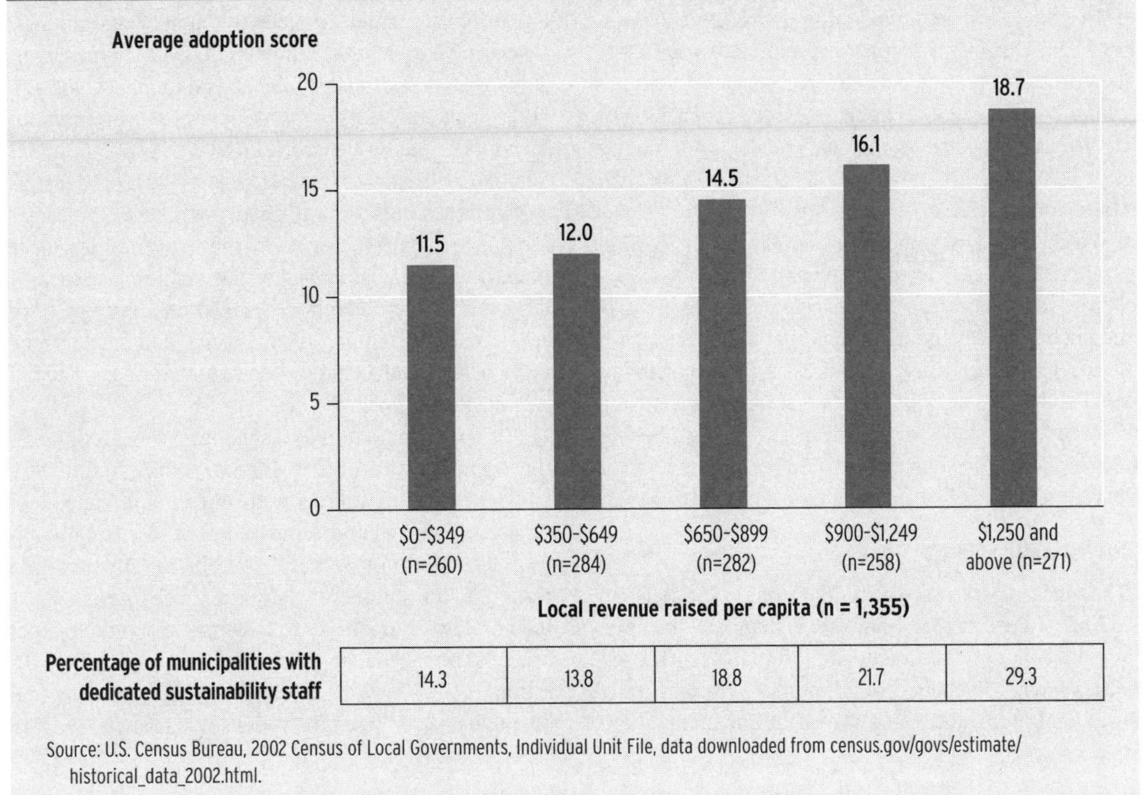

Source: U.S. Census Bureau, 2002 Census of Local Governments, Individual Unit File, data downloaded from census.gov/govs/estimate/historical_data_2002.html.

policies—an average adoption rating of 15.8% versus only 12.4% for municipalities with the mayor-council form of government (not shown).

Because smaller local governments are less able to hire needed expertise, they may seek technical assistance from community members, such as students and staff at local colleges and universities. However, our analysis, which used the proportion of college students in the local population as evidence of a college's potential role in a community, found that the presence of college students in a small municipality does not seem to affect that community's adoption of sustainability policies (not shown).

Civic Engagement Many municipalities recruit citizens to serve on advisory boards or commissions that are established to focus on particular issues. Commission members may have expertise related to the issue in question or may function as an "unbiased jury" in decisions about whether and how to create or evaluate programs. The ICMA 2010 survey specifically asked about the presence of a citizens committee, commission, or task force appointed to handle sustainability issues. Among those small communities that responded to the question (n = 1,345), the presence of such a commission correlates with an average adoption rating of 19%, compared to 13% for small communities that do not have one (not shown). The analysis suggests that citizens commissions play a strong role in policy adoption, but it is unclear whether, for example, the creation of such a commission sparks the development of sustainability policies or whether sustainability commissions are created as a response to existing community interest in developing such policies.

Growth Pressures

When small communities experience population growth, they might be expected to start thinking about sustainability, and some studies have found that they do.[9] For example, the loss of farmland to residential or commercial development, especially in places on the rural or suburban fringe, may provide the impetus for local leaders and community members to try to stop or shape growth. However, the data from the sustainability survey indicate that population growth is only weakly related to overall sustainability policy adoption and that employment growth has no impact on such policy adoption at all (not shown).

A relationship did emerge, however, between population growth and the implementation of ten sustainability policies that relate directly to growth management strategies. The planning and land use questions covered such topics as density, walkability, mixing of uses, and land conservation programs. As shown in Figure 5–3, the fastest-growing communities are more likely to adopt growth management strategies than are communities that are declining or growing more slowly.

Why might population growth render communities more likely to adopt growth management policies than sustainability policies? First, land use is the policy area in which local governments, especially in small communities, are most closely involved. Second, land use controls address issues that residents can easily see, and such policies produce results that are very local in nature. The same cannot be said of broad sustainability policies, whose benefits may not accrue solely to the community that incurs the cost but may instead benefit other communities downstream, down the road, or, in the case of greenhouse gas mitigation, around the world.

Socioeconomic Factors

While research conducted in California and published in 2009 indicates that homeownership rate, income, and educational attainment are positively correlated with a greater likelihood of adopting environmentally sustainable programs,[10] the results of our analysis are mixed. The data from the ICMA survey do not show a relationship between per capita income and the adoption of sustainability policies by small communities; however, educational attainment and homeownership rates do correlate with the adoption of sustainability policies. As shown in Figure 5–4, communities in which a higher proportion of the population has attained at least a bachelor's degree have, on average, higher rates of adoption. Two possible explanations for this are that (1) a more highly educated populace offers the technical capacity that smaller places may lack, and (2) more highly educated citizens may have a better understanding of the issues and therefore be more likely to advocate for the adoption of sustainability policies on the local level.

In the case of homeownership, the data point in the opposite direction: the relationship is not very strong, but communities with higher rates of homeownership, on average, tend to have lower sustainability policy adoption scores (Figure 5–5). One possible reason is that homeowners want to keep property tax bills as low as possible and so may discourage local officials from enacting policies that might increase municipal costs without providing appreciable fiscal or quality-of-life benefits in the short term.

Figure 5–3 Population Growth and Adoption of Growth Management Strategies among Small Communities

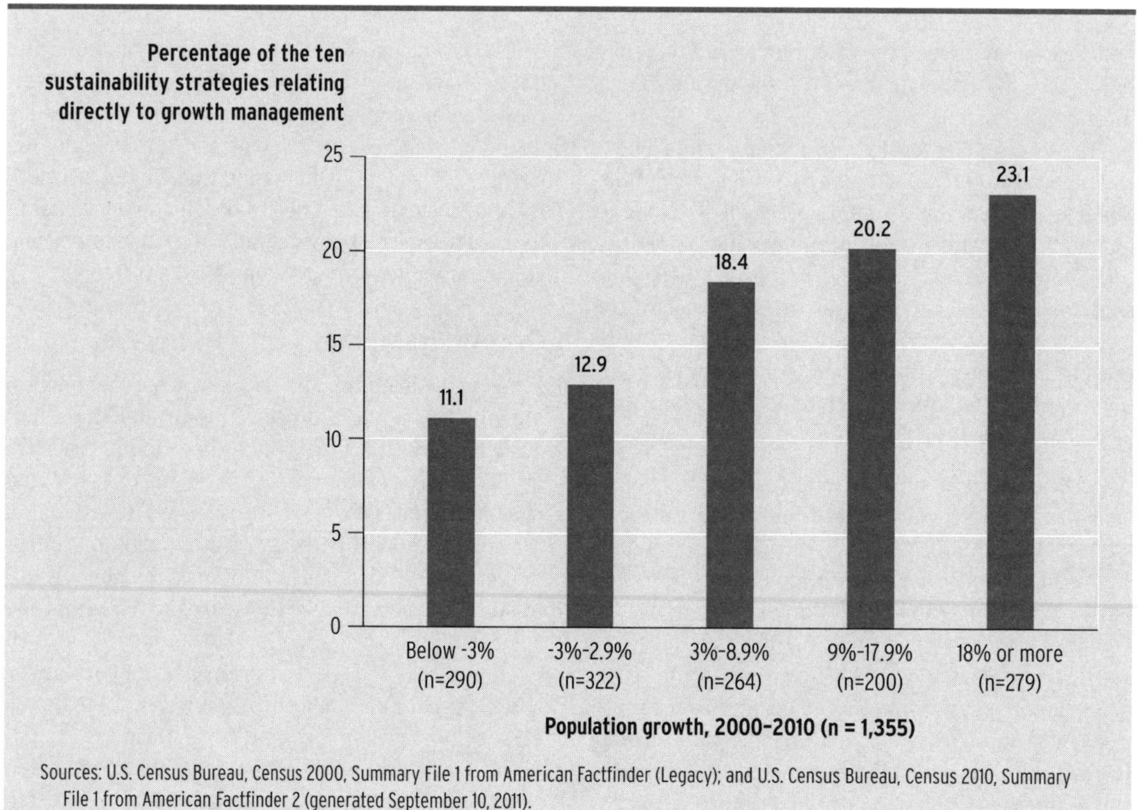

Sources: U.S. Census Bureau, Census 2000, Summary File 1 from American Factfinder (Legacy); and U.S. Census Bureau, Census 2010, Summary File 1 from American Factfinder 2 (generated September 10, 2011).

Figure 5-4 Educational Attainment and Adoption Ratings in Small Communities

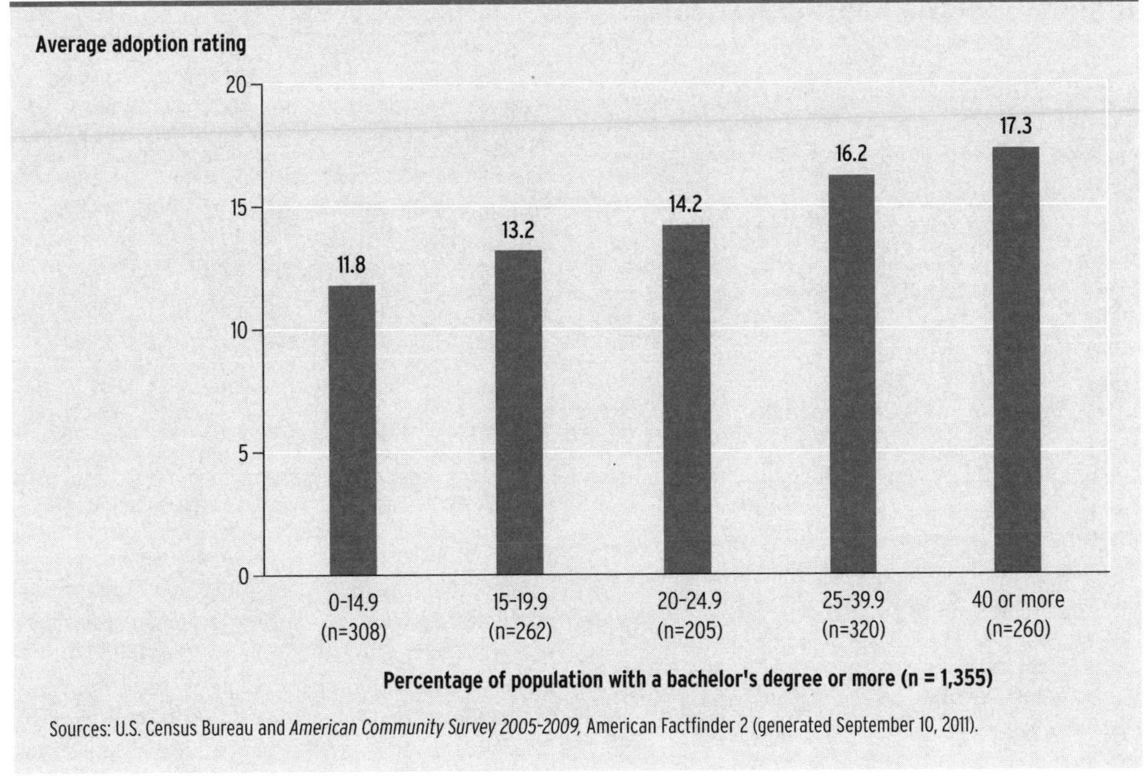

Sources: U.S. Census Bureau and *American Community Survey 2005-2009*, American Factfinder 2 (generated September 10, 2011).

Figure 5-5 Homeownership Rates and Adoption Ratings in Small Communities

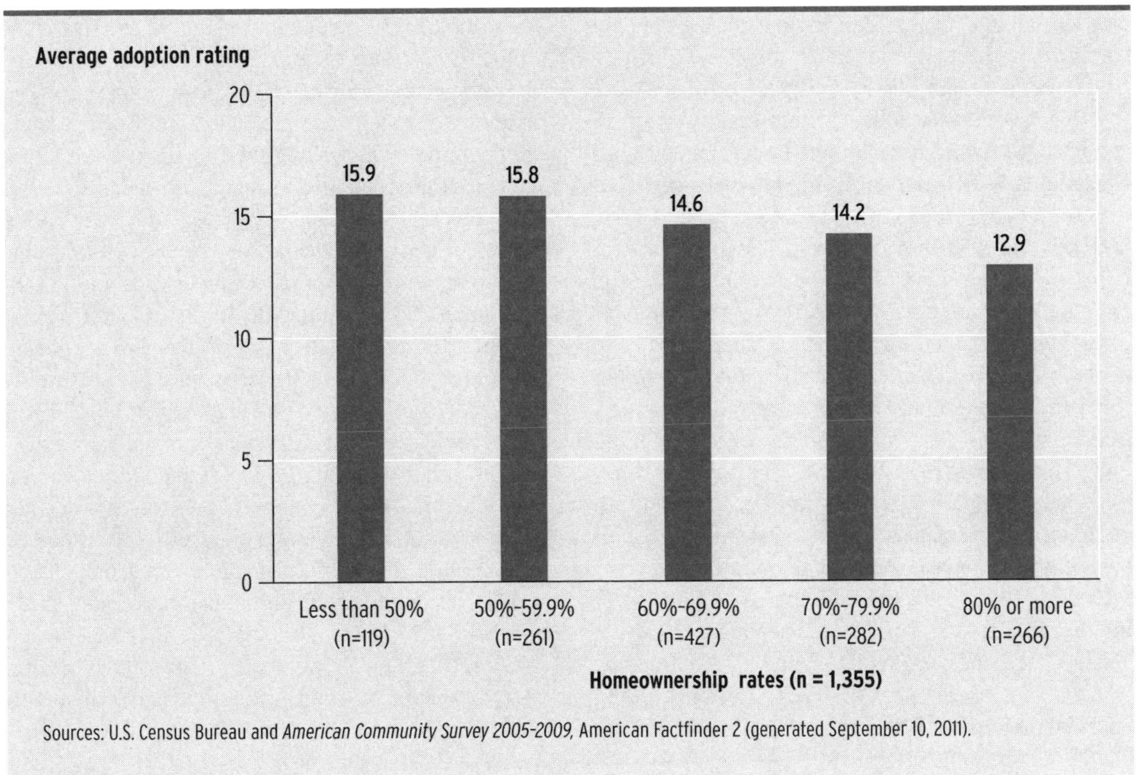

Sources: U.S. Census Bureau and *American Community Survey 2005-2009*, American Factfinder 2 (generated September 10, 2011).

Small Communities with the Highest Policy Adoption Ratings

Table 5–3 lists the ten small municipalities that scored highest in terms of sustainability policy adoption. Clearly, some small communities have succeeded in overcoming constraints that have hampered similar-sized communities. How do they do it?

Weston, Wisconsin, the number-one small community, established the New Generations initiative, which is designed to engage young people and address their identified needs, including the development of green, safe, walkable neighborhoods.[11] The village also partners with other entities—such as the federal government, local nonprofits, and private waste haulers—on sustainability programs across the community.[12] Anacortes, Washington, the number-two community on our list, focuses on framing issues in terms of local benefits, especially fiscal savings, to push sustainability. It also engages in extensive outreach efforts designed to educate residents and businesses about sustainability issues and programs, and it encourages conservation ideas from city staff. Finally, Anacortes measures outcomes and annually tracks energy usage and carbon dioxide emissions for the community as well as for city operations.[13]

These ten communities can serve as models that help other jurisdictions find simple, practical ways to become more sustainable. For instance, one area in which they have distinguished themselves from their peers is energy conservation. Nine of the top ten communities have upgraded their facilities to include energy-efficient lighting—a straightforward measure that has been undertaken by less than half of all communities with populations under 25,000 (see again Table 5–2). Seven of the top ten have upgraded to more energy-efficient building heating and cooling equipment—a move made by less than 40% of other small communities. Similarly, nine of the top ten small communities have increased the purchase of fuel-efficient vehicles, and six of those nine have added hybrid vehicles to municipal fleets. Although this is a very common strategy among bigger cities, undertaken by 84% of communities over 100,000 in population, only 33% of small communities have followed suit (Table 5–2)—possibly because of a lack of funding to purchase new vehicles or because of low vehicle turnover in small communities.

Walkability appears to be important to all ten of the highest-ranking small municipalities. All have added biking and walking trails, and all require sidewalks in new developments. These are fairly popular strategies across the board, with 57% of smaller communities building new trails and 52% requiring sidewalks (Table 5–2). These percentages might reflect the availability of funding and technical capacity for walkability projects, such as "Safe Routes to Schools" programs. A recent survey of city planners from communities of all sizes found that half of the respondents worked in communities with some kind of walk-to-school program.[14]

Table 5–3 Small Municipalities with the Highest Adoption Ratings, by Overall Adoption Score

Municipality	Population in 2010[a]	Average adoption rating
Weston, Wisconsin	14,868	58.1
Anacortes, Washington	15,778	53.7
Whitewater, Wisconsin	14,390	52.7
Ashland, Oregon	20,078	50.8
Falls Church, Virginia	12,332	50.4
Port Townsend, Washington	9,113	50.0
Dos Palos, California	4,950	49.9
Conover, North Carolina	8,165	49.8
Marquette, Michigan	21,355	49.4
Sonoma, California	10,648	49.2

a 2010 population figures are from the U.S. Census Bureau.

Conclusion

The 2010 ICMA Sustainability Survey is the first comprehensive measure of municipal sustainability policies undertaken across the country. The data make possible an analysis of the policy preferences of different kinds of communities as well as the numerous factors that influence the adoption of sustainability policies among local governments. The prevalence of sustainability policies in small municipalities is of particular interest in that these communities contain most of the U.S. population and cover the bulk of the land area.

Smaller municipalities are less likely to adopt sustainability policies than are larger, more urban municipalities. What explains the difference? Local fiscal and technical capacity is critical. Wealthier municipalities can devote staff to sustainability planning and implementation; in some places, the presence of professional management or citizen advisory boards may provide the technical expertise and/or political support needed to create and undertake sustainability policies. Interestingly, although a local government's fiscal and technical capacity is correlated with the adoption of sustainability activities, personal wealth (i.e., per capita income) is not.

Small communities are most likely to adopt sustainability policies related to recycling, energy use, and walkability. These issues are also the ones that have a direct and local impact on municipal fiscal health, boost residents' quality of life, and offer short-term political advantage for office holders. Small localities are less likely to tackle longer-term issues or those with broader impacts, such as greenhouse gas reduction planning or alternative energy generation. This finding suggests that if municipalities are to make any headway in these areas, the issues will have to be reframed so that local officials and residents can begin to see sustainability policies as directly important to their community and personal well-being.

In the absence of effective national leadership, municipalities have taken the lead in sustainability. However, that leadership is uneven, and the actions taken have been limited, especially in smaller communities. Most small municipalities, constrained by limited capacity, vision, and/or interest, have done little. As communities examine the fiscal realities in the years ahead, they may find that the adoption of policies focused on boosting environmental sustainability will save them money as well as promote economic development. Sustainability calls for as much innovation as other public services, and community leaders would perhaps do well to begin innovating sooner rather than later.

Notes

1. See, for example, "SustainLane Presents: The 2008 US City Rankings," sustainlane.com/us-city-rankings; Elizabeth Svoboda, "America's 50 Greenest Cities," *Popular Science*, February 8, 2008, popsci.com/environment/article/2008-02/americas-50-greenest-cities.
2. James H. Svara, "The Early Stage of Local Government Action to Promote Sustainability," in *The Municipal Year Book 2011* (Washington, D.C.: ICMA Press, 2011), 43–60; Michael R. Boswell, Tammy Seale, and Adrienne Greve, "Implementing Local Climate Action Plans" (paper presented at the 52nd annual conference of the Association of Collegiate Schools of Planning, Salt Lake City, Utah, October 13–16, 2011).
3. See Table 2 in "Inside the Year Book" in this volume, xii.
4. Kenneth Newton, "Is Small Really So Beautiful? Is Big Really So Ugly? Size, Effectiveness and Democracy in Local Government," *Political Studies* 30 (1982): 190–206; J. Eric Oliver, "City Size and Civic Involvement in Metropolitan America," *American Political Science Review* 94 (2000): 361–373; J. Eric Oliver, *Democracy in Suburbia* (Princeton, N.J.: Princeton University Press, 2001).
5. Rebecca Carter and Susan Culp, *Planning for Climate Change in the West*, Policy Focus Report PF024 (Cambridge, Mass.: Lincoln Institute of Land Policy, 2010), lincolninst.edu/pubs/1744_Planning-for-Climate-Change-in-the-West.
6. See note 2.
7. Svara, "Early Stage of Local Government Action."
8. Mark Schneider, Paul Teske, and Michael Mintrom, *Public Entrepreneurs* (Princeton, N.J.: Princeton University Press, 1995).
9. Stephan Schmidt and Kurt Paulsen, "Is Open-Space Preservation a Form of Exclusionary Zoning? The Evolution of Municipal Open-Space Policies in New Jersey," *Urban Affairs Review* 45 (2009): 92–118; William A. Fischel, *The Homevoter Hypothesis* (Cambridge: Harvard University Press, 2001).
10. Mark Lubell, Richard Feiock, and Susan Handy, "City Adoption of Environmentally Sustainable Policies in California's Central Valley," *Journal of the American Planning Association* 75, no. 3 (2009): 293–308; Zhenghong Tang, "How Are California Local Jurisdictions Incorporating a Strategic Environmental Assessment in Local Comprehensive Land Use Plans?," *Local Environment* 14, no. 4 (2009): 313–328.
11. Mildred Warner, "Planning for Family Friendly Communities: Case Vignettes," Linking Economic Development and Child Care Research Project (Ithaca, N.Y.: Department of City and Regional Planning, Cornell University, in collaboration with the American Planning Association, 2008), economicdevelopmentandchildcare.org/technical_assistance/planning_family_friendly/case-vignettes.pdf.
12. Weston, Wisconsin, "Sustainable Weston," westonwisconsin.org/media/Sustainable_Weston5.pdf.
13. James H. Svara, Anna Read, and Evelina Moulder, *Breaking New Ground: Promoting Environmental and Energy Programs in Local Government.* Conserving Energy and the Environment (Washington, DC: IBM Center for the Business of Government, 2011), icma .org/en/icma/knowledge_network/documents/kn/Document/302842/Breaking_New_Ground_Promoting_Environmental_and_Energy_Programs_in_Local_Government.
14. Evelyn Israel and Mildred Warner, "Planning for Family Friendly Communities," *PAS Memo,* American Planning Association (November/December 2008), planning.org/pas/memo/open/nov2008/index.htm.

6

CAO Salary and Compensation: The Big Picture

Ron Carlee
ICMA

Martha Perego
ICMA

Evelina R. Moulder
ICMA

Compensation for municipal employees has always been subject to review and debate at the local level. It became a national issue in 2009 when the *Los Angeles Times* stumbled upon the pay scandal in Bell, California, where the city manager, city council members, and at least two senior staff were exploiting the city for outrageous sums. A subsequent investigation revealed that the city manager, Robert Rizzo, had a salary of $800,000. At the time this article was being written, Rizzo was under indictment and awaiting trial. He has been expelled from ICMA.[1]

Meanwhile, several perpetual questions remain: How much should a city/county/town manager earn? What are the norms and trends? Beyond base pay, what are other appropriate ways to compensate chief appointed officials (CAOs)? ICMA guidelines for CAO pay state that the compensation of local government managers should be "fair, reasonable, transparent, and based on comparable public salaries nationally and regionally."[2] Still, the question remains: what is fair and reasonable for a local government's CAO? If that official is a city, county, or town manager, he or she serves as the chief executive officer (CEO) of a major enterprise, with more lines of business than most comparably sized private companies. If the CAO works for a mayor or county executive, he or she serves as chief operating officer, again with substantial executive responsibilities for a highly complex organization. Additionally, the actual range of services for which the CAO is responsible varies widely, as reflected in Figure 6–1.

SELECTED FINDINGS

The median salary reported for CAOs is $101,000; the mean is $109,000. Among the states with a response rate of at least 30% and more than 10 respondents, the lowest median salary reported is in Maine at $65,500 and the highest is in California at $185,501.

Sixteen percent of CAOs do not have a letter of agreement or contract, 23% do not have severance provisions, and 22% do not receive an annual performance review.

Thirty percent of CAOs are not provided with professional association memberships, and only 37% receive an allocation for professional development.

While ICMA recommends that compensation benchmarks be established in accordance with comparable local government and/or public sector agencies, there is no consensus to date on what external positions are appropriate for benchmarking CAO pay. ICMA guidelines are broad, stating that "compensation should be based on the position requirements, the complexity of the job reflected in the composition of the organization and community, the leadership needed, labor market conditions, cost of living in the community, and the organization's ability to pay."[3]

Figure 6-1 Service Delivery Responsibility for CAOs

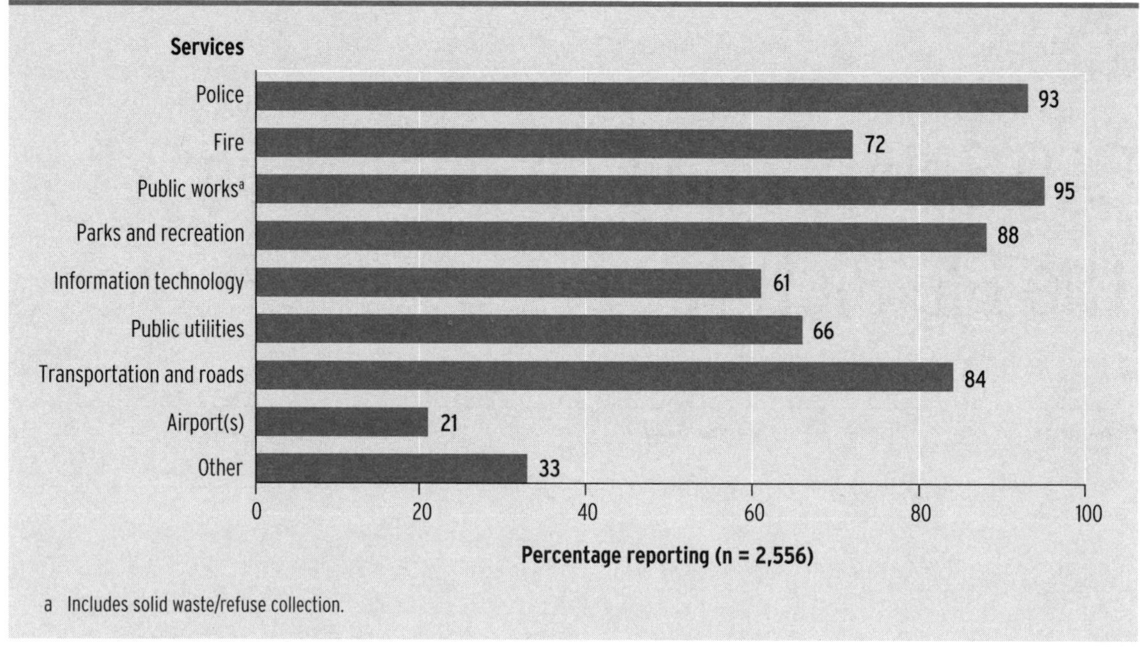

a Includes solid waste/refuse collection.

Examining new data from a 2011 national survey of local government executives in the context of the "ICMA Guidelines for Compensation," the *ICMA Model Employment Agreement*, and the ICMA Code of Ethics,[4] this article looks at compensation issues for CAOs: city, county, and town managers and administrators in local governments with the council-manager plan and the equivalent appointed positions in local governments with the mayor-council plan, town meeting, and representative town meeting. Judging from the results of this survey, it would be inaccurate to provide an unqualified, relevant amount of pay for the "average" CAO. There *is* no average CAO any more than there is an average city, county, or town. Responses show that pay practices vary widely according to the size, location, and philosophy of each local government.

Survey Methodology

The *ICMA Compensation Survey for Local Government Chief Appointed Officials* was sent to all local governments in the ICMA database for which a name is provided for the CAO position. The initial survey was mailed in February 2011, and a follow-up survey was mailed to nonrespondents in April 2011. In all, 7,084 surveys were mailed out.

For a survey of this nature, the response rate is relatively high at 36%, and the 2,556 respondents provide a substantial database (Table 6–1); however, the significant number of local governments for which no data are available limits broad generalizations.

The percentage of respondents from council-manager cities (42%) is higher by approximately 10 percentage points than that from cities with the mayor-council and commission forms of government. Among counties, the response rate is highest from those with the council-administrator form of government. This is not surprising: given that we surveyed only those local governments for which we had a name for the CAO position, respondents would reflect ICMA's membership and response rates would therefore be higher for council-manager cities and council-administrator counties.

CAO Base Salaries

In many instances throughout this article, discussion is based on the median salary; this is because the median is the midpoint and is not affected by outliers the way that the mean, or average, is affected. The median salary reported for CAOs is $101,000 (Table 6–2), which means that half the respondents earn more than this amount and half earn less.

Population Size of Local Government

The strongest association found with base salary is the population size of the local government. As one

Table 6-1 Survey Response

Classification	No. of municipalities/ counties[a] surveyed (A)	No. responding No.	No. responding % of (A)
Total	7,084	2,556	36
Population group			
Over 1,000,000	30	9	30
500,000-1,000,000	62	17	27
250,000-499,999	115	40	35
100,000-249,999	302	108	36
50,000-99,999	527	164	31
25,000-49,999	850	286	34
10,000-24,999	1,613	582	36
5,000-9,999	1,370	524	38
2,500-4,999	1,351	490	36
Under 2,500	864	336	39
Geographic division			
New England	594	206	35
Mid-Atlantic	874	233	27
East North-Central	1,146	454	40
West North-Central	835	356	43
South Atlantic	1,368	513	38
East South-Central	295	68	23
West South-Central	680	187	28
Mountain	447	184	41
Pacific Coast	845	355	42
Form of government			
Mayor-council	1,927	628	33
Council-manager	3,595	1,500	42
Commission	78	25	32
Town meeting	252	88	35
Representative town meeting	43	11	26
County commission	346	56	16
Council-administrator (manager)	623	206	33
Council-elected executive	220	42	19

a For a definition of terms, please see "Inside the *Year Book*," xii-xiv.

would expect, salaries tend to increase as the size of the local government increases (Figure 6–2).

As Table 6–3 shows, however, the range is still large within population divisions. In all population groups, the difference between the maximum and minimum salary is over $168,000. This wide variation is expected. For example, a local government with a small population could be an affluent suburb providing a wide range of services and would therefore report a higher salary, or it could be a rural community with limited services and would therefore report a lower salary. Similar explanations can be found for all other relevant variables affecting pay, such as cost of living, tenure, and years of experience in local government. Nonetheless, population size emerged in the survey as an important variable: CAOs tend to make more in larger jurisdictions than in smaller jurisdictions.

Table 6-2 CAO Base Salaries

Median salary	$101,000
Mean salary	$109,000
Bottom 20%	Less than $72,000
Top 20%	Over $142,000
Over $200,000	4%

Note: All amounts have been rounded.

In the population categories used in Table 6–3, median salaries increased by 42% between local governments with a population under 10,000 and those with a population 10,000–24,999. This is the highest percentage of increase from one population group to the next. The increases in median salaries between the other population groups are 19% and below. Also noteworthy is that median salaries are below $150,000 until populations reach 100,000 and above.

Salaries by State

While there is a wide range of pay within each state, there are clearly differences among the states. Aggregating states into regions, however, is not meaningful; the differences among states within a region are significant enough to make regional comparisons unreliable. State analysis also presents challenges because of the response rate *by* state. Although the overall response rate to the survey was 36%, the range by individual state was between 7% (Louisiana) and 59% (Nebraska).

It is also important to consider other variables when examining aggregated data at the state level. As noted, the strongest association with pay is the size of the local government. Consequently, a state's profile will be affected by the population sizes of the local governments within the state. A state in which smaller local governments outnumber larger ones can be expected to have lower salaries overall. Salaries may be slightly higher in council-manager governments, however, reflecting the higher level of responsibility that positions in such jurisdictions hold.

To examine states more closely, we considered the 30 states with a response rate of 30% or higher and more than 10 respondents; at these response rates and numbers of respondents we can have more confidence in state-to-state comparisons. Table 6–4 arrays the median CAO salaries from high to low by state. Among these states, the lowest median salary is in Maine at $65,500, and the highest is in California at $185,501.

The finding that California's salaries are the highest has been consistent since ICMA started collecting salary data in the 1980s. Notwithstanding its current economic challenges, California is home to numerous relatively affluent communities with a high cost of living, especially high housing costs. Even in California, however, CAO salaries top out under $300,000 for all communities responding to the survey.

Appendix Tables 6–A1 and 6–A2 present the minimum, mean, median, and maximum salaries for city and counties, respectively, within each state by population group. Where only one city or county reported in a population group, that record was suppressed.

Conclusions regarding Base Salaries

Because base pay is a factor of multiple variables, the ICMA survey can never be definitive in determining what a professional manager should make in a specific local government. Nonetheless, the survey collected data on several variables in addition to population size,

Figure 6–2 Median CAO Salaries

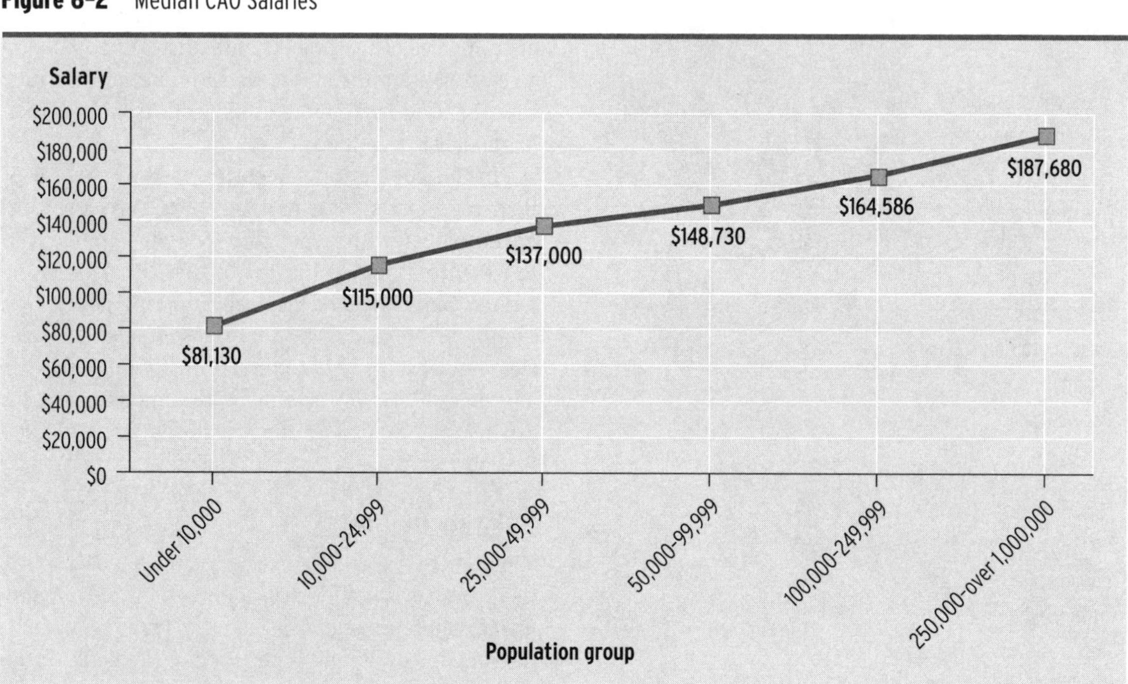

Table 6–3 Salaries by Population Size

Population	No. reporting	Mean ($)	Minimum ($)	Median ($)	Maximum ($)	Maximum minus minimum ($)
250,000-over 1,000,000	64	194,899	105,685	187,680	274,498	168,813
100,000-249,999	102	168,692	75,000	164,586	285,132	210,132
50,000-99,999	159	150,522	48,000	148,730	291,571	243,571
25,000-49,999	275	140,687	38,500	137,000	292,500	254,000
10,000-24,999	567	117,795	24,000	115,000	242,000	218,000
Under 10,000	1,298	83,855	20,000	81,130	195,727	175,727

Table 6-4 Median Salaries for Select States

State	Median salary ($)
California	185,501
Nevada	140,169
Florida	128,229
Arizona	125,000
Connecticut	121,000
Washington	120,930
Illinois	118,000
Virginia	111,000
Colorado	110,000
Texas	110,000
Alaska	107,000
Utah	105,148
South Carolina	103,000
Minnesota	101,025
Maryland	100,000
Georgia	98,548
New Mexico	98,500
North Carolina	94,250
Missouri	93,444
New Hampshire	92,000
Oregon	90,000
Wisconsin	90,000
Nebraska	87,493
Michigan	84,872
Pennsylvania	84,703
Iowa	84,450
Kansas	83,500
Delaware	75,219
Vermont	73,050
Maine	65,500

including form of government and scope of services provided, and the results provide a range that can serve as a starting point. Given the number of variables involved, ICMA's guidelines recommend that the governing body engage experts as necessary, whether contracted or in-house, "to provide the information required to establish fair and reasonable compensation levels." Such information should be obtained by applying the following steps:

1. Determine the requirements of the job and the experience needed to successfully perform the job duties.
2. Examine market conditions to learn what comparable public sector executives earn. A best practice would be to gather information using predetermined comparable benchmark local governments or public sector agencies.
3. Understand the services provided by the local government along with the nature of the current issues in the organization and in the community, and then compare these with the individual's expertise and proven ability to resolve those issues.
4. Identify the local government's current financial position, its ability to pay, and the existing policies toward compensation relative to market conditions.[5]

Contract Negotiations and Agreement

Survey results show that the negotiation of a professional manager's compensation is typically done directly by the elected officials—either the mayor, the council as a whole, or a committee of the council (75%) (not shown; from here on, unless a cited percentage is followed by a reference to a specific table or figure, the reader should understand that the datum is not shown). In some instances, however, the elected officials will use the local government attorney (11%) or human resource professional (5%) to negotiate the terms. The negotiations should result in a contract or letter of agreement. ICMA publishes a model agreement that elected officials can use as a base document (see sidebar on the following page).

Although 84% of responding CAOs reported that they have a formal contract or letter of agreement, the remaining 16% should be a source of concern. The formal approval of a compensation agreement eliminates ambiguity and is essential for providing transparency and disclosure in the public sector. Such an agreement should cover term of service, severance provisions, performance reviews, all compensation, and benefits. If the benefits for the CAO are the same as those for other employees, the agreement should say so explicitly.

Term of Service

CAOs, as executives, are typically considered at-will employees and can be separated without cause at the discretion of the council or mayor, depending on the form of government. Currently, 46% of CAOs reporting have a fixed term for their contract; for those CAOs, the most common length of term is three years.

Severance Provisions

Since most CAOs—even those with a fixed-term agreement—can be separated at any time, the ICMA model agreement recommends explicit formal severance provisions of 12 months of pay. This level of severance should serve as a deterrent to the dismissal of a CAO merely for political expediency or because of disagreement over legitimate recommendations and

History of ICMA's *Model Employment Agreement*

Over the last forty years, the use of employment agreements has been a significant trend shaping the employment relationship of local government management professionals, and ICMA has long been involved in developing and promoting such agreements.

In 1969, the ICMA Executive Board approved the concept of employment agreements, noting that "agreements of employment negotiated between managers and administrators and their employing municipalities are within the spirit of the Code of Ethics provided that such agreements do not violate the principle that the managers or administrator serves at the pleasure of its mayor and/or council and that the Executive Director be authorized to publish a report of guidelines for agreements."[1]

The first formal recommendations from ICMA were created in 1983 and focused on the importance of having a comprehensive agreement and on the need for a minimum of six months of severance protection.

Recognizing that agreements should address all terms and conditions, ICMA and The Innovation Groups published *The Public Executives Complete Guide to Employment Agreements* in 1996. The guide was the first "menu" approach for building a customized employment agreement.

A task force of members created the *ICMA Model Employment Agreement* in 2003.[2] Unlike the 1996 publication, which was designed as a broad survey of virtually all the provisions from which a manager could choose, this document recommends options for each provision that should be included in a comprehensive agreement.

The *ICMA Model Employment Agreement* is currently undergoing a review by a member task force. A revised model agreement will be available October 2012.

1 ICMA Executive Board Minutes, 1969.

2 *ICMA Model Employment Agreement* (2003), icma.org/Documents/Document/Document/5345.

administrative actions taken by the CAO. Nonetheless, the ICMA guidelines state that "severance provisions established in the employment agreement must be both reasonable and affordable so that the cost of the severance is not an impediment to fulfilling the governing body's right to terminate a manager's service, if desired."[6]

According to the 2011 survey, 77% of managers are eligible to receive severance pay, the amount of which varies mostly according to tenure. The most common amount of severance pay is approximately six months, as reported by 51% of CAOs; another 28% reported that six months is their maximum amount. Only 9% of CAOs reported a minimum severance of one year, while 16% reported one year as the maximum. As for how the severance provisions are structured, a number of variations can be found, including the amount of severance relative to the tenure of the CAO and the circumstances under which the severance provisions apply. These variations appear to be idiosyncratic rather than widespread.

Performance Reviews and Compensation Changes

The *ICMA Model Employment Agreement* recommends that CAOs have an annual performance review, with the process, format, and criteria mutually agreed upon between the CAO and the appointing authority. At a minimum, such a process should include an opportunity for both parties to prepare a written evaluation, meet and discuss the evaluation, and present a written summary of the results. The model agreement then recommends an annual compensation review for the CAO based on this evaluation.[7]

Among the CAOs responding to the survey, 78% reported that they receive an annual performance review, and 62% reported that their salaries are tied to performance; however, only 51% reported that they actually receive salary reviews. Moreover, only 57% reported that the frequency of their salary reviews is specified in their contracts/agreements.

As noted in ICMA's model agreement, CAOs should receive an increase in pay based on merit or a bonus based on performance, as documented through the review.[8] Fifty-two percent of CAOs reported eligibility for a merit increase, while only 25% reported eligibility for a bonus.

One way for CAOs to receive a compensation increase (while still maintaining an annual evaluation) is with a percentage or specified amount based on what other employees receive. The 2010 guidelines reinforce the agreement, stating that "merit adjustments or bonuses should be contingent upon performance and the overall financial position of the local government to afford additional compensation payments" and that "salary increases should be reasonably comparable to those that local government executives receive within the designated benchmark or regional market area and generally consistent with other employees."[9]

As another option, 41% of CAOs reported that they receive a cost-of-living adjustment (COLA) increase. Of those respondents, approximately one-third reported that it is included in their employment agreement, and 77% reported that they receive the same COLA percentage increase as other employees of the local government.

Compensation beyond Base Pay

Executive pay typically includes a range of benefits beyond salary. However, if the other forms of compensation are not documented in the CAO's employment contract/agreement and fully disclosed, they can be a source of conflict and public opposition; they can also be used politically. Thus, the ICMA guidelines recommend full, public disclosure of the total compensation package at the time of hire and whenever any amendments are made to the package.[10] The following are the most common and important provisions.

Pensions/Retirement In many instances, CAOs are not career employees in a single local government. As in the private sector, many are executives who serve a number of localities over their careers. Consequently, pension benefits need to be designed accordingly. ICMA's model agreement identifies several options for structuring a CAO's retirement plan, including enrollment in the local or state plan, contributions to a supplemental 457 plan, and/or participation in a 401(a) plan.[11] While additional research is required in this area, Table 6–5 shows current practices.

Insurance The most significant area of other benefits for which data specific to CAOs are not currently available is health insurance, which is highly complex and would need to be a study unto itself. *The Local Government Employee Health Insurance Benefits Survey* conducted by ICMA and CIGNA in 2011 did not differentiate among local government positions (see "Local Government Employee Health Insurance Programs, 2011" on pages 37–52 in this volume). Findings from the current survey, however, do reveal that 81% of respondents receive life insurance, 41% receive long-term disability insurance, 34% receive short-term disability insurance, and 21% receive supplemental/excess long-term disability insurance (Table 6–6). To what extent coverage in these areas is different for the CAO than for other employees was not investigated.

Table 6–5 Retirement Benefits

Retirement benefits	Percentage reporting (n = 2,556)
Defined benefit plan	60
Defined contribution plan	36
Deferred comp (IRS Section 457 Plan)	47

Car Directly related to the CAO's ability to carry out the business of local government, the model agreement recommends that the CAO be provided with a car or car expense allowance,[12] a provision reported by 60% of the CAOs (Table 6–6).

Professional Development Of special interest to ICMA is the growth and development of the CAO. When asked which provisions for professional development they receive, 70% of CAOs reported professional association memberships, 37% reported professional development expense allocation, and 19% reported educational expenses (Table 6–6).

Housing and Moving Expenses Among the challenges to a local government in selecting the best CAO—and to a CAO in securing the most appropriate position—is the high cost of relocation. The devaluation of residential property in many communities has exacerbated the problem. Many homeowners in the United States are under water with their mortgages, which makes relocation without housing assistance financially impossible. As reported in this survey, only 2% of CAOs are currently receiving some form of housing assistance (Table 6–6), which by necessity may become more common in the future. Moving expenses were reported by 21% of CAOs, which is common provision for most CEOs in the private sector and nonprofit organizations.

Technology Expenses The position responsibilities typically require that the CAO be available 24/7 in case of emergency. Forty-four percent of CAOs reported an allowance to cover the cost of cell phones, computers, and other technology that may be required (Table 6–6).

Leave Like pensions and health insurance, leave is another complex area that will require more analysis

Table 6-6 Other Benefits

Other benefits	Percentage reporting (n = 2,556)
Insurance	
Life insurance	81
Long-term disability insurance	41
Short-term disability insurance	34
Supplemental/excess long-term disability insurance	21
Excess life insurance	10
Car expenses/allowance	60
Professional development	
Professional association memberships	70
Professional development expense allocation	37
Educational expenses	19
Social club memberships	16
Housing and moving	
Housing assistance in the form of loans	1
Housing assistance in the form of down-payment assistance	1
Moving expenses	21
Technology allowance (cell phone, computer, etc.)	44

in the future. Issues include the type and amount of leave received, and provisions to either cash out leave annually or be paid for leave upon termination (either at retirement or before). As with pensions and health insurance, leave is a complex issue for local government employees at all levels.

The model agreement recommends that the CAO "be credited with sick and vacation leave equal to the highest annual accrual provided to all other employees" and thereafter annually accrue leave "at the highest rate provided to the other employees."[13] In addition, it is recommended that the CAO accrue leave without limit and be compensated for accrued leave at termination.[14]

Leave becomes a compensation issue only to the extent that the provisions for the CAO differ from those for other employees. Respondents reported the following provisions:

- Twenty percent of CAOs receive "executive leave" of 10 days a year, on average; 19% reported that they can cash out executive leave. Of note, the majority of respondents who receive executive leave are in California.
- Average annual leave is 22 days a year; 44% of CAOs can cash out some amount of annual leave.
- Average sick leave is 14 days; 25% of CAOs can cash out sick leave.
- Forty-two percent of CAOs receive a payment for unused sick leave when they end their employment with the local government.

At this point we do not fully know the extent to which these provisions apply to other employees as well. Moreover, the details of these provisions require further exploration regarding accrual rates over time, accrual balance limits, maximum amounts that can be cashed out annually or at separation, and other practices that vary among local governments.

Summary and Conclusions

Among the CAOs responding to the survey, executive pay overall appears to be consistent with historical trends for the profession. The base mean salary of approximately $109,000 (not shown) is not excessive when compared with the mean salary of $204,650 for chief executives of companies and enterprises as reported by the U.S. Bureau of Labor Statistics in its 2010 national estimates.[15] Moreover, we found no evidence of excessive salaries and benefits or of the inappropriate practices that contributed to the unethical conduct exhibited in Bell, California.

Nevertheless, additional work is required to obtain universal reporting and the level of transparency needed to ensure continued public confidence in the profession and in local government. Additional research is also required to better understand compensation beyond base pay, including pensions, health insurance, and leave provisions—all of which are areas of relevance for all local and state employees.

For members of the profession, critical findings are that 16% of CAOs do not have a letter of agreement or contract, 23% do not have severance provisions in their contracts, and 22% do not receive an annual performance review. These are the practices that are most important and should apply to all CAOs. The formal agreement, adopted by the elected officials and made available to the public, is the most important vehicle to ensure transparency in executive compensation. Severance provisions protect both the CAO and the elected body; ICMA recommends severance of at least one year's base salary, although the most common provision is for six months of severance pay. Annual reviews are essential for feedback and should be the basis for compensation increases, consistent with what the local government can afford and what is provided to its other employees.

We also note that 30% of CAOs are not provided with professional association memberships. While ICMA clearly has a vested interest in this provision, the ability of CAOs to network with peers is important for their professional development and growth. Of even greater concern is the finding that only 37% of CAOs receive an allocation for professional development. Professional development in a rapidly changing society is critical for all employees, not just CAOs. For communities to be truly competitive, their employees need to be current, with the CAO setting the example.

ICMA will continue the salary survey on an annual basis, refining the methodology to help ensure a complete picture of CAO pay in local governments. Comments and recommendations from CAOs and other researchers are encouraged.

Notes

1. "High Salaries Stir Outrage in Bell," *Los Angeles Times*, latimes.com/news/local/bell/ (last accessed 12/20/2011).
2. "ICMA Guidelines for Compensation" (2010), 1, icma.org/Documents/Document/Document/302085.
3. Ibid.
4. Ibid., *ICMA Model Employment Agreement* (2003), icma.org/Documents/Document/Document/5345, and ICMA Code of Ethics (n.d.), icma.org/en/icma/ethics/code_of_ethics.
5. "ICMA Guidelines for Compensation," 1–2.
6. Ibid., 2.
7. *ICMA Model Employment Agreement*, 7.
8. Ibid., 1–2.
9. "ICMA Guidelines for Compensation," 2.
10. Ibid., 3.
11. *ICMA Model Employment Agreement*, 6–7.
12. Ibid., 3–4.
13. Ibid., 3.
14. Ibid., 6.
15. Bureau of Labor Statistics, "Occupational Employment Statistics: May 2010 National Occupational Employment and Wage Estimates, United States," bls.gov/oes/current/oes_nat.htm#11-0000.

Appendix Table 6-A1 City Salaries by Population Group within States

State	No. reporting	Base salary			
		Minimum ($)	Mean ($)	Median ($)	Maximum ($)
Alabama					
50,000-99,999	2	161,000	163,000	163,000	165,000
5,000-9,999	3	47,528	99,176	118,000	132,000
Under 2,500	2	40,000	89,347	89,347	138,694
Alaska					
5,000-9,999	3	107,000	120,667	120,000	135,000
2,500-4,999	4	104,000	112,500	107,000	132,000
Arizona					
100,000-249,999	3	180,000	181,500	180,000	184,500
25,000-49,999	5	135,013	155,103	147,500	178,000
10,000-24,999	6	109,000	139,733	127,500	181,400
5,000-9,999	7	6,000	112,536	113,000	140,250
2,500-4,999	10	85,000	98,135	90,000	141,421
Under 2,500	2	80,000	88,500	88,500	97,000
Arkansas					
25,000-49,999	2	107,000	118,500	118,500	130,000
California					
250,000-499,999	2	234,996	248,444	248,444	261,891
100,000-249,999	16	174,161	235,264	229,678	285,132
50,000-99,999	23	175,086	212,551	214,000	291,571
25,000-49,999	38	163,400	199,818	199,250	285,000
10,000-24,999	42	112,000	169,556	168,000	242,000
5,000-9,999	24	45,000	130,830	125,825	195,000
2,500-4,999	11	72,192	121,383	95,000	195,727
Under 2,500	7	82,224	130,503	106,000	189,600
Colorado					
100,000-249,999	3	190,571	197,743	193,482	209,175
25,000-49,999	3	140,000	166,113	153,338	205,000
10,000-24,999	7	106,000	139,233	145,000	167,042
5,000-9,999	11	90,000	112,746	107,000	135,000
2,500-4,999	8	92,415	126,075	121,800	169,651
Under 2,500	19	57,300	81,262	79,560	110,000
Connecticut					
25,000-49,999	6	120,000	127,750	123,000	149,000
10,000-24,999	11	58,000	124,640	127,842	152,000
5,000-9,999	3	75,370	101,495	114,114	115,000

Note: Where only one city or county reported in a population group, that record was suppressed.

State	No. reporting	Base salary			
		Minimum ($)	Mean ($)	Median ($)	Maximum ($)
Delaware					
5,000-9,999	3	68,000	99,635	104,000	126,904
Under 2,500	8	35,000	62,770	65,000	83,721
Florida					
100,000-249,999	5	132,500	168,647	154,000	205,000
50,000-99,999	11	133,100	173,935	170,693	210,140
25,000-49,999	14	125,000	168,372	160,500	235,000
10,000-24,999	36	90,000	133,265	132,457	195,000
5,000-9,999	15	56,000	101,136	106,000	142,600
2,500-4,999	19	26,000	89,536	90,000	160,000
Under 2,500	13	45,000	84,913	90,000	113,730
Georgia					
100,000-249,999	2	132,584	161,580	161,580	190,575
25,000-49,999	4	117,000	125,820	125,000	136,280
10,000-24,999	15	85,000	115,647	110,490	147,000
5,000-9,999	15	65,000	97,592	7,309	151,000
2,500-4,999	14	38,000	74,658	76,448	112,190
Under 2,500	5	56,000	69,800	60,000	100,000
Idaho					
5,000-9,999	2	92,920	99,760	99,760	106,600
2,500-4,999	4	40,000	73,931	79,000	97,723
Illinois					
100,000-249,999	2	121,222	142,111	142,111	163,000
50,000-99,999	9	101,000	159,801	170,000	183,700
25,000-49,999	20	127,575	166,652	164,100	225,000
10,000-24,999	33	40,000	126,247	127,613	203,000
5,000-9,999	24	65,000	110,481	104,750	181,193
2,500-4,999	22	36,000	87,945	81,763	143,000
Under 2,500	8	58,000	87,577	70,914	177,000
Indiana					
5,000-9,999	2	73,000	79,500	79,500	86,000
Under 2,500	3	54,000	64,400	67,200	72,000
Iowa					
50,000-99,999	2	160,000	179,422	179,422	198,844
25,000-49,999	3	106,054	115,951	115,000	126,800
10,000-24,999	9	81,595	119,568	117,504	151,922
5,000-9,999	24	62,541	90,143	91,009	114,016
2,500-4,999	17	51,655	75,236	73,000	113,556
Under 2,500	17	39,000	55,925	56,664	75,000

Note: Where only one city or county reported in a population group, that record was suppressed.

State	No. reporting	Base salary			
		Minimum ($)	Mean ($)	Median ($)	Maximum ($)
Kansas					
25,000-49,999	5	122,990	127,554	125,000	133,000
5,000-9,999	12	75,520	92,934	91,594	137,000
2,500-4,999	23	45,000	76,633	77,147	108,637
Under 2,500	12	35,000	59,092	58,282	75,000
Kentucky					
10,000-24,999	5	84,000	104,303	107,816	120,000
2,500-4,999	2	75,000	78,150	78,150	81,300
Maine					
10,000-24,999	7	98,200	104,672	102,612	113,000
5,000-9,999	14	48,500	83,835	82,950	117,900
2,500-4,999	24	43,000	64,900	62,087	110,196
Under 2,500	17	34,320	57,925	50,000	99,000
Maryland					
50,000-99,999	2	165,000	182,227	182,227	199,454
10,000-24,999	6	84,150	109,292	109,500	142,000
5,000-9,999	5	82,000	112,788	100,000	173,404
2,500-4,999	6	60,000	73,955	65,614	100,000
Under 2,500	4	22,000	61,541	71,824	80,517
Massachusetts					
25,000-49,999	5	125,000	147,337	156,183	169,000
10,000-24,999	28	79,185	124,514	130,664	149,739
5,000-9,999	14	72,363	97,212	95,500	125,000
2,500-4,999	8	51,580	86,365	80,967	132,500
Under 2,500	2	37,711	68,856	68,856	100,000
Michigan					
100,000-249,999	2	137,317	139,659	139,659	142,000
50,000-99,999	3	112,700	122,567	125,000	130,000
25,000-49,999	9	86,900	113,752	108,000	145,000
10,000-24,999	27	75,400	98,189	99,284	124,500
5,000-9,999	27	37,000	89,382	90,000	139,900
2,500-4,999	39	49,500	75,591	72,500	111,000
Under 2,500	29	40,000	59,323	58,000	79,000
Minnesota					
50,000-99,999	8	114,000	134,720	135,230	154,569
25,000-49,999	8	108,540	131,211	134,570	141,000
10,000-24,999	16	100,300	114,849	113,442	130,000
5,000-9,999	17	77,875	98,195	97,000	112,000
2,500-4,999	23	61,000	86,791	85,160	107,000
Under 2,500	16	47,840	63,753	62,000	81,996

Note: Where only one city or county reported in a population group, that record was suppressed.

State	No. reporting	Base salary			
		Minimum ($)	Mean ($)	Median ($)	Maximum ($)
Mississippi					
10,000-24,999	2	52,000	67,565	67,565	83,130
Missouri					
25,000-49,999	7	118,709	139,647	140,400	158,980
10,000-24,999	13	67,500	106,782	101,600	145,100
5,000-9,999	18	62,650	96,257	97,969	145,948
2,500-4,999	13	44,000	65,972	62,000	100,000
Under 2,500	7	42,250	55,066	51,000	74,000
Montana					
50,000-99,999	2	100,000	109,000	109,000	118,000
5,000-9,999	2	83,116	91,558	91,558	100,000
Nebraska					
10,000-24,999	6	96,000	111,259	112,700	125,000
5,000-9,999	8	72,500	86,902	89,550	96,000
2,500-4,999	6	73,418	83,530	85,314	92,000
Under 2,500	8	40,500	51,283	50,000	63,000
Nevada					
50,000-99,999	2	140,169	163,085	163,085	186,000
5,000-9,999	2	105,000	118,500	118,500	132,000
New Hampshire					
25,000-49,999	4	110,000	122,476	119,951	140,000
10,000-24,999	6	93,730	112,977	115,500	127,856
5,000-9,999	12	53,000	82,191	87,000	101,500
2,500-4,999	6	55,000	67,581	66,079	82,500
Under 2,500	3	50,000	65,660	63,500	83,480
New Jersey					
50,000-99,999	4	113,559	150,890	149,500	191,000
25,000-49,999	9	82,500	160,454	155,000	292,500
10,000-24,999	13	55,000	137,081	142,371	165,000
5,000-9,999	9	45,000	103,723	104,000	150,046
2,500-4,999	8	21,000	90,001	93,100	140,000
Under 2,500	2	63,863	90,682	90,682	117,500
New Mexico					
50,000-99,999	2	128,500	139,250	139,250	150,000
25,000-49,999	3	106,000	109,333	111,000	111,000
10,000-24,999	3	80,000	88,753	81,090	105,170
5,000-9,999	2	90,000	92,500	92,500	95,000

Note: Where only one city or county reported in a population group, that record was suppressed.

State	No. reporting	Base salary			
		Minimum ($)	Mean ($)	Median ($)	Maximum ($)
New York					
10,000-24,999	8	97,410	148,114	163,000	191,000
5,000-9,999	10	68,690	122,979	145,500	175,000
2,500-4,999	4	49,000	84,003	72,787	141,440
North Carolina					
100,000-249,999	4	164,172	175,668	178,750	181,000
50,000-99,999	5	141,110	168,367	169,000	192,400
10,000-24,999	13	100,000	114,059	113,500	128,919
5,000-9,999	19	63,000	98,929	92,389	139,000
2,500-4,999	27	40,000	78,522	80,000	110,477
Under 2,500	21	39,000	70,761	63,000	106,600
North Dakota					
10,000-24,999	2	90,000	102,000	102,000	114,000
Ohio					
25,000-49,999	8	82,825	128,427	128,917	180,000
10,000-24,999	19	71,127	106,748	106,000	152,069
5,000-9,999	18	68,135	99,376	101,970	146,000
2,500-4,999	13	30,000	76,397	72,150	128,000
Under 2,500	6	38,480	45,062	45,000	51,594
Oklahoma					
10,000-24,999	8	72,000	99,777	102,001	135,000
5,000-9,999	2	90,254	102,627	102,627	115,000
2,500-4,999	11	51,119	74,374	72,000	101,000
Under 2,500	2	49,375	55,042	55,042	60,709
Oregon					
50,000-99,999	3	147,000	154,367	152,000	164,100
25,000-49,999	5	125,000	141,676	138,960	167,418
10,000-24,999	17	106,344	123,621	120,000	148,000
5,000-9,999	13	83,280	99,938	98,000	126,000
2,500-4,999	15	55,000	82,225	81,228	116,000
Under 2,500	33	22,000	54,127	53,695	93,184
Pennsylvania					
50,000-99,999	2	97,584	145,292	145,292	193,000
25,000-49,999	12	94,700	122,404	117,220	182,000
10,000-24,999	43	56,065	100,800	99,575	148,525
5,000-9,999	36	20,000	5,025	70,601	145,000
2,500-4,999	36	30,888	66,806	66,300	102,000
Under 2,500	8	35,000	63,348	54,994	111,647

Note: Where only one city or county reported in a population group, that record was suppressed.

State	No. reporting	Base salary			
		Minimum ($)	Mean ($)	Median ($)	Maximum ($)
Rhode Island					
25,000-49,999	3	111,394	123,465	122,000	137,000
10,000-24,999	3	103,000	109,090	105,500	118,771
South Carolina					
10,000-24,999	5	91,083	104,701	100,034	124,800
5,000-9,999	7	68,000	88,072	82,000	112,500
2,500-4,999	5	40,000	84,275	83,375	130,000
Under 2,500	4	55,000	70,967	67,433	94,000
South Dakota					
10,000-24,999	2	111,714	116,132	116,132	120,550
5,000-9,999	2	85,904	93,517	93,517	101,130
Under 2,500	2	50,000	63,500	63,500	77,000
Tennessee					
50,000-99,999	2	126,000	133,000	133,000	140,000
10,000-24,999	8	65,000	113,410	112,300	163,530
5,000-9,999	6	73,424	98,918	94,000	131,193
2,500-4,999	3	45,000	71,750	75,000	95,250
Under 2,500	4	20,000	41,172	44,000	56,687
Texas					
250,000-499,999	2	172,000	193,000	193,000	214,000
100,000-249,999	8	167,000	198,074	195,636	232,000
50,000-99,999	5	170,000	181,380	178,000	197,000
25,000-49,999	17	96,000	154,839	160,000	201,251
10,000-24,999	24	95,400	135,413	131,038	207,190
5,000-9,999	26	56,000	102,352	107,000	157,141
2,500-4,999	42	35,000	88,423	82,000	159,000
Under 2,500	16	30,000	68,761	64,500	114,715
Utah					
25,000-49,999	4	115,625	131,281	129,750	150,000
10,000-24,999	8	86,000	111,246	113,835	125,000
5,000-9,999	8	75,000	100,695	99,890	135,980
2,500-4,999	3	82,500	90,974	87,125	103,296
Under 2,500	3	47,350	65,979	63,000	87,588
Vermont					
10,000-24,999	2	107,500	114,750	114,750	122,000
5,000-9,999	8	61,000	78,799	80,818	98,060
2,500-4,999	5	50,000	67,604	60,400	100,000
Under 2,500	3	56,000	62,864	56,493	76,100

Note: Where only one city or county reported in a population group, that record was suppressed.

State	No. reporting	Base salary			
		Minimum ($)	Mean ($)	Median ($)	Maximum ($)
Virginia					
50,000-99,999	2	151,902	160,951	160,951	170,000
25,000-49,999	4	128,625	146,188	151,563	153,000
10,000-24,999	12	97,500	131,943	133,045	166,000
5,000-9,999	10	76,500	97,570	94,000	139,000
2,500-4,999	10	46,000	82,388	85,800	106,113
Under 2,500	11	42,000	65,126	68,000	82,000
Washington					
25,000-49,999	4	142,320	151,792	146,000	172,848
10,000-24,999	16	106,000	132,061	128,870	162,154
5,000-9,999	19	90,000	118,267	120,000	150,000
2,500-4,999	9	76,898	97,267	98,976	120,000
Under 2,500	2	68,000	76,500	76,500	85,000
West Virginia					
50,000-99,999	2	72,000	104,842	104,842	137,683
Wisconsin					
25,000-49,999	3	102,445	117,148	122,000	127,000
10,000-24,999	16	75,000	100,931	102,762	119,890
5,000-9,999	22	64,000	88,966	90,260	111,000
2,500-4,999	16	63,591	75,445	75,000	105,000
Under 2,500	13	50,000	69,918	66,699	95,000
Wyoming					
5,000-9,999	2	91,800	103,900	103,900	116,000

Note: Where only one city or county reported in a population group, that record was suppressed.

Appendix Table 6-A2 County Salaries by Population Group within States

State	No. reporting	Base salary			
		Minimum ($)	Mean ($)	Median ($)	Maximum ($)
Alabama					
50,000-99,999	2	51,740	65,041	65,041	78,342
10,000-24,999	3	48,000	56,583	51,750	70,000
California					
Over 1,000,000	3	250,000	259,353	253,562	274,498
500,000-1,000,000	3	182,000	235,408	250,224	274,000
250,000-499,999	4	162,683	213,474	224,000	243,212
100,000-249,999	2	168,996	209,498	209,498	250,000
50,000-99,999	2	160,000	169,000	169,000	178,000
Colorado					
250,000-499,999	2	156,523	158,262	158,262	160,000
10,000-24,999	3	83,000	110,362	119,000	129,086
5,000-9,999	2	100,850	109,925	109,925	119,000
Florida					
250,000-499,999	6	145,000	168,667	175,000	180,000
100,000-249,999	3	125,425	175,142	170,000	230,000
25,000-49,999	2	92,700	117,850	117,850	143,000
10,000-24,999	2	96,000	99,000	99,000	102,000
Georgia					
500,000-1,000,000	3	200,000	231,605	228,000	266,815
100,000-249,999	4	124,000	135,000	133,000	150,000
50,000-99,999	4	90,000	128,707	138,664	147,500
25,000-49,999	3	50,400	88,867	106,200	110,000
10,000-24,999	15	57,289	84,389	83,000	109,000
5,000-9,999	3	42,000	47,667	50,000	51,000
Illinois					
25,000-49,999	4	73,902	82,142	74,500	105,664
Kansas					
250,000-499,999	2	178,597	183,139	183,139	187,680
50,000-99,999	2	94,000	114,000	114,000	134,000
25,000-49,999	2	88,000	96,500	96,500	105,000
Kentucky					
50,000-99,999	2	114,000	124,500	124,500	135,000
Louisiana					
100,000-249,999	2	91,314	120,657	120,657	150,000

Note: Where only one city or county reported in a population group, that record was suppressed.

State	No. reporting	Base salary			
		Minimum ($)	Mean ($)	Median ($)	Maximum ($)
Maine					
25,000-49,999	3	55,000	65,500	65,500	76,000
Maryland					
100,000-249,999	2	155,671	160,336	160,336	165,000
Michigan					
100,000-249,999	3	115,316	126,468	120,146	143,943
50,000-99,999	4	82,500	99,506	90,755	134,014
25,000-49,999	6	61,161	84,029	86,872	98,503
Minnesota					
100,000-249,999	2	150,000	153,000	153,000	156,000
50,000-99,999	2	128,752	131,376	131,376	134,000
25,000-49,999	2	105,000	107,900	107,900	110,800
10,000-24,999	6	66,953	83,006	85,096	92,888
Mississippi					
25,000-49,999	2	77,200	101,600	101,600	126,000
Nevada					
25,000-49,999	2	90,891	113,446	113,446	136,000
New Mexico					
25,000-49,999	3	85,000	92,333	90,000	102,000
10,000-24,999	4	56,343	83,936	84,700	110,000
New York					
100,000-249,999	2	106,085	118,043	118,043	130,000
50,000-99,999	6	85,000	114,483	115,150	138,600
North Carolina					
100,000-249,999	6	126,690	158,860	162,326	198,935
50,000-99,999	7	90,000	117,507	107,849	172,200
25,000-49,999	5	70,000	107,774	109,850	146,520
10,000-24,999	5	80,701	92,801	94,000	102,306
Ohio					
100,000-249,999	4	90,688	106,172	102,500	129,000
Oregon					
100,000-249,999	2	137,652	145,326	145,326	153,000
10,000-24,999	2	65,532	82,016	82,016	98,500

Note: Where only one city or county reported in a population group, that record was suppressed.

State	No. reporting	Base salary			
		Minimum ($)	Mean ($)	Median ($)	Maximum ($)
South Carolina					
250,000-499,999	3	133,737	169,229	169,950	204,000
100,000-249,999	4	159,650	168,409	168,410	177,165
50,000-99,999	3	103,000	113,700	113,100	125,000
Virginia					
250,000-499,999	2	238,960	250,063	250,063	261,166
50,000-99,999	9	126,510	158,644	157,443	188,288
25,000-49,999	11	99,291	126,994	125,000	165,000
10,000-24,999	8	73,060	101,483	103,900	140,000
5,000-9,999	4	80,000	98,000	93,500	125,000
Wisconsin					
100,000-249,999	3	118,535	140,087	138,935	162,790
50,000-99,999	2	101,275	109,138	109,138	117,000
25,000-49,999	6	87,392	98,646	94,445	116,917
10,000-24,999	2	82,500	91,063	91,063	99,625

Note: Where only one city or county reported in a population group, that record was suppressed.

7

E-Government 2011: Trends and Innovations

Donald F. Norris
University of Maryland, Baltimore County

Christopher Reddick
University of Texas at San Antonio

Electronic government (e-government) has been with us for nearly two decades and has spread rapidly across the globe. All national, most if not all state, and nearly all local governments now offer information and services electronically 24/7/365 through official government websites. This article reports the findings from a survey of U.S. local governments to present a snapshot of the place of e-government in the nation as of 2011.

SELECTED FINDINGS

The most important reason that local governments give for adopting e-government is to provide citizens with access to local government information (98%). Accordingly, most online offerings are information and communication rather than interactive services and transactions.

Among local governments that reported facing barriers, more than half (67%) cited the lack of financial resources. However, it appears that a rapidly growing number of local governments are adopting cloud computing, which enables them to reap the benefits of computing power easily and cost-effectively without the expense of purchasing, maintaining, operating, and upgrading it.

Relatively few governments reported changes occurring as a result of e-government, but most of the reported changes have been positive–most notably, improved customer service (87%) and improved local government communication with the public (78%).

Methodology

The questionnaire used for this survey was based in part on the 2004 ICMA local e-government survey.[1] Before developing the 2011 instrument, we asked a number of local information technology (IT) directors and chief information officers (CIOs) to review the 2004 instrument and make recommendations based on their knowledge of recent e-government developments and trends.* Armed with their suggestions, we worked cooperatively with the ICMA survey research staff to write the 2011 questionnaire. While many of the questions we used are identical to those used in the 2004 ICMA survey, we added a number of new questions and, to keep the length of the instrument manageable, deleted others.

*We wish to acknowledge and express our appreciation to the following local government officials who reviewed the 2004 survey instrument and provided comments and suggestions that we then used in developing the 2011 instrument. Any errors or omissions are those of the authors and in no way reflect on these officials or their advice: Michael Cannon, chief information officer (CIO), Rockville, Maryland; Ira Levy, director of technology and communication services, Howard County, Maryland; David Molchany, deputy county executive (previously CIO), Fairfax County, Virginia; Elliot Schlanger, CIO, State of Maryland (previously CIO, Baltimore, Maryland); Paul Thorn, information technology manager, Annapolis, Maryland.

In the spring of 2011, ICMA mailed the survey to all municipal governments with a population of 10,000 or greater and to all county governments that have elected executives or appointed managers (a total of 4,452 governments). It sent a second mailing to local governments that had not responded to the first mailing, and it also provided an online option for completing the survey. Most respondents (1,020) returned paper surveys, while 306 completed the online version.

Approximately 30% of the sample responded to the 2011 survey (Table 7-1). In terms of population, larger local governments—those with populations of 250,000 and greater—were overrepresented because of a much higher response rate (40%); medium-sized governments (25,000–249,999) were also overrepresented with a response rate of 33%; and smaller governments (those under 25,000) were underrepresented with a response rate of 26%. As for other areas of classification, cities responded to a greater degree than counties; and council-manager jurisdictions, local governments in the West, and central cities were overrepresented, while mayor-council and council-elected executive jurisdictions and local governments in the Northeast were underrepresented.

At 30%, the response rate to the 2011 survey is somewhat lower than the response rates to earlier ICMA e-government surveys (50% in 2000; 53% in 2002; and 42% in 2004). ICMA has noticed a decline in response to its surveys in recent years and attributes this, in part, to the "Great Recession" and resultant local staff cutbacks, which have left local governments with fewer resources to devote to completing surveys.[2]

Reasons for Adopting E-Government

It is well established that local governments have adopted e-government rapidly and somewhat extensively over the past two decades. An important question is why they did so. As shown in Figure 7-1, the main reason that local governments have adopted e-government is to provide access for citizens—access to local government information (98%), to local government itself (90%), to local elected officials (70%), and to appointed officials (67%). Two other reasons offered by substantial percentages of respondents are to save money (69%) and to facilitate citizen participation (65%). These findings are consistent with those from a 2005 study, which found that local governments adopt e-government mainly to provide information and services online and also to provide citizens with access to local government officials.[3]

Table 7-1 Survey Response

Classification	No. of municipalities/ counties[a] surveyed (A)	Respondents	
		No.	% of (A)
Total	4,452	1,326	30
Cities	3,302	1,021	31
Counties	1,150	305	26
Population group			
Over 1,000,000	33	15	46
500,000-1,000,000	73	25	34
250,000-499,999	117	48	41
100,000-249,999	370	153	41
50,000-99,999	630	211	34
25,000-49,999	1,062	312	29
10,000-24,999	2,167	562	26
Geographic region			
Northeast	999	198	20
North-Central	1,234	361	29
South	1,417	460	33
West	802	307	38
Metro status			
Central	858	323	38
Suburban	2,318	685	30
Independent	1,276	318	25
Form of government			
Mayor-council	1,197	232	19
Council-manager	1,883	742	39
Commission	70	17	24
Town meeting	106	22	21
Representative town meeting	46	8	17
Council-administrator (manager)	735	229	31
Council-elected executive	415	76	18

Note: This survey was sent to all city-type governments with a population of 10,000 and greater and to all counties. Of the counties under 10,000 in population, so few responded (40) that they are not included in the analysis. The responses from the smaller governments are included in the summary of the survey that is available on the ICMA website. Therefore, readers who compare the data from this chapter to that summary will note there are small, almost always insubstantial differences between the two data sets.

a For a definition of terms, please see "Inside the *Year Book*," xii-xiv.

Figure 7-1 Reasons for Providing E-Government Services

Reasons	Percentage reporting (n = 1,235)
Citizen access to local government information	98
Citizen access to the local government	90
Citizen access to elected officials	70
Save money	69
Citizen access to appointed officials	67
Citizen participation in government/e-democracy	65
Produce revenue	17
Other	5

Local E-Government Functionality

Following David Coursey and Donald Norris in their 2008 article based on the data from the 2004 survey,[4] we divided local e-government offerings into two categories: (1) information and communication and (2) transaction-based services. The former categories, the "low-hanging fruit," are inarguably easier and less costly to automate and manage on websites. The latter, because of their greater complexity, are more difficult and more costly to offer.

Online Services

Respondents were asked whether their local governments offer various services online. The data in Table 7-2 show that large percentages of local governments offer various information and communication applications via their websites: nine such services are offered by at least half of responding local governments—several by large majorities—and one is offered by 45%. However, the remaining seven information and communication services have been adopted by 17% or less of local governments. Compared to the findings from 2004,[5] these show that local governments, not surprisingly, are offering more basic e-government information and communication applications than ever before.

As for transaction-based services, the adoption rates are generally lower. Only three of these services have been adopted by at least half of the responding local governments (requests for services, 58%; payment of utility bills, 53%; requests for records, 50%) (Table 7-2). Two other services (registration for recreational facilities/activities and payment of fines and fees) have adoption rates that range between 41% and 48%. All other services have been adopted by smaller percentages of respondents. Again, transaction-based services are more difficult and more costly to automate on local websites, which is likely the most important reason that local governments have been slower to adopt them.

Respondents were also asked to rate, on a scale of 1 to 5, whether the applications and services provided through the local government website involve mostly one-way communication to citizens or are mostly interactive/transaction oriented. Slightly more than half the respondents (53%) reported that their e-government applications and services are mostly one-way communication to citizens; about one-third (31%) said that their applications and services are about half and half; and 16% said that they are mostly two-way communication. These findings are consistent with the notion that e-government remains primarily about delivering services and information one way. But there is some evidence, at least from these respondents, that local e-government may be moving, albeit slowly, in the direction of greater interactivity and transactional capability.

The provision of information and services online is, by definition, e-government. An important question is whether—and to what extent—local governments have moved away from traditional service provision methods in favor of online provision. For each service they provide online, respondents were asked whether those same services are also provided

Table 7-2 Online Local E-Government Services

Services	No. reporting (A)	Offer online No.	Offer online % of (A)
Information and communication			
Council agenda/minutes	1,250	1,169	94
Codes/ordinances	1,237	1,124	91
Forms that can be downloaded for manual completion (e.g., voter registration, building permits, etc.)	1,238	1,097	89
Employment information/applications	1,246	1,096	88
Communication with individual elected and appointed officials	1,227	843	69
Geographic information systems (GIS) mapping/data	1,209	784	65
E-newsletters sent to residents/businesses	1,177	754	64
E-alerts	1,226	739	60
Streaming video	1,246	632	51
Video on demand	1,226	557	45
Mobile apps (iPhone or Droid)	1,173	199	17
Customer relationship management (CRM)/311	1,133	195	17
Interactive voice response (IVR)	1,130	189	17
Podcasts	1,143	133	12
Moderated discussions	1,157	84	7
Instant messaging (IM)	1,166	83	7
Chat rooms	1,153	32	3
Transaction-based services			
Requests for services, such as pothole repair	1,210	700	58
Payments of utility bills	1,148	613	53
Requests for local government records	1,201	597	50
Registration for use of recreational facilities/activities, such as classes and picnic areas	1,192	571	48
Payments of fines/fees	1,171	474	41
Delivery of local government records to the requestor	1,180	433	37
Payments of taxes	1,160	417	36
Completion and submission of permit applications	1,180	398	34
Completion and submission of business license applications/renewals	1,158	256	22
Property registration, such as animal, bicycle registration	1,134	142	13
Voter registration	1,121	101	9

in person, on paper (e.g., paper forms and/or mail), and/or by phone. This question did not include services that only have online options (e.g., streaming video, podcasts, chat rooms, etc.).

As shown in Table 7-3, local governments continue to provide traditional delivery options for all online services for which a traditional option is available. However, for most of these services, there is some degree of drop-off in the use of traditional methods. That drop-off is much greater, on average, for information and communication services than for transaction-based services. This could be because of relatively lower adoption rates of the latter and/or citizen resistance to abandoning the more traditional methods. An early prediction for e-government was that moving citizens away from traditional methods of dealing with government to online services would make processes more efficient, thereby saving governments money. While the data in Table 7-3 suggest that local governments have in fact begun to make strides—in some cases, substantially—toward the goal of replacing more traditional service delivery methods with online services, other data do not confirm that money savings have necessarily resulted (see "Changes as a Result of E-Government" further on in this article).

Table 7-3 Provision of Traditional Service Methods in Addition to Online Services

Services	No. offering service online (A)	Also provide service In person % of (A)	On paper % of (A)	By phone % of (A)
Information and communication				
Council agenda/minutes	1,169	55	55	13
E-newsletters sent to residents/businesses	754	26	35	7
Codes/ordinances	1,124	51	52	14
Forms that can be downloaded for manual completion (e.g., voter registration, building permits, etc.)	1,097	70	59	14
Employment information/applications	1,096	61	56	17
Communication with individual elected and appointed officials	843	47	39	36
Geographic information systems (GIS) mapping/data	784	44	36	13
Transaction-based services				
Requests for services, such as pothole repair	700	69	50	61
Payments of utility bills	613	86	78	46
Requests for local government records	597	74	69	31
Registration for use of recreational facilities/activities, such as classes and picnic areas	571	76	63	49
Payments of fines/fees	474	83	72	31
Delivery of local government records to the requestor	433	70	64	22
Payments of taxes	417	86	74	27
Completion and submission of permit applications	398	76	68	19
Completion and submission of business license applications/renewals	256	75	65	16
Property registration, such as animal, bicycle registration	142	60	58	16
Voter registration	101	59	55	15

Use of Social Media

Just a few years ago, social media essentially did not exist at all or were not in use in the world of local government. Since then, however, the worldwide adoption of social media has skyrocketed. In 2011, according to the *New York Times*, Facebook (launched in February 2004) had more than 800 million subscribers and Twitter (unveiled in March 2006) had more than 200 million users.[6] With such a rapid worldwide uptake, we sought to determine whether local governments in the United States have adopted social media as part of their e-government offerings.

About two-thirds (68%) of respondents reported that they have adopted at least one social medium (not shown)—this, in less than seven years after Facebook arrived and less than five years after Twitter. Among those local governments that reported using social media, 92% subscribe to Facebook, 70% have adopted Twitter, slightly under half (45%) post on YouTube, one in five (20%) blog, and 16% use Flickr (Figure 7-2). By almost any standard, the adoption of social media by U.S. local governments has been extraordinary.

To determine the nature of that usage, the survey again asked respondents to rate, on a scale of 1 to 5, the extent to which social media are used mostly as one-way communication from the government outward or mostly as two-way communication between the government and its citizens. Of the 833 local governments that responded to the question, 64% said mostly one-way while only 14% said mostly two-way; the remaining 23% reported that it was somewhere in between (not shown). These findings should not be surprising for at least two reason that have already been noted: (1) most e-government applications are mostly one-way communication and (2) local government adoption of social media is a relatively new phenomenon.

Cloud Computing

Cloud computing is the use of the Internet by one organization to access (for a fee, of course) what is essentially the excess computing capacity of another

Figure 7-2 Local Government Use of Social Media

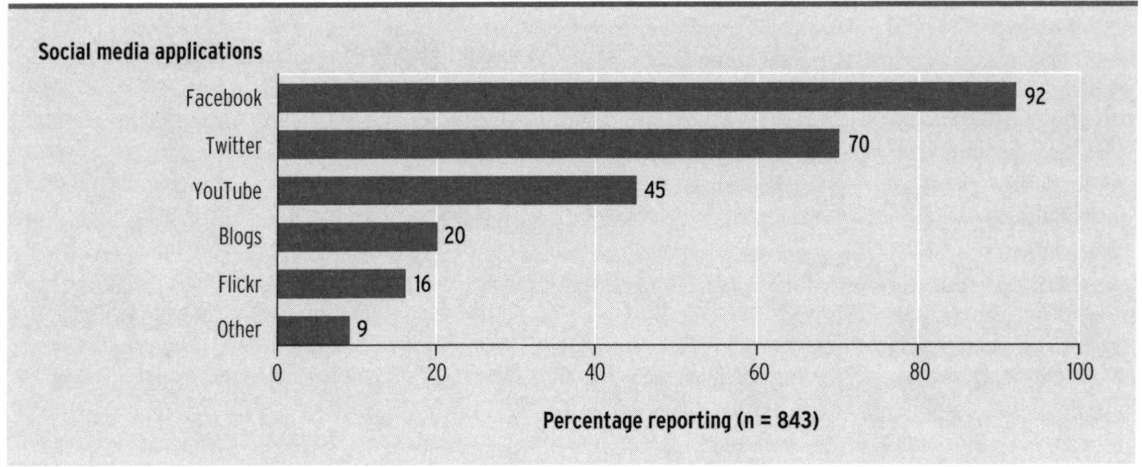

organization in lieu of developing additional capacity in-house. Perhaps the first example of the commercialization of the cloud (i.e., the Internet) came in 2006, when Amazon.com rolled out Amazon Web Services.[7] By providing access to applications, computing power, storage, e-mail, and other functionality, the cloud offers local governments a potentially easy and cost-effective opportunity to reap the benefits of computing power that they do not own and do not have to maintain, operate, and upgrade.

As shown in Table 7-4, slightly more than a quarter of local governments (27%) reported that they use cloud computing. On the one hand, this is not a very substantial proportion of local governments. On the other hand, since cloud computing is so recent, such an uptake by U.S. local governments represents quite a rapid adoption of this technological innovation. Given the rapidity of adoption, we expect that substantially more governments will use cloud computing in coming years. Among local governments that use cloud computing, the data show that they use it for such purposes as software applications (67%), offsite storage (29%), e-mail (22%), office tools (13%), main storage (13%), and computer power (11%).

Table 7-4 Cloud Computing in Local Governments

	No. reporting	Percentage
Does your local government use cloud computing? (n = 1,240)		
Yes	335	27
No	905	73
If yes, what is cloud computing used for? (n = 331)		
Software apps	222	67
Offsite storage	97	29
E-mail (e.g., Google mail)	74	22
Desktop office tools (e.g., Google apps)	43	13
Main storage	43	13
Computer power	35	11
Other	54	16

Barriers to Adopting E-Government

Although local governments have significantly expanded their e-government offerings, not all local governments offer a wide range of e-services, and the more transaction-oriented or interactive a service, the less likely that it will be adopted. Why might this be so? Clearly, one reason might be the existence of barriers to adoption, a conclusion found by previous studies.[8]

Respondents were shown a list of 21 barriers to e-government initiatives and asked to identify the top five barriers that their local governments have encountered. It is noteworthy that only one of the barriers—lack of financial resources—was reported by more than a majority of local governments in 2011 (Table 7-5). That lack of financial resources continues to be a barrier to local e-government deployment should not be surprising: historically (at least since the first ICMA e-government survey in 2000), it has been listed as a barrier by a large percentage of respondents, many of whose budgetary constraints have been compounded by the recent recession.

Only one additional barrier was reported by a sizeable percentage of local governments: lack of technology/web staff in the IT department (46%).

Three barriers were reported by about 30% of respondents while four were reported by between 23% and 27%. Of the remaining 12 barriers on the list, 6 were reported by less than 10% of local governments. When asked to single out the most important barrier (a question not asked in 2004), a plurality of respondents (42%) cited a lack of financial resources, while 13% cited a lack of technology/web staff in the IT department—responses that essentially mirror the findings shown in Table 7-5.

Table 7-5 Barriers to Local E-Government Initiatives

Barriers	No. reporting	Percentage
Total reporting	1,241	100
Lack of financial resources	835	67
Lack of technology/web staff in the IT department	571	46
Issues regarding security	380	31
Issues relating to convenience fees for online transactions	372	30
Difficulty justifying return on investment	357	29
Lack of technology/web staff in the operating departments	334	27
Lack of technology/web expertise in the operating departments	284	23
Staff resistance to change	283	23
Need to upgrade technology (PCs, networks, etc.)	279	23
Issues regarding privacy	232	19
Website does not accept payment by credit card	225	18
Lack of information about e-government applications in the operating departments	213	17
Lack of collaboration among departments	206	17
Lack of resident/business interest/demand	177	14
Lack of technology/web expertise in the IT department	173	14
Inadequate bandwidth	100	8
Lack of support from elected officials	93	8
Lack of information about e-government applications in the IT department	86	7
Resident/business resistance to change	55	4
Lack of support from top administrators	54	4
Other	102	8

Changes as a Result of E-Government

To begin to assess the impact of e-government, we presented respondents with a list of 16 possible changes in local government as a result of e-government and asked them to identify those changes that their governments have experienced. Perhaps the first thing to notice is that 90% of respondents reported at least some change (not shown). The second, however, is the limited number of changes they experienced, a finding that is consistent with previous studies.[9] Only four changes were reported by at least half of the respondents: improved customer service (87%), improved communication with the public (78%), increased efficiency of business processes (52%), and increased time demands on IT staff (50%) (Table 7-6). One change was reported by 46% of local governments; four by between 30% and 39%; three by between 20% and 29%; and four by less than 10%.

Table 7-6 How E-Government Has Changed Local Government

Changes	No. reporting	Percentage
Total reporting	1,192	100
Changes reported		
Improved customer service	1,032	87
Improved local government communication with the public	933	78
Increased efficiency of business processes	616	52
Increased time demands on IT staff	592	50
Increased citizen contact with elected and appointed officials	552	46
Changed the role of departmental staff	465	39
Decreased transaction times	448	38
Changed the role of IT staff	414	35
Reengineered/reengineering business processes	403	34
Reduced time demands on departmental staff	345	29
Increased time demands on departmental staff	329	28
Reduced administrative costs	292	25
Reduced the number of departmental staff	94	8
Reduced time demands on IT staff	64	5
Generated revenue from fees, advertising	59	5
Reduced the number of IT staff	38	3

The third noteworthy finding is that although many of the changes listed on the survey instrument were not reported, those that were reported most often are generally positive. Still, some expected or desired changes do not appear to be occurring—for example, reduced IT staffing (3%), generated revenue (5%), reduced time demands on IT staff (5%), and reduced departmental staff (8%). Moreover, two changes reported by these local governments are clearly negative: increased time demands on IT staff (50%) and increased time demands on departmental staff (28%).

Respondents were then asked to indicate which of the listed positive and negative changes were the most significant. The top two positive changes, with nearly indistinguishable response rates, were improved communication with the public and improved customer service (35% each) (not shown). Only 11% cited increased efficiency of business operations. The most significant negative changes reported were increased time demands on IT staff (53%) and increased time demands on departmental staff (24%) (not shown). The changed role of departmental staff came in third but with only 6% of governments reporting it.

Local E-Government Management

The survey also examined how e-government is organized and managed. Nearly 6 in 10 local governments (59%) reported that they have a separate IT department responsible for e-government (not shown). Those that do not were asked which individual or department has this responsibility, and of the 485 who responded to this question, one-third (34%) named the city/county manager/chief administrative office, 23% named the chief technology officer/IT department, and 13% named the public information office (Figure 7–3). These data show considerable diversity among local governments regarding the location of e-government management.

When asked which individual or department has day-to-day responsibility for the overall management of the local government website, about one-third of respondents (32%) reported that management responsibility lies with the CIO or IT department; one in five (20%) named the public information office; slightly fewer (19%) located that responsibility in the city or county manager's or CAO's office; and just 11% cited the chief technology officer (Figure 7–4). As with e-government management in general, these findings show considerable diversity in local website management.

Asked whether they have a dedicated webmaster, nearly two-thirds (62%) of local government respondents reported that they do (not shown). In addition, almost all local governments (95%) allow individual departments to have their own web pages on the local government website, and of those, 82% reported that department web pages are required to conform to a "look and feel" consistent with that of the local government website (not shown).

Figure 7-3 Department/Office Responsible for Management of E-Government

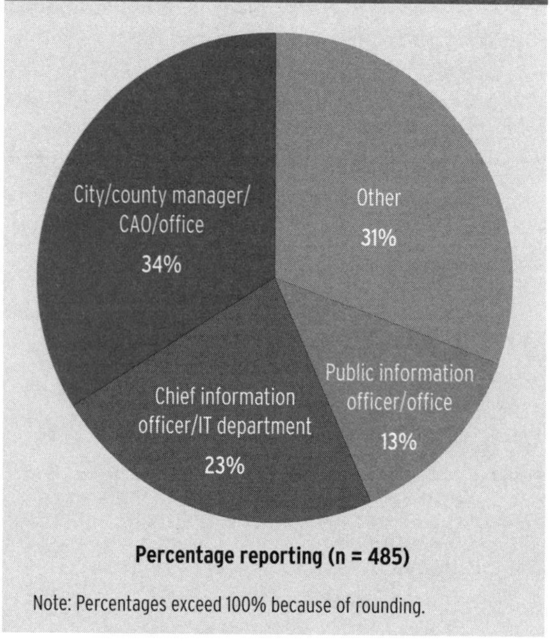

Note: Percentages exceed 100% because of rounding.

Figure 7-4 Department/Agency Responsible for Daily Management of Local Government Website

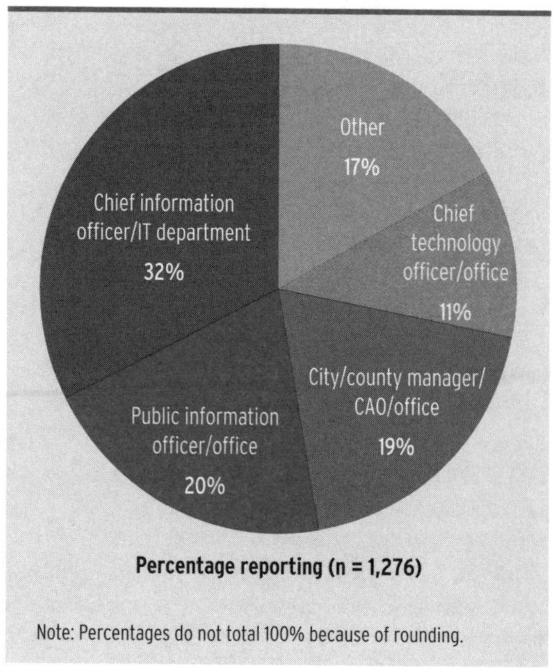

Note: Percentages do not total 100% because of rounding.

It is somewhat common for organizations to develop policies to govern their websites and/or to address matters that affect website users. The survey presented respondents with a list of 10 areas in which local governments have policies or procedures affecting their websites and site users, and it asked them to indicate which were applicable to their local governments. Of those areas, six—providing links to other governments, use of social media, providing links to community organizations, website security, website privacy, and providing links to nonprofits—were identified by between 53% and 65% of local governments (Figure 7–5). Only one-third or less have adopted policies in the remaining four areas. These findings suggest that local governments, by and large, have adopted formal policies to help them manage their websites and to assist site users.

In theory, if not always in practice, planning can be important to a local government's ability to implement online applications as well as to the success or failure of those applications. Prior studies of local government planning for IT and e-government, however, have revealed little or no planning,[10] and the data from this survey are consistent with those findings. As shown in Table 7–7, less than half of local governments (49%) have a formal IT plan, although where such plans exist, the great majority of them

Table 7–7 Planning for Local E-Government

	No. reporting	Percentage
Does your local government have a formal information technology plan? (n = 1,259)		
Yes	615	49
No	644	51
If yes, does this plan include e-government? (n = 615)		
Yes	506	82
No	109	18

(82%) do include e-government as a component. These findings suggest that most local governments are not following sound management practice with regard to planning for e-government.

Local governments have several options in terms of how they might acquire e-government applications. In the 2011 survey, respondents were shown a list of six options, and the largest percentage (64%) reported the in-house development of e-government applications by local staff (Figure 7–6). Next came outsourcing to application service providers (50%), followed closely

Figure 7–5 Policies on Local Government Website

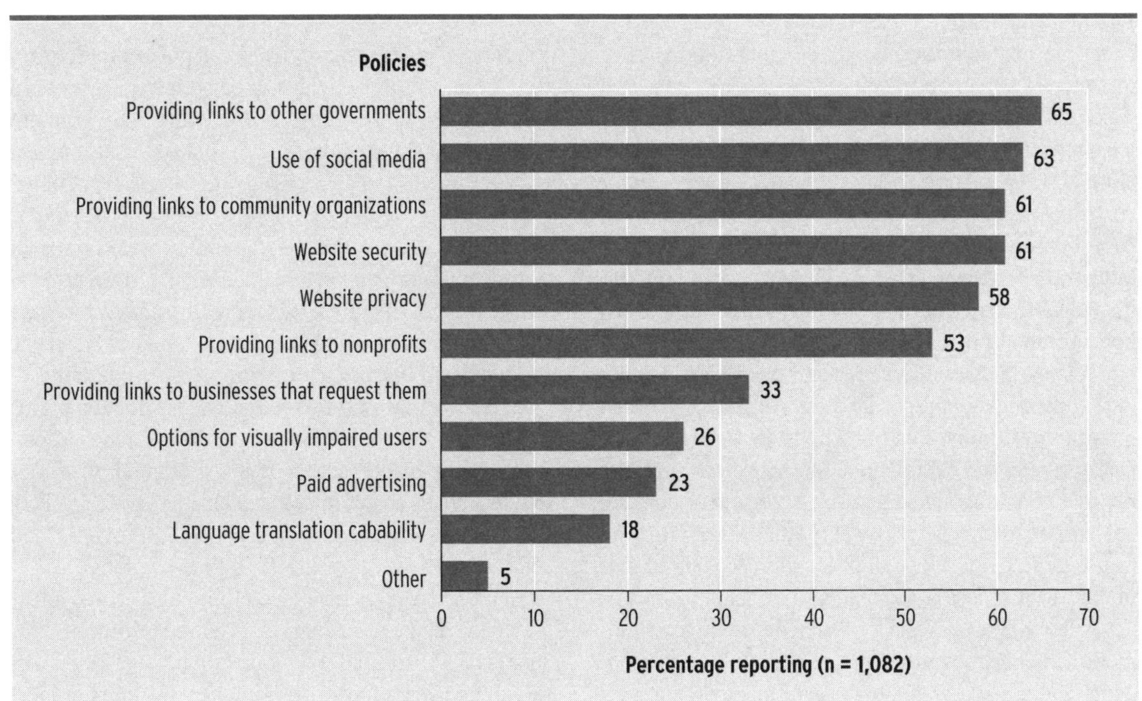

Figure 7-6 How Local E-Government Services Are Acquired

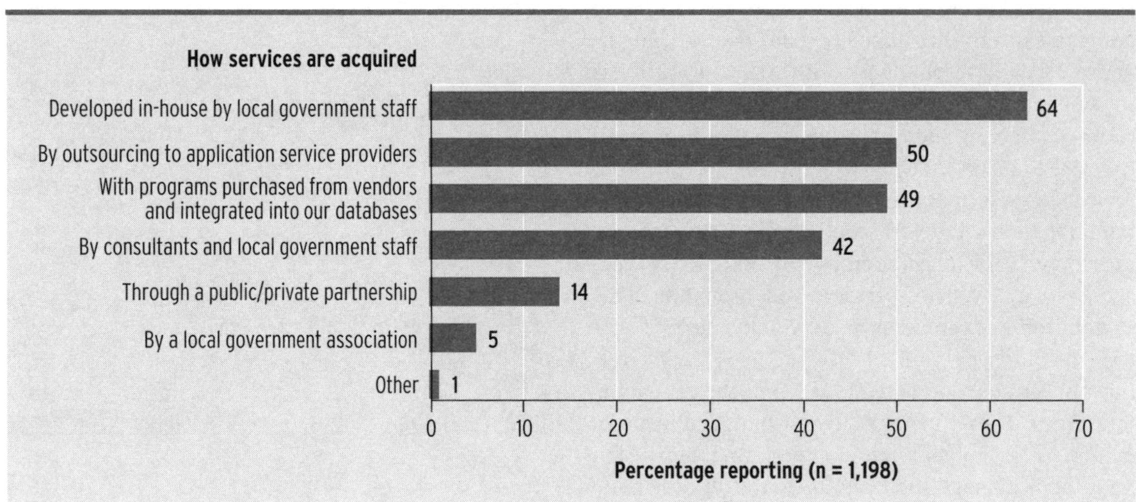

by purchasing programs from vendors (49%). Used to a much smaller degree are public-private partnerships (15%) and local government associations (5%).

Respondents were also asked which of the six methods is used most commonly for e-service application development, and same three options led in the responses: in-house by local government staff (35%), outsourced to application service provider (22%), and with programs purchased from vendors and integrated into their databases (21%) (not shown).

E-Government Financing

The final area of interest addressed in the 2011 survey is e-government financing. Respondents were asked to choose from among three options the one that best describes the e-government budget process in their local governments. More than three-quarters of respondents (78%) reported that their local governments do not have a separate budget item for e-government (not shown). Among those that do have a separate budget, 18% reported that the IT department prepares it, while 4% reported that each department develops and submits its own budget.

When asked what revenue source or sources their local governments use to fund e-government, the vast majority of respondents (94%) checked general fund revenues (Figure 7–7). Other, although not especially notable, funding sources for e-government include enterprise funds (18%), utility funds (15%), and transaction fees (15%). All other sources were identified by 10% or less of local governments reporting.

As for where the local governments obtain cost estimates for their e-government projects, 76% of respondents identified IT solution vendors (not shown), which should not be terribly surprising since the vendors who sell these products and services are in a superior position to know their costs. After that, the most frequently cited source for cost estimates is other local governments (42%), which is also not surprising because local governments often ask their peers who have implemented similar projects for cost estimates. A nearly equal percentage (41%) reported that they develop cost estimates in-house. Only 12% use research organizations (e.g., PTI, Gartner and the like) to obtain cost estimates for e-government projects.

Conclusions

Responses to this survey of local governments provide evidence of the widespread adoption and use of e-government across the country. The e-government survey in 2004 found that nearly all local governments in the United States, regardless of size, had adopted e-government but were mainly using it to provide information and services, along with a limited range of transactions and interactions.[11] Today, U.S. local governments are offering a greater array of information, services, transactions, and interactions online. However, the provision of information and services continues to overshadow that of transactions and interactions. This is partly, if not mainly, because information and services represent the "low-hanging fruit" and are easier and less costly to automate on websites. It is also likely that rates of adoption are greater for information and services than for interactions and transactions.

The 2011 survey also looked into local government adoption of more recent e-government innovations, such as social media and cloud computing. Responses reveal amazing adoption rates, with two-thirds of local

Figure 7-7 Financing E-Government

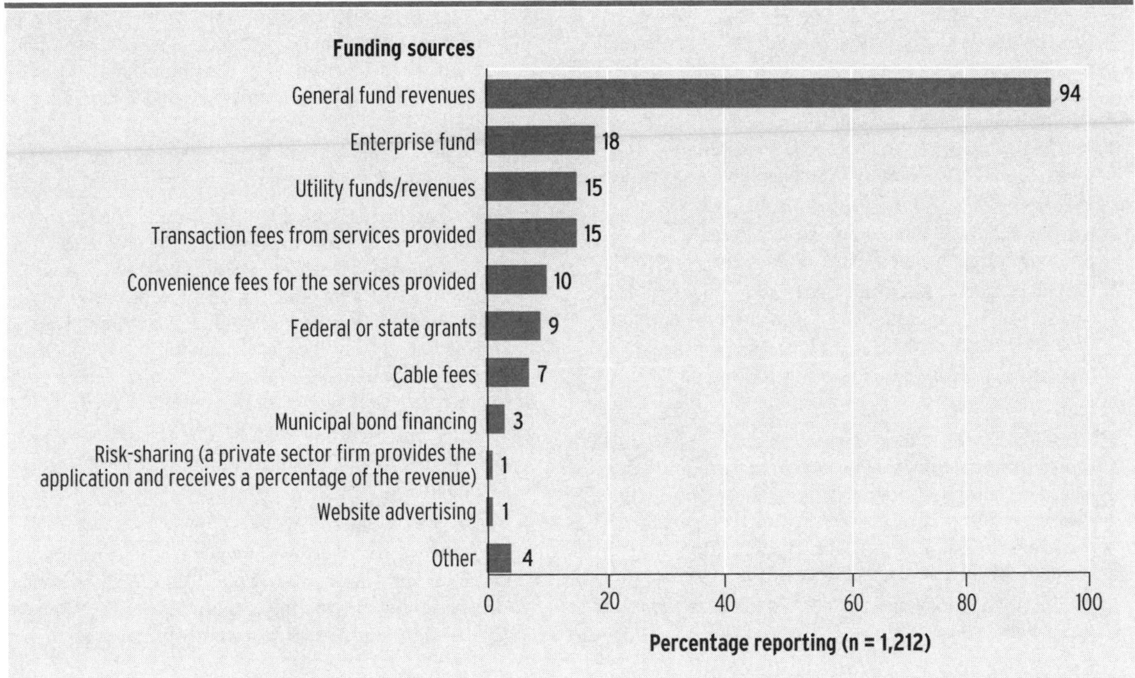

governments having adopted social media and over a quarter having adopted cloud computing; however, it is too early to assess the impacts of this trend. Clearly, more research into local government use of these technologies will be needed to understand the ramifications.

Local governments continue to confront a number of barriers in adopting e-government. However, the survey data suggest two important findings. First, the number one barrier to adoption of e-government among local governments continues to be lack of funding, as has been the case over the past decade. Second, only one other barrier came close to being cited by half of the respondents, and only two of the remaining barriers were identified by 30% or more. This would suggest that, with the additional years of experience and presumably more success, fewer governments are encountering barriers to the adoption of e-government. One final note about barriers that should be heartening to local governments is that very few respondents reported a lack of support for e-government from elected or top appointed officials.

One important question that was asked for the first time in the 2011 survey is why local governments adopt e-government. To paraphrase the real estate business, e-government is all about access (rather than location). And this means access to local government information, to the local government itself, and to local officials. This confirms Norris's findings from 2005.[12] Two other important reasons that respondents gave for providing e-government are to save money and to facilitate citizen participation or e-democracy. While it is not possible to know from this one question what respondents had in mind when they cited these reasons, it seems significant that local governments today consider saving money and citizen participation to be important reasons for providing online services.

Despite what local governments say about their motivations for adopting e-government or the impacts that online services and applications have produced, the data clearly show that, at the end of the day, local e-government in the United States remains very decidedly about delivering services and information along with, to a lesser extent, facilitating some transactions and interactions. But there is virtually no evidence that e-government has transformed governments, changed relationships between the governments and the governed, or led to electronic democracy. As is the case with earlier studies on this topic,[13] we expect that another examination of e-government in five or ten years will find e-government patterns and results strikingly similar to those that have been reported here—except, perhaps, in the area of local government use of social media. However, for this to be an exception, local governments will have to dramatically move from one-way (government to citizen) use of social media to make it a truly two-way endeavor.

Notes

1. See, for example, David Coursey and Donald F. Norris, "Models of E-Government: Are They Correct? An Empirical Assessment," *Public Administration Review* 68, no. 3 (2008): 523–536; David Coursey, "E-Government: Trends, Benefits, and Challenges," in *The Municipal Year Book 2005* (Washington, D.C.: International City/County Management Association, 2005), 14–21.
2. Evelina Moulder, director of survey research, ICMA, personal communication, November 7, 2011.
3. Donald F. Norris, "Electronic Democracy at the American Grassroots," *International Journal of Electronic Government Research* 1, no. 3 (2005): 1–14.
4. Coursey and Norris, "Models of E-Government."
5. Ibid.
6. "Facebook," *New York Times,* December 14, 2011, topics.nytimes.com/top/news/business/companies/facebook_inc/index.html; "Twitter," *New York Times,* December 14, 2011, topics.nytimes.com/top/news/business/companies/twitter/index.html?scp = 1-spot&sq = Twitter&st = Search (accessed January 21, 2012).
7. "About AWS," Amazon Web Services, 2011, aws.amazon.com/what-is-aws/.
8. See, for example, Coursey and Norris, "Models of E-Government"; Donald F. Norris and M. Jae Moon, "Advancing E-Government at the Grass Roots: Tortoise or Hare?" *Public Administration Review* 65, no. 1 (2005): 64–75.
9. See for example, Coursey and Norris, "Models of E-Government."
10. See, for example, Donald F. Norris and Lori A. Demeter, "Computing in American City Governments," in *The Municipal Yearbook 1999* (Washington, D.C.: International City/County Management Association, 1999); Stephen H. Holden, Donald F. Norris, and Patricia D. Fletcher, "Electronic Government at the Local Level: Progress to Date and Future Issues," *Public Productivity and Management Review* 26, no. 3 (2003): 1–20.
11. Coursey and Norris, "Models of E-Government"; see also Coursey, "E-Government: Trends, Benefits, and Challenges."
12. Norris, "Electronic Democracy at the American Grassroots."
13. Donald F. Norris, "E-Government 2020: Plus ça change, plus c'est la meme chose," *Public Administration Review* 70 (special issue) (December 2010): S180–S181; Coursey and Norris, "Models of E-Government."

8

Award-Winning Innovations in 2011: Exploring the Boundaries of Transformation

Karen Thoreson
Alliance for Innovation

James H. Svara
Center for Urban Innovation, Arizona State University

Four years into the "Great Recession," it is no surprise that citizens across the United States are weary of bad economic news and a dreary forecast for recovery. That sentiment is particularly resonant among local governments, which felt the precipitous drop in sales and income tax revenue early. Property taxes fell more slowly, but lower revenues will be a continuing drag for many years forward as housing prices slowly rebound. Four out of five cities made personnel cuts in 2010, two out of three cities cut jobs in 2011, and it is estimated that local government has lost over 500,000 jobs since peak levels in 2009.[1]

In the *ICMA State of the Profession 2009* survey, most managers indicated that they were taking short-term steps—for example, making across-the-board cuts, imposing furloughs, and eliminating vacant positions—rather than significantly changing their organizations, rethinking their approaches to service delivery, or revising their long-term strategic plans.[2] The same pattern was in evidence last year as local governments generally pursued cuts rather than creative solutions to cope with the fiscal crisis. But there were important exceptions.

In 2011, the Alliance for Innovation, a national nonprofit that promotes the adoption of new approaches in local government, hosted its third BIG IDEAS event in Fort Collins, Colorado, and opened the meeting with a panel presenting discussion papers on the future of local government. One paper advocated a fundamental reassessment of what local government does and how it delivers its core services. Saying that "the 'vending machine' is broken"—that government can no longer

SELECTED FINDINGS

The Fairfax County, Virginia, public-private partnership office converted a potentially polarizing project into an ecosystem restoration project that enlisted volunteer groups who work and care for the natural environment.

Belleville, Illinois's Buy Belleville First campaign uses an informational approach and a discount program both to educate Belleville's citizens about the importance of sales tax revenue to the city's budget and to increase patronage and revenues for local businesses.

Lethbridge, Alberta, implemented a "deconstruction" program involving the selective dismantlement and harvesting of building components for reuse, recycling, and waste management, and saved 10,448 tons of construction waste in the first six deconstruction projects.

be the sole provider of services to passive citizens—it proposed a shift to focus on core mission, linking a changed workforce to new technology, shared services, nongovernmental solutions, and authentic civic engagement as ways to start adaptively building a new model.[3] A second paper did not necessarily disagree with that assessment but saw little evidence that the proposed shifts being advocated would emerge. As evidence from previous recessions and cutback periods has shown, "even the shock of the Great Recession is unlikely to change the pattern of gradual rather than dramatic change."[4] A third paper argued that the primary challenge is changing the internal workings of local government so that elected officials and professional staff will work together to address highly complex problems in a shifting external environment.[5]

These views of the future provide a backdrop for examining the award-winning programs of 2011. Despite the decline in resources and successive rounds of cuts, local government officials and citizens across North America keep coming up with new ideas. Some of these ideas are direct responses to fiscal pressures, and some reflect a recognition of the new realities and new ways of doing the work of local government that the first BIG IDEAS paper suggested. Others, however, are creative new approaches intended to make government more effective in addressing community problems, more efficient in delivering services, and better able to ensure that the workforce of today and tomorrow will be ready to serve. By highlighting some of the most noteworthy approaches, this article encourages other governments to consider them, modify them, and make them work in their own communities.

For the past four years we have reviewed hundreds of award-winning programs to ascertain: *What leading-edge ideas are being implemented in local governments across the continent?* The 21 cases presented in 2012 represent a wide range of North American communities, from cities as small as 4,500 in population to cities exceeding 8 million. The featured innovations fall into five broad categories: new connections to leverage results, citizens as volunteers, organization and finance, sustainability, and solving uncommon local problems. The article then examines key features of the highlighted cases and reviews lessons learned from them.

Alliance for Innovation and ICMA Awards for Best Practices

More than 220 submissions and 50 award winners were reviewed for this article. These included Innovation Case Studies and top-ranking award submissions from the Alliance for Innovation, recipients of ICMA honors, winners of the National Civic League's All-America City Award, and recipients of the Innovation in American Government Award from the Ash Center at Harvard University.

New Connections to Leverage Results

Local governments are finding ways to involve a wider range of players in delivering service, planning for the future, and saving tax dollars.

Comprehensive Citizen Engagement

Windsor Heights, Iowa (pop. 4,860)[6]
ICMA Strategic Leadership and Governance Award

Starting in 2000, Windsor Heights made a commitment to undertake activities that inform, educate, and involve citizens through a variety of media and creative ways. The Takin' It to the Streets program, in which the city council holds meetings literally on a neighborhood street and serves refreshments afterward, not only promotes citizen involvement but also encourages neighbors to get to know each other. The Community Coffee Club, in which the city administrator and a council member invite citizens to join them for coffee once a month at a local coffee shop, enables local officials to meet with citizens and keep all parties current on community events. The city reports that these sustained efforts to connect with citizens *where they are* have resulted in increased interaction between citizens and local officials at both formal and informal meetings, greater citizen access to and confidence in their local government, and broadened perspectives among citizens of their community's future.

Arlington Urban Design Center

Arlington, Texas (pop. 365,438)
2011 TLG Innovation Study, Alliance

With the opening of new sports facilities and its selection as the site for the Super Bowl in 2011, Arlington was undergoing a significant amount of development activity. To capitalize on this surge of reinvestment, the city's Community Development and Planning Department collaborated with the University of Texas's School of Urban and Planning Affairs to create a unique studio staffed with six graduate students studying architecture, landscaping, and urban planning. The Arlington Urban Design Center (AUDC) was established in July 2009 to create public awareness about the importance of sustainable urban design and its impact on quality of life, the environment, and economic investment. Directed by city employees, the AUDC strives to provide high-quality urban design solutions at no cost to its clients. To date, 22 projects have been completed, including the construction of affordable housing, streetscape and signage improvements, and commercial facelifts. The AUDC is located inside city hall near the main public entrance, which sends a clear message that the city highly values design and wants to make the service accessible to all citizens.

Water Regional Utility Partnership

Round Rock, Texas (pop. 99,887)
2011 TLG Innovation Study, Alliance

After completing a utility study in 2005 that analyzed the costs of accessing various sources of water—from lakes to the north and west to aquifers to the east—with and without partners, Round Rock concluded that going solo was much more expensive than working with partners, and it initiated a partnership with two other cities, Leander and Cedar Park. Located just north of Austin, the three cities had each secured rights from the Lower Colorado River Authority to access water in nearby Lake Travis. Leander and Cedar Park were already accessing water from Lake Travis through separate treatment and distribution systems.

One goal of Round Rock's regional utility partnership was to finance and build the infrastructure necessary to secure long-term water supplies for three of the fastest-growing cities in Texas. Together they created the Brushy Creek Regional Utility Authority, which secured below-market financing from the Texas Water Development Board. The design and construction of a 106-million-gallon-per-day water treatment and distribution system, to be constructed in four phases, is projected to cost an estimated $327 million. Just as important was the goal to achieve significant savings in design and construction costs by building one regional system instead of three stand-alone municipal systems. To this end, the project is expected to save approximately 33% of current costs, or up to $100 million.

Fairfax County Restoration Project

Fairfax County, Virginia (pop. 1,081,726)
2011 TLG Innovation Study, Alliance

When the Virginia Department of Transportation MegaProjects began land clearing for the High Occupancy Toll (HOT) Lanes project on the Capital Beltway (I-495), local environmental and civic organizations became concerned. Preconstruction work required the removal of many native plants as well as old-growth quality forest around the existing highway, which would result in damage to and loss of wildlife habitats. Citizens approached the Office of Public Private Partnerships with the idea of replicating an environmental restoration initiative that had been undertaken in New York. The result was the Fairfax County Restoration Project (FCRP), whose purpose is to restore ecosystem functions in Fairfax County through collaboration with public, private, and volunteer organizations. It strengthens efforts already under way in each sector by identifying opportunities to share volunteers, education initiatives, and resources, and it includes a collaborative website and events calendar.

As construction of the HOT lanes began, FCRP member organizations rescued seedlings and plant material at two construction sites and cultivated them for future planting. Current efforts focus on reaching out to homeowners affected by the construction and educating them on sustainable practices for land use and landscaping. To this end, the FCRP holds educational forums and workshops for citizens, homeowners associations, and civic associations on the benefits of using native plantings and water runoff management. It has also helped to develop a community garden laboratory and a living classroom for teaching students about the environment.

Citizens as Volunteers

Regular citizens can make significant contributions to their communities and cost-effectively change how local governments operate and succeed.

Novi Youth Council

Novi, Michigan (pop. 55,224)
2011 TLG Innovation Study, Alliance

The Novi Youth Council brings together teens from more than five high schools to develop goals, create initiatives, and enhance the community. When first formed, the council was given a blank slate upon which to look at projects to pursue. After brainstorming, the members decided that they wanted to break out of the "typical" youth council model of being a social venue for teens and instead make an impact on the community. They chose to focus on

- Promoting drug prevention within schools
- Bridging the gap between teens and seniors
- Providing education on teen depression and suicide.

With an annual budget of only $500, this 19-member council is significantly improving various health and wellness aspects of community life through such innovative programs as "Addicted to Movies . . . not Drugs," "Project Sticker Shock," "It's OUR Novi," and an intergenerational "prom." In so doing, it is having a profound impact on citizen engagement and community spirit, thereby serving as a model program for local governments of all sizes.

West Vancouver Community Centre

West Vancouver, British Columbia (pop. 44,058)[7]
2011 TLG Innovation Study, Alliance

In 2009, the city of West Vancouver took a bold step regarding its newly constructed $40 million, 83,000-square-foot community center, which includes community programming space and an adjoining 40,000-square-foot aquatic center with a combined operating budget of $6.7 million. Rather than run it as a municipal operation, the city entered into a joint operating agreement with a newly formed nonprofit. The West Vancouver Community Centre Services Society, a membership organization governed by a board of directors who reside in the community, is responsible for the operation and budgeting oversight of all services and programs that take place in the facility. Focused on sustainability, accessibility, collaboration, and multidimensional integration, the buildings and the community governance model is designed to take West Vancouver's blend of community services to the year 2050 and beyond, with the community at the helm.

Caring for the Kenai

Kenai, Alaska (pop. 7,100)
All-America City Award

In 2008, the Kenai River in South-Central Alaska was designated as a Category 5 river—an impaired water body in accordance with the federal Clean Water Act. Caring for the Kenai (CFK) is an ongoing environmental awareness contest that brings together the entire community of Alaska's Kenai Peninsula and offers over $25,000 in cash awards to area schools and local students. CFK poses the question, "What can I do, invent, create or improve to better care for the environment of the Kenai Peninsula or improve the area's preparedness for natural disaster?" Over 500 students research, experiment, and conduct interviews to learn about an environmental issue they wish to solve. Working with community and business leaders, government agencies, and policy makers, CFK students generate new and inventive ideas to address environmental challenges, learn about the practical application of their ideas, and gain real-world experience implementing their projects. Parents learn about CFK when students discuss and work on their projects at home. Local media assist in getting the message out to the public. Industry, government, educators, regulators, and private citizens collaborate to promote both educational and environmental innovations. CFK is one of three community-based environmental programs recognized in the Kenai All-America City Award.

NYC Service

New York City, New York (pop. 8,175,133)
Ash Center Top 25 Innovations in American Government

NYC Service is Mayor Michael Bloomberg's program to leverage citizen service as a core strategy to respond to local needs. Launched in April 2009, the program introduces "impact volunteerism": targeting local needs, using best practices, and measuring impact. This is accomplished through identifying volunteer opportunities for local nonprofit organizations and sharing those opportunities with the public. Using a sophisticated website, NYC Service has identified community building, neighbors in need, education, health, emergency preparedness, and the environment as priority areas in which New Yorkers can volunteer their time. In all, the mayor reports that the program's three primary goals have been met: channeling volunteers to address the city's greatest needs, making New York the easiest place in which to volunteer, and promoting service as a core part of what it means to be a citizen.

Organization and Finance

Focusing internally on planning, organizational development, and leadership training and externally on citizen involvement can improve the bottom line and produce excellent results.

Challenges, Solutions, and Innovations Alliance (CSI Alliance)

Sarasota County, Florida (pop. 379,448)
2011 TLG Innovation Study, Alliance

Difficult economic times have created a "new normal" for local governments. While most government leaders recognize the need for honest discussions with employees, understanding how best to engage employees on emotionally laden topics is another matter. In confronting today's challenges, Sarasota County Government (SCG) is philosophically committed to the Networked Talent Model, in which all levels of an informed and engaged workforce participate in generating solutions and making decisions to achieve a common goal. Over the years, county employees have taken advantage of opportunities to learn together through such tools as award and recognition programs, team assessments, and broadbanding, which have supported positive cultural change. The success of these past efforts set the stage in January 2009 for SCG to take its employee engagement practices to the next level. Through the Challenges, Solutions, and Innovations Alliance (CSI Alliance), SCG actively engages a large, cross-functional group of employees in thinking creatively to meet enterprise-wide challenges with no- to low-cost solutions. Employee workgroup successes to date include transparency in the payroll and benefit system, revisions to the downtown parking plan, and other time- and money-saving solutions.

Buy Belleville First

Belleville, Illinois (pop. 44,478)
All-America City Award

The Buy Belleville First campaign is a twofold effort designed to educate Belleville's citizens about the importance of buying goods within their own community and to increase patronage and revenues for local businesses. The two components are an informational campaign and the "Belleville First" discount program. For the first component, community volunteers hand-delivered letters to the 17,000 households within the city's corporate limits, describing what sales tax revenues mean to the city's budget and reminding them that the more they buy in Belleville, the more sales tax comes to the city for police and fire protection, roadway repairs and construction, city services, etc. For the second component, participating merchants offer discounts to those holding a Belleville First card; the Belleville Main Street organization coordinates the program and produces the cards; and the city promotes the program to residents and visitors. Since its inception, the Buy Belleville First campaign has gained momentum and become more successful than originally anticipated.

"I Value" Campaign

Hampton, Virginia (pop. 137,436)
2011 Havlick Alliance for Innovation Award

In January 2010, the new city manager of Hampton faced the task of balancing the upcoming fiscal year 2011 budget while confronting an approximate $19 million shortfall. Knowing that maximum community input was necessary to help her make the tough decisions ahead, she wanted to make community involvement in the budget process a top priority. To accomplish this, the city took an innovative approach by pulling together a team comprising marketing, communication, and technology professionals throughout the organization. The team quickly embarked on the most extensive community involvement project the city had ever undertaken. Blending some of the best traditional citizen-outreach practices with an array of Internet-based engagement tools, including live online chats and electronic polling, the "I Value" campaign largely involved having citizens rate their city services in terms of "needs" and "wants." Beyond engaging the community on all levels, the campaign helped the city manager produce a balanced budget with little community dissent. Since the first year of the process, "I Value" has included citizen feedback on the capital budget as well as on the operating budget.

Changing the Public (and Internal) Perspective of Local Government

Montgomery, Ohio (pop. 10,251)
ICMA Strategic leadership and Governance Award 2011

In 2001, in order to create a better work environment for employees and a more productive system of government for residents, Montgomery instituted the High Performing Organization (HPO) business model throughout its departments. The city studied the HPO theory of three distinct phases of work and tailored the third phase, the Networked Talent Model, to fit its specific needs. This model assumes that work is holistic in nature and is done by teams of employees who demonstrate the leadership, management, and technical skills to work effectively together toward common goals. The changes improved not only the work environment but also organizational capacity, individual employee skills, and the quality of employee teamwork. Some specific results include revised hiring practices, new human resource performance tools, and the implementation of an annual organizational culture tool.

Sustainability

A wealth of new approaches is being developed to make communities more sustainable.

Greening Lakewood Business Partnership

Lakewood, Colorado (pop. 142,980)
All-America City award

The Learning Source in Lakewood operates one of the largest adult literacy programs in the United States. When it learned that its utility costs for its one-story brick building were higher than those for a 50-unit, multifamily complex, the organization sought energy-efficiency expertise from the community. This sparked the formation of the Greening Lakewood Business Partnership (GLBP). GLBP's mission is to bring energy efficiency to older, existing office and commercial buildings in Lakewood while providing job training, particularly for military veterans returning from overseas. The partnership includes the city of Lakewood, which works with the utility company, banks, and the state to help fund energy-efficient retrofits; Red Rocks Community College, which created a program for students to train in energy auditing and provides free audits to businesses under the supervision of experts in the field; the Alameda Gateway Community Association, which continues the discussion with Lakewood businesses; Veterans Green Jobs, which mobilizes the military veterans to enter the Red Rocks program; the Jefferson County Workforce Center, which coordinates funding for the students' paid internships; and the Better Business Bureau, which markets the partnership. As for the Learning Source, GLBP has helped it reduce its monthly heating bills from $3,500 to $200.

Lethbridge Deconstruction Initiative

Lethbridge, Alberta (pop. 87,882)[8]
2011 TLG Innovation Study, Alliance

Buildings, like everything else, have a life cycle. For the past four years, Facility Services in Lethbridge has taken responsibility for mitigating the environmental impact that occurs when a city facility or community building has reached the end of its useful life and is destined to be removed. Unlike demolition, in which a site is cleared of its building by the most expedient means, deconstruction in this context is the selective dismantlement and harvesting of building components, specifically for reuse, recycling, and waste management. The process, which is known as "waste streaming," involves identifying and assessing various building elements prior to deconstruction so that they can be reconverted into useful building material and diverted accordingly. Hazardous materials are properly abated to render a safe and clean site, and prearranged "homes" are found for remaining usable materials before work is even started. The successful contractor is generally awarded salvage of all materials, which helps generate funds to offset deconstruction and disposal costs. In adopting deconstruction as a responsible means of building disposal, the city has, to date, successfully diverted 10,448 tons of construction and demolition waste—or the equivalent volume of 70 average 2,000-square-foot houses—from entering local landfills.

Oro Valley Energy Efficiency and Solar Project

Oro Valley, Arizona (pop. 41,011)
2011 TLG Innovation Study, Alliance

The Oro Valley Energy Efficiency and Solar Project has created a long-range plan that is producing substantial savings for the town, but the real triumph of this project is the innovative mix of financing that was used to pay for it. The $4 million project is self-funded through federal energy bonding, an Energy Efficiency and Conservation Block Grant, local utility incentives, and energy savings. Each financing source is uniquely bundled into a funding vehicle known as Energy Performance Contracting, a strategic, design-build energy plan that funds itself by virtue of its own savings and is increasingly being used in energy-related projects. In this project, the newly applied and/or installed technologies and operating procedures will generate cost reductions to ensure that 100% of project costs are recovered over the next 10 years, and these savings will be used to retire the debt service created to initiate the program. The utility company Arizona Public Service Energy Services has guaranteed both energy and operational cost reductions to mitigate the risks typically associated with the traditional approach of financing new projects.

Solving Uncommon Local Problems

Out-of-the-box thinking can yield unanticipated opportunities for communities to solve problems that are specific to them.

Local Job-Generation Stimulus Programs

Sunnyvale, California (pop. 140,081)
2011 TLG Innovation Study, Alliance

St. Lucie County, Florida (pop. 277,789)
ICMA Strategic Leadership and Governance Award

As the "Great Recession" began to unfold, both Sunnyvale, California, and St. Lucie County, Florida, determined that rather than wait for the federal government to start a stimulus program, each would create its own. In Sunnyvale, the goal was to undertake $60 million in low-interest, bond-funded capital improvement projects. Sunnyvale Works! required the city to reinvent its capital improvement project processes by finding new ways to expedite procedures, using staff to better advantage, and accelerating what it takes to get a project under construction. As a result, Sunnyvale changed the way it does business, becoming more agile, breaking down internal departmental barriers, and adopting methods that have permitted the city to expand the original $60 million in projects to more than $80 million without increasing its costs.

In 2009, St. Lucie County had one of the highest unemployment rates and one of the highest foreclosure rates in the country. To help put residents back to work and boost the local economy, the county developed a comprehensive stimulus program consisting of many small "shovel-ready" projects and local-preference ordinances. Projects ranged from a $4,000 canoe dock to a $6.6 million road-widening project. In the end, the stimulus plan helped to create just over 500 jobs and provided work projects to a number of local businesses.

We Are Legal Graffiti

Fort Worth, Texas (pop. 727,575)
All-America City Award

Standard-issue weapons to fight graffiti in Fort Worth produced little results, but when two high school art teachers joined with students from rival high schools, they were able to turn things around. We Are Legal (WAL) is a voluntary, student-driven, non-scholastic effort that redirects the time and talents of central-city and predominately Hispanic youth to producing well-conceived and approved art. Each youth signs a contract in which he or she pledges to no longer paint illegally. With no more than guidance from the teachers and support from a growing number of community organizations and businesses, WAL students—would-be criminals who were fined for tagging—have transformed themselves into Fort Worth's Pop Surrealism Post Modern Urban Art Movement. They also are transforming the community by adorning walls with murals rather than graffiti. And their work is paying off. Still-active taggers respect the wall murals that the students have painted by not tagging the work. With a 33% decline in graffiti, particularly in the neighborhood from which most WAL students come, Fort Worth has become a more attractive place to live.

Public Service Areas in Philadelphia

Philadelphia, Pennsylvania (pop. 1,526,006)
2011 TLG Innovation Study, Alliance

In 2010, Philadelphia established the Public Service Areas Model for Sustainable Change in High Crime Neighborhoods as a pilot program to bring a citizen-centric, coordinated approach to improving public safety in challenged neighborhoods. The process began by canvassing residents to learn what they thought could be done to make their neighborhoods safer, and then by having a coordinated team of public and nonprofit agencies deliver the resources necessary to turn those ideas into concrete action. During the first phase of the program, crimes were reduced by 17%. Since the program began, 85 parcels in the pilot area have been cleaned, dangerous buildings have been destroyed, programs for schoolchildren have been established, new recreation programs are in place, and nonprofits are delivering health programs for seniors and job training programs for residents. The residents, many of whom had lost all faith in the "system," are now engaged, which most believe is the key to the program's success.

Foreclosure Prevention Partnership Program

Las Vegas, Nevada (pop. 583,756)
2011 TLG Innovation Study, Alliance

Ninety percent of Nevada's foreclosures are located in the southern part of the state, which includes unincorporated Clark County and the cities of Las Vegas, North Las Vegas, and Henderson. Southern Nevada experienced 71,000 foreclosures from January 2008 to June 2010, representing more than 11% of its housing stock. Las Vegas continues to lead the nation in foreclosures, with 1 in every 80 homes receiving a foreclosure filing in June 2010.

Funds provided for the Neighborhood Stabilization Program through the Housing and Economic Recovery Act (HERA) and the American Recovery and Reinvestment Act (ARRA) assist local governments only in reducing the number of already foreclosed properties, but neither HERA nor ARRA provides foreclosure intervention and prevention services. Thus, the city of Las Vegas created the Foreclosure Prevention Partnership Program (FPPP) to bring together government agencies, housing counseling agencies, lenders, and nonprofit organizations to combat the foreclosure crisis. The program uses a dual approach: educational forums and Freehomeaid.org, a foreclosure prevention counseling services website. (The website was originally named StopNVForeclosures.org but was changed when FPPP learned that many of its potential clients were being lured to unscrupulous sites when searching the Internet for foreclosure help. That change alone increased traffic on the website by twofold.) At no cost to the homeowner, the forums and the website provide educational materials, tools to prevent foreclosure, and an online system designed to streamline the foreclosure case submission process.

Powered Paragliders in Palm Bay

Palm Bay, Florida (pop. 103,190)
2011 Muehlenbeck Award for Innovation, Alliance

In 2009, the Palm Bay police department created a first of its kind for its Search Operations Aerial Response (SOAR) unit: an ultralight classified aircraft called a Powered Paraglider (PPG). The PPG, which consists of a small, two-cycle motor worn on the back of a pilot and a parachute-type "wing" capable of lifting the pilot and motor into the air, provides a low-cost option for a police agency that is unable to purchase or maintain more conventional forms of aviation. The PPG was never intended to replace commonly used forms of police aviation, such as airplanes or helicopters; rather, it supplements these aircraft by providing an aerial platform that is portable (weighing about 60 pounds), easily deployable from any open field, inexpensive to operate (as little as $5 per hour), and able to remain airborne for up to four hours (with a three- to five-gallon fuel capacity) as long as wind and weather conditions are favorable.

In addition, the PPG is legally permitted to operate below the 1,000-foot minimum altitude for general aviation. Flying between 20 and 30 mph (depending on wind direction), the glider can cover up to 70 miles. The "low and slow" principle allows it to have both maneuverability and an unobstructed view of objects on the ground. An officer operating a PPG can cover a larger area more thoroughly and in a shorter amount of time than can multiple officers in patrol cars or on foot. Using radio contact with the officers on the ground, the pilot can direct them to specific locations to further investigate any sightings made from the air.

Lessons Learned

The cases described here are not the only ones that have been recognized by the Alliance for Innovation, ICMA, the Ash Center, and All-America City Program, but they do exemplify new approaches that have been crafted to solve enduring or perplexing local problems. In previous years we have noted that innovative organizations share certain characteristics, such as inclusive leadership within the staff or with elected officials, convergence of motivation to make something happen, willingness to be creative and take risks, internal and external collaboration, and a strong connection to engagement with citizens. These elements are present in the organizations featured here, but there are also programmatic characteristics that link these 21 award-winning efforts.

Complex Partnerships

Enduring partnerships nearly always represent an equation in which the sum exceeds the value of the individual parts. Arlington, Texas's AUDC program brought together university design students with residents and businesses to make the community a more desirable and attractive place. The city placed the program's front door on the first floor of city hall to promote its interest in great, affordable design for the city center. The Fairfax County, Virginia, Office of Public Private Partnerships was able to convert a potentially polarizing project into an ecosystem restoration initiative that enlisted volunteer groups who work and care for the natural environment. In a state often known for rugged individualism, Round Rock, Texas, looked beyond the simplicity of building its own utility and instead partnered with Leander and Cedar Park to combine the water rights of all three jurisdictions into a single system, saving nearly $100 million for the local governments and ratepayers. Lakewood, Colorado, used the community's energy-efficiency expertise not only to retrofit the Learning Source literacy building but also to create the Greening Lakewood Business Partnership, which is bringing energy efficiency to existing offices and commercial buildings while providing job training for veterans and energy education for students.

Borderless Internal and External Collaboration

Collaboration is defined as "the work and activity of a number of persons who individually contribute to the efficiency of the whole" and also "the state of having shared interests or efforts."[9] Both definitions apply to a number of the cases cited. The West Vancouver Community Centre in British Columbia was bold in blurring the boundaries between the public and private sectors when it entered into an agreement with a nonprofit organization to operate a brand-new $40 million community center. Sarasota County, Florida, and Montgomery, Ohio, each undertook extensive cross-team training to allow employees to come up with unexpected solutions to lingering problems that the regular work groups had not successfully tackled. Budget woes led Hampton, Virginia's new city manager to enlist the city staff and community to help pare expenses and raise revenues in ways that enhance the city rather than diminish it. Philadelphia, Pennsylvania, developed cross-department teams made up of public safety, code compliance, recreation, and other staff to join with residents in beautifying the neighborhood, decreasing crime, and connecting with nonprofits to increase access to services.

Authentic Engagement

No longer does including residents in public sector deliberations simply mean holding public hearings or posting notices in the local newspaper. Today local governments across the country and around the world are discovering the power, creativity, and commitment of their residents. Windsor Heights, Iowa, made a game-changing commitment to be accessible to residents, holding council meetings in neighborhoods and hosting coffee clubs in local cafés. Three cities sought to involve youth in efforts to solve local problems: Kenai, Alaska, created an environmental awareness contest to invent better ways to care for the environment; Novi, Michigan, established a nontraditional teen council; and Fort Worth, Texas, engaged art teachers and taggers to transform polarizing graffiti into community murals. Other communities addressed their citizens' needs in separate but equally important ways through education and action: Las Vegas, Nevada, recognized that foreclosures were being addressed only after the fact and set up prevention programs to help homeowners avoid losing their homes; New York City built a user-friendly website where thousands of volunteer opportunities are cataloged and easily accessed; and Belleville, Illinois, helped its citizens understand how their shopping patterns affect city services.

Using Ingenuity to Get Remarkable Results

It has been said that innovation without measuring results is simply play. In this competitive and financially challenging environment, local governments cannot afford to be investing in programs that do not achieve their potential. Oro Valley, Arizona, put that notion to work when it translated energy savings into a $4 million energy bond structured so that the debt service is repaid through the savings earned from new technology and new operating procedures. Sunnyvale, California, and St. Lucie County, Florida, took existing resources and created their own local "stimulus" programs, completing future-year capital projects early and creating local construction jobs within their communities. Lethbridge, Alberta, made destruction constructive by implementing a "waste streaming" process and saving 10,448 tons (9,478 metric tonnes) of construction waste in the first six deconstruction projects. Palm Bay, Florida, decided to "fly slow and low" with new technology that expands its traditional police aviation capability by allowing officers to investigate larger areas more thoroughly and in a less time-consuming manner.

Conclusion

In the continuing hard times of 2012, local governments are using innovation not only to fill gaps and save money, but also to build partnerships, engage citizens, and solve perplexing problems. The governments featured in this article are exploring the boundaries of transformation in local government. Doing so is hard and successes may be rare, but the cases provided here can give other governments ideas and inspiration to emulate and build upon.

Notes

1. Christopher W. Hoene and Michael A. Pagano, "City Fiscal Conditions in 2011," *Research Brief on America's Cities* (Washington, D.C.: National League of Cities, September 2011), 6 – 7, nlc.org/find-city-solutions/research-innovation/finance/city-fiscal-conditions-in-2011.
2. Gerald J. Miller, "Weathering the Local Government Fiscal Crisis: Short-Term Measures or Permanent Change?" in *The Municipal Year Book 2010* (Washington, D.C.: ICMA Press, 2010), 33–36.
3. Frank Benest et al., "What Is the Future of Local Government? A White Paper Intended to Provoke a Needed Conversation" (presented at the Alliance for Innovation, BIG IDEAS: The Future of Local Government, Fort Collins, Colo., October 14–16, 2011), transformgov.org/en/knowledge_network/documents/kn/document/302595/the_future_of_local_government.
4. David N. Ammons, Karl W. Smith, and Carl W. Stenberg, "Local Governments in the Wake of the Great Recession: Are Big Changes Ahead?" (presented at the Alliance for Innovation, BIG IDEAS: The Future of Local Government, Fort Collins, Colo., October 14–16, 2011), 4, transformgov.org/en/learning/bigideas.
5. John Nalbandian, Michael Wilkes, Amanda Kaufman, "Bridging the Gap: Leadership Challenges from the Midwest" (presented at the Alliance for Innovation, BIG IDEAS: The Future of Local Government, Fort Collins, Colo., October 14–16, 2011), transformgov.org/en/learning/big_ideas.
6. Unless otherwise noted, all populations are 2010 estimates from the U.S. Census Bureau.
7. Thomas Brinkhoff, "City Population," July 1, 2010, citypopulation.de/Canada-BritishColumbia.html#Stadt_gross.
8. City of Lethbridge, *Lethbridge Census 2011: Count Yourself In* (Lethbridge, Alberta: City Clerk's Office, June 20110, lethbridge.ca/City-Government/Census/Documents/2011%20Final%20Census%20Report.pdf.
9. *Merriam-Webster Thesaurus Online,* s.v. "Collaboration," accessed December 31, 2011, merriam-webster.com/thesaurus/collaboration.

9

Public Pensions Face Record Pace of Change

Elizabeth K. Kellar
Center for State and Local Government Excellence

Local governments face growing challenges in funding their pension obligations, in large part because of the financial crisis of 2008–2009. The economic downturn reduced the value of equities in all retirement plans, causing an increase in the unfunded liabilities of state and local public sector defined benefit (DB) plans.[1] How large are the unfunded liabilities? For the 126 public pension plans in the Public Plans Database, the 2010 unfunded liability was $0.8 trillion.[2] It is important to note, however, that these plans have a total of $2.7 trillion in assets, which means that most of them have enough time to make the changes necessary to return to a sound financial footing.

SELECTED FINDINGS

The 126 plans in the Public Plans Database have $2.7 trillion in assets and an aggregate liability of $0.8 trillion, and are 77% funded.

Efforts to improve funding levels for public pensions face delays from several sources, including continued economic uncertainty and legal barriers.

Local governments that want to improve pension funding should (1) focus on recruiting and retaining good employees (rather than on simply cutting costs), (2) use independent experts to evaluate assumptions, (3) ensure that pension boards include key stakeholders and possess significant financial expertise, and (4) encourage the necessary changes at the state level–and, if that fails, take local action.

Despite two years of good investment returns since the 2008 financial meltdown, a number of factors will make it difficult to quickly restore healthy pension funding levels:

- Economic uncertainties continue. Traditionally, state and local governments recover from recessions more slowly than the private sector—a pattern that has held true during the current recession, which is the deepest since the Great Depression. The federal government's stimulus package, the American Recovery and Reinvestment Act (ARRA), helped state and local budgets through fiscal year (FY) 2011, but that support has largely ended. With Congress considering spending cuts, the resulting reductions in federal aid are likely to increase pressures on state and local budgets.
- Legal barriers prevent instantaneous changes. Pension benefits are protected by state law, state constitutions, contractual agreements, or all three;

as a result, significant change often takes years and requires careful planning, good communication, and a highly competent board of trustees. Because of the difficulty of adjusting current benefit arrangements, governments that choose to do so usually focus on new hires; many also negotiate with current employees to increase employee contributions to pensions. Such changes do strengthen pension funding, but the positive financial effects may not be evident for many years.

- Most DB pension plans recognize gains and losses over a three- to five-year period, so the 2008–2009 losses will be "smoothed" over a number of years. In other words, pension liabilities will continue to increase until the 2008–2009 losses are fully recognized. While the gains of 2010 and 2011 have helped, they have not been large enough to make up for the losses.

Economic Realities Prompt a Focus on Benefits

Long-term fiscal constraints on state and local governments mean that pay and benefits packages will be subject to continuing scrutiny. Since September 2008, when local government employment peaked, over half a million jobs have been shed. (The losses have been split evenly between public education and general local government.) As 2011 came to a close, the private sector had begun to add jobs, but the downward trend in public sector employment continued, especially at the local level.

In keeping with historical trends, state and local governments are recovering more slowly from the recession than is the private sector. One bright spot is in the area of state income tax revenues: according to the *Fiscal Survey of the States: Fall 2011*, these revenues are beginning to recover in some states.[3] Nevertheless, tax revenues vary widely among the states. In Alaska and North Dakota, for example, revenues more than doubled in the third quarter of 2011 when compared with the same period in 2010. Iowa and Delaware, in contrast, reported lower revenues than they had the previous year.[4]

Overall, neither state nor local revenues have returned to their 2008 levels: sales and property tax revenues, for example, remain flat. Meanwhile, costs have increased, largely because of growing demand for government-subsidized services, such as Medicaid, for the unemployed.[5] The ARRA, which provided $120 billion to states in FY 2010 and $98 billion in FY 2011, has largely come to an end, and the additional federal financial support for state Medicaid programs ended in June 2011.[6] In short, state government budgets will remain tight—and state budget woes inevitably increase fiscal pressures on local governments. A complicating factor for local governments is that their largest source of revenue is the property tax: because property assessments are typically done every three years, the downturn in property values is now hitting affected communities in full force. Tight revenues intensify the focus on reducing benefit costs.

Despite the current pension worries, DB plans are in better shape today than they were in the 1970s, when governments often funded pensions on a pay-as-you-go basis. In 1986, when the Governmental Accounting Standards Board provided guidance on pension funding and accounting standards, governments gained greater awareness of the need for consistent contributions; as a result, most plans were on their way to sound funding by the end of the 20th century.[7]

Political Pressure for Pension Reform

Because of the fragile economy, states have had little appetite to shore up pension plans by raising taxes. Instead, states have been adjusting plan designs to improve funding levels. The National Conference of State Legislatures reports that in the first six months of 2011, 25 states enacted significant revisions to at least one state retirement plan. And between January 2010 and September 2011, states enacted these revisions:[8]

- Twenty-seven increased employee contributions.
- Twenty increased the age and length-of-service requirements for normal retirement.
- Eighteen revised cost-of-living provisions.
- Fourteen lengthened the period that is used to calculate final average salary, which serves as the base for pension benefits.[9]

Although the pace of change has intensified, many of the concerns about pension funding date back to the 2001 recession. It was not until 2008, however, when public and private retirement plans experienced severe investment losses, that there was sufficient political will to make potentially unpopular adjustments to many public pension plans.

Public Pension Plans: Substantial Assets and Wide Variation

Two points can help put concerns about public pension plans into perspective: First, state and local pension assets are held in trust, which means that the pension assets are overseen by an independent board of trustees and are not part of the operating budget. Moreover, as noted earlier, the 126 plans in the Public Plans Database have $2.7 trillion in assets—a significant sum;[10] as of 2010, these plans were 77% funded and had an aggregate liability of $0.8 trillion.[11]

Second, pension funding varies widely from place to place. For example, many observers might assume that all local governments in fiscal distress have poorly funded pension plans—but they would be wrong. A case in point is Kalamazoo, Michigan, a city that has lost much of its economic base and faces dire budgetary pressures. Nonetheless, Kalamazoo's independent municipal DB pension plan remains fully funded because of excellent governance, expert investment advice, and sound funding policies. In the 1990s, times were good; but instead of taking a "pension holiday," the government continued to pay into the fully funded plan. Thanks to that strategy, the plan became "overfunded" and was better able to weather the economic downturns of the past decade.[12]

Illinois offers another example: of its four large, statewide public pension plans, three are significantly underfunded—but one plan, the Illinois Municipal Retirement Fund (IMRF), is more than 80% funded. Why the difference? The practices of the IMRF are not exotic, but they do illustrate the importance of funding discipline. The IMRF is funded by investment returns (59%), employer contributions (27%), and employee contributions (14%). Employers make their required contributions in both good times and bad, in part because the IMRF board is authorized to enforce collections from all participating governments. The employer contribution for the other three statewide pension plans, in contrast, depends on an appropriation from the state legislature, which has failed to consistently make the annual required contributions to the plans.[13]

Like 70% of public sector pension plans, the IMRF uses the "entry-age normal" approach for funding and reporting purposes; this approach recognizes a larger accumulated pension obligation for active employees and requires a larger contribution than the "projected unit credit" method.[14] The IMRF also assumes an annual return of 7.5% on investments, and it did not adjust that assumption between 1995 and 1999, when the stock market experienced high growth. Despite the economic downturn that began in 2008, the future of the IMRF is strong.

In March 2010, in an effort to improve the funding status of all statewide plans, the Illinois General Assembly enacted legislation that will affect all new employees; among its provisions, the legislation calls for

- Increasing the vesting period from 8 to 10 years
- Increasing the normal retirement age for full pension benefits from 60 to 67, with a minimum of 10 years of service
- Increasing the earliest retirement age for a reduced pension from 55 to 62, with a minimum of 10 years of service
- Increasing the amount of time used to calculate the final rate of earnings from 4 to 8 years[15]
- Capping eligible wages for retirement benefits at $106,800, adjusted for inflation
- Changing the annual automatic noncompounding pension increase (i.e., the cost-of-living adjustment) from 3% of the amount originally specified to half of the consumer price index or 3%, whichever is less.

Poorly funded pension plans face a difficult road ahead; nonetheless, changes such as these will help to establish more sustainable funding paths.

Pension Reform: What Works?

Policy makers often want an instant "fix" for an underfunded pension plan, but the reality is that getting pension funding back on track may take years, especially if outdated policies or other legal barriers stand in the way of change. For example, if a government wants to close down its DB plan and shift employees to a defined contribution (DC) plan, it will have to administer and fund two plans at once: the existing pension plan, for current employees and retirees, and the new plan, for new hires. Not only is it more expensive to administer two separate plans, but the government's contributions to the closed plan will increase because no new employees will be contributing to it.

If a DB plan is poorly funded, or if a government wants to adjust its plan for other reasons related to specific human resource goals, the experiences of other local governments offer some valuable lessons:

- *Focus on the government's ability to recruit and retain good employees.* When Gwinnett County, Georgia, decided that it wanted to attract a wide range of workers, it made an unusual move: it began by conducting a marketing study, which revealed that a move to a DC plan would appeal to younger professionals and to those who did not anticipate a career with a single government.

Since implementing the new plan four years ago, the county has benefited from cost savings; its ability to recruit workers has also improved.[16] Nevertheless, there are concerns that the transition to a DC plan (and the resulting drop in assets for those nearing retirement) may require workers whose jobs include significant physical demands to remain in their jobs past the age that they or the government might have anticipated.[17] In keeping with standard practice, the county continues to conduct annual benefit reviews to ensure that its compensation and benefits package remains competitive with that of the three other governments in the Atlanta metropolitan area.[18]

- *Use independent experts to evaluate assumptions—and, if changes are needed, communicate fully and broadly.* Until 2000, the Houston Municipal Employees Pension System (HMEPS) was adequately funded. In 2001, after an actuary hired by HMEPS estimated that the city's contributions would grow from 10% to 15% of payroll, the city council approved benefit increases. But after a second study, conducted in 2003, found that benefit funding would amount to 50% of payroll, city officials realized that major changes were needed. Armed with the new, reliable data, officials communicated clearly with employees and residents to help them understand the proposed adjustments. The process took time and required state legislation, but by 2004, Houston had gained voter approval to change certain pension provisions.[19] Houston's pension funding level, which was below 50% in 2003, is now approaching 70%.[20]
- *Ensure that pension boards include key stakeholders and that the members have financial expertise.* When Gwinnett County created a new pension board in 2007, it looked for individuals with significant financial expertise. Employees hold two of the seven board seats, which has been important in the board's relationship with county employees. As part of its 2005 reforms, Houston also made an effort to increase the financial expertise of its board.[21]
- *Encourage the necessary changes at the state level—and, if that fails, take the appropriate steps at the local level.* In California, most local governments lowered the retirement age and adjusted the formula used to calculate pensions over a decade ago, leading to larger pension payouts. The result, according to Rod Gould, city manager of Santa Monica, is that "pension costs for most California municipalities are likely to increase 25% or more in the next three years."[22] Since it has become clear that these decade-old decisions are not affordable, the League of California Cities and other groups have adopted principles for pension reform. While the league would ultimately like the state legislature to address pension reform, it has identified steps that local governments can take in the meantime, in the course of collective bargaining, that will lead to better-funded pensions.[23]

Conclusion

Financial independence in retirement is an important societal goal, and retirement security has been particularly important in the public sector, where employees have traditionally accepted lower compensation in exchange for a secure retirement. There is general agreement that the generation that earns retirement benefits should pay for them. Some pension plans, however, are not being funded according to that principle—in some cases because of actions that could have been avoided. First, a few public employers took routine "pension holidays" and failed to make their required contributions year after year. The holidays proved costly for those plans, a few of which are less than 50% funded today. Second, some governments relied on poor data or granted benefit improvements that later proved unaffordable. Third, the economic woes of the past decade have been so severe that even many well-managed pension plans have had to make adjustments to ensure sound funding levels.

As governments struggle to catch up on their pension obligations, new hires often receive less generous benefits, which may not provide sufficient income replacement when they retire. If this occurs, will these employees have a DC plan or other savings plan that will enable them to reach their retirement income goals? And if local governments have more modest benefit packages, will they still be able to attract and retain the people they need?

Pension reform often begins with an effort to cut costs. But a better starting point is to identify the government's human resource goals and then develop a financially responsible way to achieve them. The balance between what governments pay in salaries and what they pay in deferred compensation may change, but the goal remains the same: governments need qualified, dedicated employees—and a compensation package that meets their needs.

Notes

1. In a defined benefit (DB) plan, the type of plan in which most public employees participate (and to which both they and their employers contribute), the employer promises retirees that they will receive a specified amount, which is determined through a formula that takes into account both salary and years of service). Hence, employers bear the investment risk. Public employee contributions to DB plans average 5% of salary, whereas private sector employees make no contributions to DB plans (if they have one); such plans are funded entirely by employers. Private sector workers are more likely to participate in defined contribution (DC) plans—individual retirement accounts to which employers contribute specified amounts (usually 8% of salary) and employees typically contribute 3% of salary. Although both DB and DC plans accumulate assets through investment earnings, employees with DC plans bear the investment risk: they do not have a guaranteed monthly retirement income from their employer. About 30% of public employees (mostly police officers, firefighters, and teachers) do not participate in social security; these employees typically contribute 8% to their DB plans (Center for State and Local Government Excellence [CSLGE], *State & Local Pensions: An Overview of Funding Issues and Challenges* [Washington, D.C.: CSLGE, January 2011]).
2. Alicia H. Munnell et al., *The Funding of State and Local Pensions in 2010* (Boston: Center for Retirement Research at Boston College, May 2011), crr.bc.edu/images/stories/slp_17_508.pdf.
3. National Governors Association (NGA) and National Association of State Budget Officers (NASBO), *The Fiscal Survey of States: Fall 2011; An Update of State Fiscal Conditions* (Washington, D.C.: NGA and NASBO, 2011), nasbo.org/LinkClick.aspx?fileticket=y%2fqdEfO cPfs%3d&tabid=65.
4. Lucy Dadayan, "States Post Another Strong Quarter in Tax Collections" (Albany: Nelson A. Rockefeller Institute of Government, State University of New York at Albany, December 8, 2011), rockinst.org/newsroom/data_alerts/2011/12-08.aspx.
5. Christopher W. Hoene and Michael A. Pagano, "City Fiscal Conditions in 2011" (Washington, D.C.: National League of Cities, September 2011), nlc.org/news-center/press-room/press-releases/2011/city-fiscal-conditions-2011.
6. NGA and NASBO, *Fiscal Survey of States: Fall 2011*.
7. The Governmental Accounting Standards Board is scheduled to release new, voluntary pension reporting standards in 2012. However, because the proposed guidelines address pension accounting but do not include standards for reporting pension funding, it will be more difficult than ever for state and local governments to determine how to budget for pension obligations and to assess whether funding is on track.
8. Ronald K. Snell, "Pensions and Retirement Plan Enactments in 2011 State Legislatures" (Washington, D.C., and Denver, Colo.: National Conference of State Legislatures, September 30, 2011), ncsl.org/documents/employ/PensionEnactmentsSept30-2011.pdf.
9. Many state and local governments are making even more significant changes to their retiree health benefits, which are far less well funded than pension plans.
10. Munnell et al., *Funding of State and Local Pensions in 2010;* and "Public Plans Database" (Boston and Washington, D.C.: Center for Retirement Research at Boston College and CSLGE), pubplans.bc.edu/pls/htmldb/f?p=198:3:2290981529480329.
11. This represents a decline from 79% in 2009, which stems from two sources: "smoothing" losses in the value of equities that occurred in 2008, and the difficulties that state and local governments have had contributing the full amount of their annual required contributions. Munnell et al., *Funding of State and Local Pensions in 2010*.
12. Hannah McKinney (comments made at the Fiscal Future of the Local Public Sector Conference, Washington, D.C., June 2–3, 2011).
13. CSLGE, *Illinois Municipal Retirement Fund* (fact sheet) (Washington, D.C.: CSLGE, January 2011).
14. In *The Funding of State and Local Pensions: 2009–2013* (Boston: Center for Retirement Research at Boston College, April 2010), crr.bc.edu/images/stories/Briefs/slp_10.pdf, Alicia H. Munnell, Jean-Pierre Aubry, and Laura Quinby explain the distinctions between the two methods as follows: "Suppose a plan sponsor needs to contribute $15,000 for a particular employee who will retire in five years, and that the sponsor fully funds the cost specified by either method. Under projected unit credit, the sponsor recognizes and funds, say, $1,000 in the first year, $2,000 in the second year, $3,000 in the third year, $4,000 in the fourth year, and $5,000 in the fifth year. Under entry-age normal, an actuary would level the contributions over the five-year period so that the sponsor would recognize and pay a normal cost of $3,000 per year. . . . Up to the point of retirement, the entry-age method recognizes a larger accumulated pension obligation for active employees and requires a larger contribution than the projected unit credit" (Munnell, Aubry, and Quinby, *State and Local Pensions*, 3).
15. Pension rules vary and can have a significant effect on retirement compensation. For example, pensions may be based on average salary throughout an employee's career, on average salary for the last three or more years of service, or on the last year of salary.
16. Christine Becker et al., *Strengthening State and Local Government Finances: Lessons for Negotiating Public Pension Plan Reforms* (Washington, D.C.: CSLGE, September 2011), slge.org/vertical/Sites/%7BA260E1DF-5AEE-459D-84C4-876EFE1E4032%7D/uploads/Strengthening_S__L_Govt_Finances_Sept_2011_12-031.pdf.
17. Ibid.
18. Ibid.
19. Among the key modifications to the 2001 contract that were negotiated after the May 2004 election were (1) an increase in the employee contribution rate for certain employees from 4% to 5% of salary; (2) a reduction in the cost-of-living adjustment from 4% to 3% for retirees

hired before January 1, 2005, and from 4 to 2% for retirees hired on or after January 1, 2005; (3) a reduction in the plan multiplier for certain employees from 4.25% to 2.5% for 20 years of service; (4) an increase in the retirement eligibility age; and (5) a transfer of a $300 million note from the city to HMEPS (ibid., 36 – 37).

20. Ibid., 35–37.

21. Becker et al., Strengthening State and Local Government Finances.

22. Rod Gould, "The League Steps Up on Pension Reform," Western City, November 2011, 14, westerncity.com/Western-City/November-2011/The-League-Steps-Up-on-Pension-Reform/.

23. Gould, "Pension Reform."

10

Police and Fire Personnel, Salaries, and Expenditures for 2011

Evelina R. Moulder
ICMA

Continuing the trend identified in 2010 when police and fire departments, like other local government departments, saw their budgets reduced, police and fire pensions in 2011 have been on the table in some communities while other communities have considered increasing the police and fire personnel share of health insurance premiums. Some local governments have also reduced the numbers of police and fire personnel, and some are exploring shared and contracted services to save costs.

The statistics in this annual article are not intended to be used for benchmarking, which requires that many factors be considered to identify localities of similar characteristics, such as population density, vulnerability to natural disasters, and the like. Rather, these statistics are meant to provide a general picture of police and fire personnel and expenditures for each year.

SELECTED FINDINGS

The average entrance salaries are $43,978 for police and $40,333 for fire personnel. The average maximum salaries for police and fire personnel are $62,323 and $55,904, respectively.

The average maximum salary including longevity pay for police officers is $70,451. These salaries vary significantly by geographic division: East South-Central cities show the lowest average maximums while Mid-Atlantic and Pacific Coast cities show the highest.

Per capita average overtime expenditures were $12.24 for police and $9.38 for fire departments.

The average per capita total departmental expenditures 2011 were $283.65 for police and $194.17 for fire departments.

Methodology

The data in this research were collected from responses to ICMA's annual *Police and Fire Personnel, Salaries, and Expenditures* survey, which was mailed in February 2011 to 3,301 municipalities with populations of 10,000 or more (Table 10–1). A second survey was sent to those local governments that did not respond to the first. Respondents had a choice of completing and submitting the survey on the web or by mail. A total of 1,170 jurisdictions submitted surveys for an overall response rate of 35%, which is slightly lower than last year's response rate: a smaller percentage of municipalities under 250,000 in population responded in 2011.

The survey response patterns are presented in Table 10–1 by population group, geographic region, and geographic division. There is variation in the response patterns by population size, with a low of 22% in cities with over 1,000,000 population (two cities—Phoenix and San Antonio—responded in this population group) and a high of 39% in cities with

Table 10-1 Survey Response

Classification	No. of municipalities[a] surveyed (A)	Respondents	
		No.	% of (A)
Total	3,301	1,170	35
Population group			
Over 1,000,000	9	2	22
500,000-1,000,000	23	9	39
250,000-499,999	36	10	28
100,000-249,999	180	61	34
50,000-99,999	419	134	32
25,000-49,999	786	283	36
10,000-24,999	1,848	671	36
Geographic region			
Northeast	897	194	23
North-Central	928	360	39
South	847	361	43
West	629	255	41
Geographic division			
New England	352	74	21
Mid-Atlantic	545	120	22
East North-Central	680	235	35
West North-Central	249	125	50
South Atlantic	387	184	48
East South-Central	169	55	33
West South-Central	290	122	42
Mountain	163	63	39
Pacific Coast	466	192	41

a For a definition of terms, please see "Inside the *Year Book*," xii-xiv.

a population of 500,000–1,000,000. The patterns by geographic division show that New England and Mid-Atlantic jurisdictions were the least likely to complete the questionnaire (21% and 22%, respectively), while South Atlantic and West North-Central jurisdictions were the most likely to do so (48% and 50%, respectively).

Administration

Respondents were asked several questions about service provision and delivery. Virtually all the jurisdictions responding to the 2011 survey (96%) indicated that they provide police services, and 84% reported that they provide fire services (not shown)—figures that have remained almost identical for several years. Twenty jurisdictions reported having a public safety department. To be counted among these respondents, a city had to report "public safety department" as the type of service for both police and fire (see sidebar above).

Cities Reporting a Public Safety Department (Consolidated Police and Fire)

Ceres, CA	Gladstone, MO
Eustis, FL	Maryville, MO
North Palm Beach, FL	Mexico, MO
Bainbridge, GA	Sikeston, MO
Storm Lake, IA	Cayce, SC
East Grand Rapids, MI	North Augusta, SC
Escanaba, MI	North Myrtle Beach, SC
Grand Haven, MI	Spartanburg, SC
Gross Pointe Park, MI	Mitchell, SD
Holland, MI	Ashwaubenon, WI

These data on cities that provide police and fire services do not necessarily mean that all these cities actually deliver each service: 5% of jurisdictions reported contracting with another government for police service delivery (Figure 10–1). The highest percentage of cities reporting this arrangement is in the Pacific Coast division (19%) (not shown). Among the 43 cities that do not provide police services, 39 answered the question about how the services *are* provided, and of those, the majority (28), all of which are under 250,000 in population, reported that the county provides the service (not shown). Three cities reported a regional police service; one reported a special district.

Of the cities that provide fire protection services, the majority (64%) reported having a full-time paid or a full-time and part-time paid fire department, 17% reported a combination of paid and volunteer fire personnel, 12% reported an all-volunteer fire department, and the remaining cities said they contract out for such services or provide them in some other way (Figure 10–1). Among the 187 cities that do not provide fire services, 166 provided information on how the services *are* provided, and of those, 57% reported that services are provided by a special district, and 27% indicated that the county provides the service (not shown). Regional fire services were reported by 7%.

Figure 10-1 Type of Service, 2011

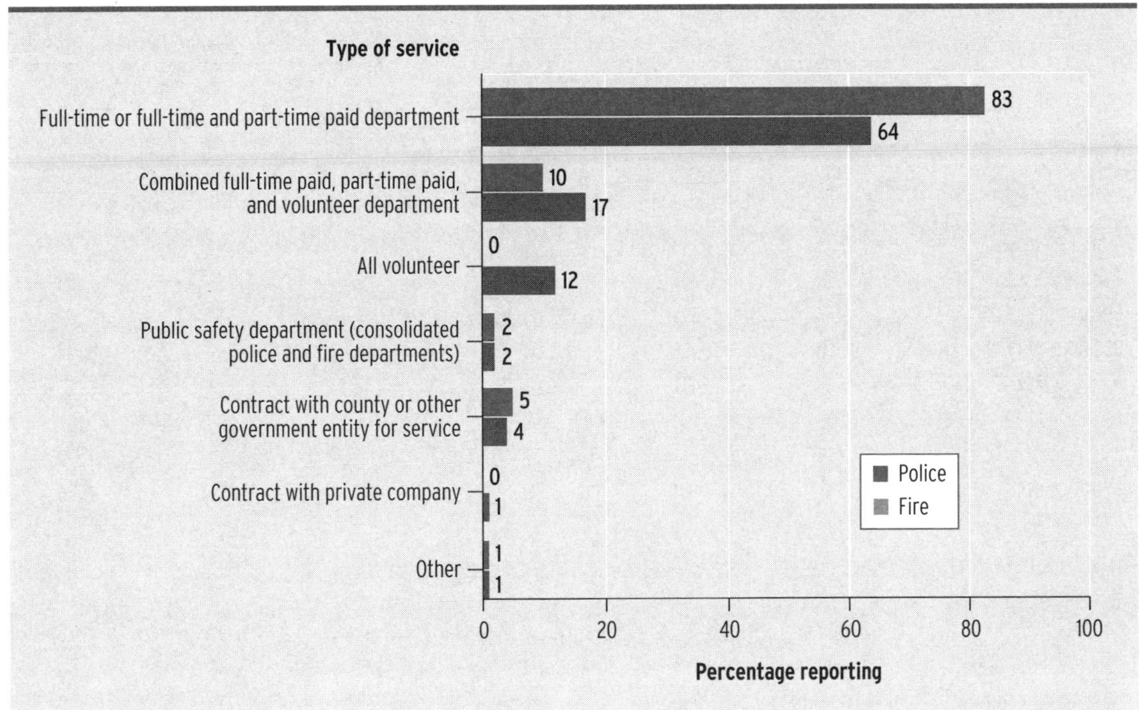

Personnel

The average size of the full-time paid workforce for both police and fire departments is presented in Table 10–2. The data include both uniformed and civilian, or nonuniformed, personnel. The average number of total police department employees, 117, represents a slight increase over the average number reported in 2010, which was 114. The average number of fire personnel is 80, compared with 76 in 2010. As with all averages in this article, these fluctuate depending on which cities report information each year. Using the average number of personnel per capita normalizes the data. When the per capita per 1,000 population is calculated, the average per capita drops slightly for police even though the overall average is slightly higher. The average number of full-time paid police personnel per 1,000 population is 2.69; that of fire personnel is 1.70.

The average numbers of full-time police personnel by population category in 2011 have decreased somewhat from the 2010 figures. The average for the two cities over 1,000,000 in 2011 is 3,786, compared with 3,870 in 2010. For cities in the 500,000–1,000,000 population group, the eight reporting cities in 2011 show an average of 1,833 police employees compared with 1,931 for the five reporting cities in 2010.

The patterns for fire departments are similar to those for police departments (Table 10–2). Cities in the population group of 500,000–1,000,000 show an average of 953 fire employees in 2011, compared with 1,105 in 2010. Continuing down in population, the average for communities in the 10,000–24,999 population group in 2011 is 29, almost identical to the average in 2010.

With the exception of cities in the 10,000–24,999 population group, per capita figures per 1,000 population show slightly lower numbers of full-time paid fire personnel in 2011 than in 2010. The cities under 100,000 population show higher numbers of fire personnel per capita than the larger cities show.

The cross-sectional patterns by geographic division indicate that municipalities in the West South-Central division have the highest average number of full-time police employees (231) and that those in the Mid-Atlantic division have the lowest (53) (Table 10–2). Regarding full-time paid fire employees, the highest average number is also in the West South-Central division (134), and the lowest is again in the Mid-Atlantic division (39). For both the police and fire departments, the East South-Central and South Atlantic divisions show the highest average numbers of full-time paid personnel per 1,000 population; for police, the lowest number of full-time paid personnel per 1,000 population is in

Table 10–2 Full-Time Paid Personnel, 2011

	Police			Fire		
Classification	No. of cities reporting	Mean	Per capita per 1,000 population	No. of cities reporting	Mean	Per capita per 1,000 population
Total	1,001	117	2.69	791	80	1.70
Population group						
Over 1,000,000	2	3,786	3.23	2	1,786	1.53
500,000–1,000,000	8	1,833	2.85	9	953	1.52
250,000–499,999	10	1,050	3.00	9	567	1.54
100,000–249,999	46	401	2.67	46	229	1.48
50,000–99,999	108	162	2.37	98	109	1.61
25,000–49,999	244	92	2.58	207	61	1.70
10,000–24,999	583	44	2.78	420	29	1.75
Geographic division						
New England	71	60	2.33	58	55	1.77
Mid-Atlantic	102	53	2.24	44	39	1.36
East North-Central	208	84	2.30	177	58	1.40
West North-Central	117	80	2.39	90	55	1.20
South Atlantic	154	130	3.77	130	89	2.50
East South-Central	49	129	3.51	48	83	2.48
West South-Central	113	231	3.03	107	134	1.84
Mountain	53	161	2.81	45	104	1.53
Pacific Coast	134	146	2.20	92	91	1.24

the Pacific Coast division followed closely by the Mid-Atlantic division, while for fire, the lowest number is in the West North-Central division, followed closely by the Pacific Coast division.

Figure 10–2 shows the changes over ten years in the average number of full-time employees per 1,000 population for both services.

Table 10–3 presents the average numbers of full-time uniformed, or sworn, personnel in police and fire departments as of January 1, 2011. Among reporting cities, these numbers are 89 for police departments and 78 for fire departments, higher than the 2010 averages (88 and 74, respectively). For the two cities reporting with over 1,000,000 in population, the average number of sworn police personnel reported in 2011 is 2,953. Predictably, the remaining averages are consistently correlated with the population size of the responding jurisdictions: the police department averages range from 1,289 for cities of 500,000–1,000,000 to 35 for cities of 10,000–24,999. The figures per 1,000 population show a high of 2.52 for cities over 1,000,000 in population cities and a low of 1.80 for cities of 50,000–99,999.

It is important to recognize that fluctuations in averages within population groups from year to year depend on the population size of the responding jurisdictions. If, in a given year, most of the respondents have populations at the high end of the range—that is, closer to 249,999 than to 100,000—it will usually result in a higher average number of personnel.

The West South-Central division shows the highest average numbers of sworn full-time police personnel (170), while the Mid-Atlantic and New England divisions show the lowest (44 and 54, respectively) (Table 10–3). When per capita per 1,000 population figures are reviewed, the South Atlantic (2.98) and East South-Central (2.74) divisions are the highest, and the Pacific Coast division is the lowest (1.52), which was also the case in 2010 and 2009. For fire personnel, the East South-Central division shows the highest average number of uniformed personnel per capita (2.44), followed closely by the South Atlantic division (2.28), while the West North-Central and Pacific Coast divisions show the lowest (1.09 and 1.16, respectively).

Figure 10-2 Police and Fire Trends in Employees per 1,000 Population, 2001-2011

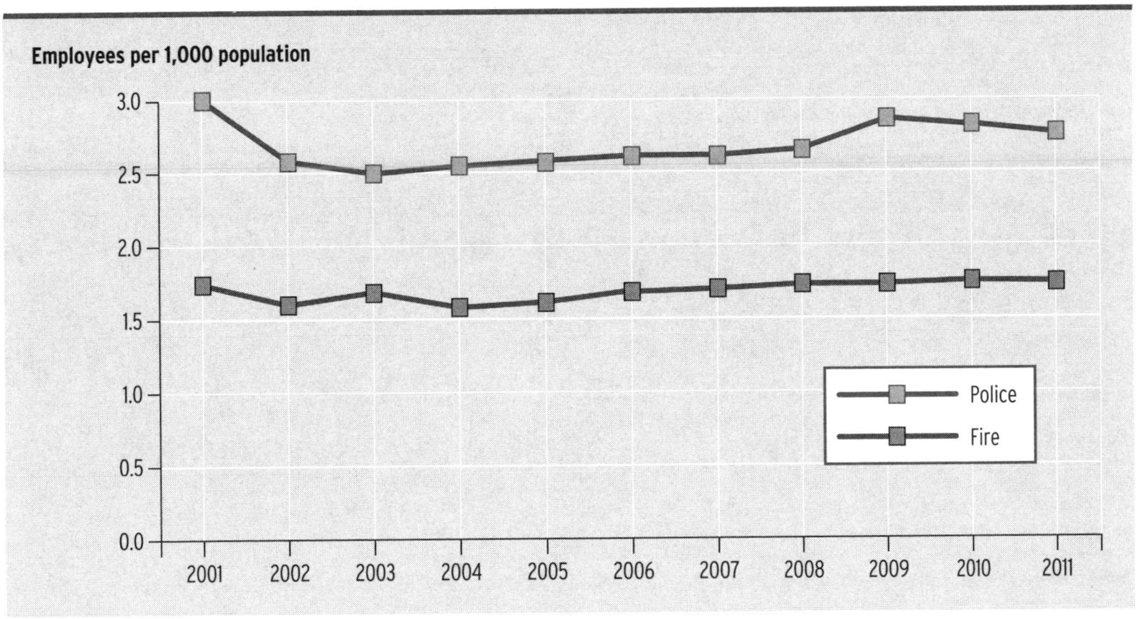

Table 10-3 Uniformed Sworn Personnel, 2011

	Police			Fire		
Classification	No. of cities reporting	Mean	Per capita per 1,000 population	No. of cities reporting	Mean	Per capita per 1,000 population
Total	993	89	2.08	737	78	1.63
Population group						
Over 1,000,000	2	2,953	2.52	2	1,684	1.44
500,000-1,000,000	8	1,289	1.96	9	890	1.43
250,000-499,999	10	808	2.30	9	490	1.34
100,000-249,999	47	286	1.89	47	213	1.38
50,000-99,999	107	123	1.80	95	103	1.52
25,000-49,999	245	70	1.96	193	58	1.63
10,000-24,999	574	35	2.19	382	28	1.69
Geographic division						
New England	70	54	1.93	51	56	1.77
Mid-Atlantic	100	44	1.90	31	45	1.53
East North-Central	205	69	1.82	164	59	1.36
West North-Central	113	63	1.87	83	49	1.09
South Atlantic	152	100	2.98	126	82	2.28
East South-Central	50	100	2.74	47	82	2.44
West South-Central	114	170	2.18	103	131	1.77
Mountain	55	94	2.02	45	95	1.38
Pacific Coast	134	103	1.52	87	85	1.16

Table 10-4 Minimum Crew per Fire Apparatus, 2011

	Pumpers		Ladders		Rescue units	
Classification	No. of cities reporting	Average minimum crew	No. of cities reporting	Average minimum crew	No. of cities reporting	Average minimum crew
Total	561	3.2	534	3.0	429	2.5
Population group						
Over 1,000,000	2	4.0	2	4.0	1	2.0
500,000-1,000,000	7	4.0	8	4.0	7	3.1
250,000-499,999	8	3.8	8	3.6	6	3.3
100,000-249,999	39	3.6	39	3.5	30	2.7
50,000-99,999	77	3.2	76	3.1	60	2.5
25,000-49,999	154	3.0	146	3.0	114	2.2
10,000-24,999	274	3.1	255	3.0	211	2.6
Geographic division						
New England	29	3.0	25	2.8	25	2.3
Mid-Atlantic	44	3.5	42	3.6	34	3.4
East North-Central	100	3.2	97	3.0	89	2.4
West North-Central	63	3.3	60	3.2	53	2.8
South Atlantic	107	3.0	103	2.7	74	2.3
East South-Central	35	3.1	33	2.9	27	2.3
West South-Central	82	3.2	77	3.0	58	2.4
Mountain	30	3.3	32	3.5	21	2.4
Pacific Coast	71	3.0	65	3.2	48	2.4

Staffing Requirements for Fire Personnel

Both reporting jurisdictions with a population of 1,000,000 and over reported minimum staffing requirements, as did 80% of reporting jurisdictions overall (not shown). The responses by geographic division indicate that the majority of jurisdictions in all areas of the country except the Mid-Atlantic division have a minimum requirement, and that more than 90% of cities in the South Atlantic, Pacific Coast, East South-Central, and West South-Central divisions have requirements or policies advising minimum staffing per shift. This pattern is similar to that reported in previous surveys.

The average minimum staffing for apparatus—pumpers, ladders, and other equipment—is presented in Table 10-4. For pumpers, ladders, and rescue units, the average minimum crew is generally higher among larger cities.

Hours Worked per Shift

Several questions were asked regarding the average number of hours worked per week and per shift for both services. The results, which are not displayed, are as expected. Approximately 74% of jurisdictions reported that their police department employees work 40 hours a week, and 17% reported a 42-hour workweek. Fire departments had more varied responses to the workweek question: 38% indicated that their workweek is 56 hours, and only 6% reported a 40-hour workweek. Twenty-two percent reported a 50- to 54-hour workweek in 2011.

The average number of hours worked per shift also varies between the services. Thirty-six percent of the cities indicated that their police officers work an 8-hour shift, and 57% reported 10- or 12-hour shifts (not shown). Fire departments, on the other hand, are most likely to have 24-hour shifts (78%), virtually unchanged from 2010.

Table 10-5 Police Officers' Annual Base Salary, January 1, 2011

	Entrance salary					Maximum salary					No. of years to reach maximum	
Classification	No. of cities reporting	Mean ($)	First quartile ($)	Median ($)	Third quartile ($)	No. of cities reporting	Mean ($)	First quartile ($)	Median ($)	Third quartile ($)	No. of cities reporting	Mean
Total	987	43,978	36,166	42,900	50,367	971	62,323	51,271	60,769	70,888	813	8
Population group												
Over 1,000,000	2	39,998	39,553	39,998	40,443	2	63,950	62,635	63,950	65,264	2	20
500,000-1,000,000	7	52,807	46,414	48,648	51,906	7	75,082	70,252	72,516	74,908	8	11
250,000-499,999	9	48,447	39,864	45,905	59,509	9	65,977	56,359	63,383	74,568	8	9
100,000-249,999	49	48,549	38,810	48,641	54,059	49	68,610	62,296	68,680	77,781	42	9
50,000-99,999	105	47,443	39,048	47,724	54,264	104	66,888	57,465	66,302	76,222	91	9
25,000-49,999	241	44,995	37,080	44,470	51,240	241	63,674	52,504	61,360	72,010	207	8
10,000-24,999	574	42,364	35,078	41,467	48,364	559	60,115	48,984	57,928	67,884	455	8
Geographic division												
New England	70	44,500	40,012	44,020	48,116	70	57,183	50,709	55,349	61,675	68	8
Mid-Atlantic	100	47,734	40,196	47,080	54,807	102	81,649	68,559	79,594	93,593	105	6
East North-Central	210	46,874	41,658	47,320	51,710	204	63,926	56,359	63,621	71,500	201	7
West North-Central	112	39,830	34,554	40,184	44,880	112	55,214	47,562	57,181	63,487	90	8
South Atlantic	153	35,595	31,614	34,301	38,108	144	55,836	47,372	53,652	60,185	59	14
East South-Central	51	30,455	26,780	31,016	33,242	51	45,382	37,952	45,529	50,291	40	14
West South-Central	112	40,493	34,691	40,027	46,742	108	54,403	45,463	55,388	64,780	86	11
Mountain	50	44,177	37,596	42,916	48,696	50	62,507	53,422	62,836	70,686	39	10
Pacific Coast	129	57,911	50,736	57,221	63,990	130	73,876	64,807	74,525	81,850	125	6

Salary and Longevity Pay

Tables 10–5 through 10–8 present various salary and longevity pay data for full-time police officers and firefighters.

Minimum and Maximum Salaries

Tables 10–5 and 10–6 present detailed entrance and maximum salary data for police officers and firefighters, respectively, as well as the average number of years required for each to reach the maximum. In addition to the measures of central tendency (mean and median) for the salary data, the first and third quartiles are included to indicate the degree of dispersion. The annual base salaries are the entrance salaries paid to sworn police officers or firefighters within their first 12 months of employment. Each reported amount excludes uniform allowances, holiday pay, hazardous duty pay, and any other form of additional compensation. The maximum is the highest annual base salary paid to uniformed personnel who do not hold any promotional rank.

The median entrance salary for police personnel is $42,900 and the mean is $43,978 (Table 10–5). The median maximum salary for police is $60,769 and the mean is $62,323. The entrance salary for firefighters tends to be lower than that for police, with a median of $39,209 and a mean of $40,333 (Table 10–6). The maximum fire salary median and mean are $54,596 and $55,904, respectively. For both police and fire, the mean is higher than the median salary. This indicates that some higher salaries are positively skewing the mean.

The highest average entrance salaries for police and fire personnel are found in the Pacific Coast division. The highest average maximum salaries for police personnel are found in the Mid-Atlantic division, followed by the Pacific Coast division. For fire personnel, the highest average entrance salary is in the Pacific Coast division. The lowest average entrance and maximum salaries for both police personnel and firefighters are all found in the East South-Central division. For both services, the difference between the highest

Table 10-6 Firefighters' Annual Base Salary, January 1, 2011

	Entrance salary					Maximum salary					No. of years to reach maximum	
Classification	No. of cities reporting	Mean ($)	First quartile ($)	Median ($)	Third quartile ($)	No. of cities reporting	Mean ($)	First quartile ($)	Median ($)	Third quartile ($)	No. of cities reporting	Mean
Total	706	40,333	32,956	39,209	46,646	693	55,904	46,500	54,596	64,032	540	8
Population group												
Over 1,000,000	2	44,468	42,834	44,468	46,102	2	65,082	60,633	65,082	69,531	0	
500,000-1,000,000	8	47,488	40,848	44,838	47,740	8	69,254	60,838	66,128	73,379	9	8
250,000-499,999	8	45,274	38,229	43,526	50,002	8	62,700	54,420	58,296	65,223	6	11
100,000-249,999	44	44,227	35,851	43,166	51,094	43	61,862	53,807	61,578	68,654	39	8
50,000-99,999	86	43,456	36,912	43,084	49,652	84	61,427	53,062	61,887	69,062	71	8
25,000-49,999	193	41,764	34,419	40,247	47,417	192	57,667	48,376	55,940	63,887	155	8
10,000-24,999	365	38,084	30,718	36,984	44,000	356	52,425	43,314	51,388	60,614	260	8
Geographic division												
New England	53	42,861	38,712	43,003	45,860	50	53,562	48,396	52,811	55,679	42	6
Mid-Atlantic	33	39,639	33,756	39,662	43,496	35	65,317	52,373	64,098	80,158	32	7
East North-Central	157	43,872	38,497	43,128	49,559	156	59,096	51,465	59,960	66,677	149	7
West North-Central	72	37,333	32,122	36,238	44,225	73	51,886	45,776	51,892	58,053	54	8
South Atlantic	122	32,332	28,240	31,782	34,856	116	50,110	42,289	48,638	55,802	43	13
East South-Central	49	29,450	25,813	29,394	32,007	48	43,047	36,323	43,722	48,936	37	15
West South-Central	101	38,394	32,602	37,905	44,214	98	51,433	42,763	52,194	60,341	72	9
Mountain	35	40,467	35,885	39,790	44,725	34	57,376	49,893	56,486	62,083	26	10
Pacific Coast	84	55,213	49,092	53,372	59,086	83	71,086	64,020	69,874	76,302	85	5

and lowest average entrance salaries among the geographic divisions is substantial: $27,456 for police and $25,763 for fire. The difference between the highest and lowest average maximum salaries among the geographic divisions for police is $36,267, compared with $28,039 for firefighters.

For both police and fire services, an average of eight years of service is required to reach the maximum salary.

Longevity Pay

Longevity pay is defined as compensation beyond the regular maximum salary based on number of years of service. Longevity serves as an economic incentive to decrease employee turnover and reward those employees who have already achieved the maximum salary and now have limited opportunities for promotion. Longevity pay can be administered in several ways—a flat dollar amount, a percentage of the base salary, a percentage of the maximum pay, or a step increase in the basic salary plan.

Tables 10–7 and 10–8 show a range of longevity pay data for police and firefighter personnel, respectively. The tables cover whether personnel can receive longevity pay, the maximum salary they can receive including longevity pay, and the average number of years of service that is required for them to receive longevity pay.

Sixty percent of all police departments reporting have a system that awards longevity pay to their personnel (Table 10–7). The Mid-Atlantic and West South-Central divisions show the highest percentages of cities with longevity pay for police personnel (93% and 92%, respectively).

The average maximum salary including longevity pay for police officers is $70,451. The figures range from a low of $60,528 for cities with a population of 250,000–499,999 to a high of $74,884 for cities with a population of 50,000–99,999. Geographic divisions show a clear disparity in this regard. Once again, cities in the East South-Central division show the lowest average maximum at $46,189, while the highest

Table 10-7 Longevity Pay for Police Officers, January 1, 2011

		Personnel can receive longevity pay				Maximum salary including longevity pay					No. of years of service to receive longevity pay	
	No. of cities reporting	Yes		No								
Classification	(A)	No.	% of (A)	No.	% of (A)	No. of cities reporting	Mean ($)	First quartile ($)	Median ($)	Third quartile ($)	No. of cities reporting	Mean
Total	1,024	619	60	405	40	480	70,451	55,516	66,237	78,325	586	6
Population group												
Over 1,000,000	2	2	100	0	0	1	72,000	72,000	72,000	72,000	2	1
500,000-1,000,000	8	6	75	2	25	5	74,149	70,348	74,312	75,955	6	5
250,000-499,999	10	3	30	7	70	2	60,528	57,600	60,528	63,455	3	6
100,000-249,999	47	27	57	20	43	22	73,186	65,770	70,994	79,214	26	6
50,000-99,999	109	67	62	42	39	48	74,884	61,720	69,956	85,064	61	7
25,000-49,999	254	166	65	88	35	139	73,581	57,014	66,706	79,554	157	6
10,000-24,999	594	348	59	246	41	263	67,758	52,400	62,798	73,286	331	6
Geographic division												
New England	71	53	75	18	25	43	60,901	54,594	59,585	65,473	50	7
Mid-Atlantic	109	101	93	8	7	84	90,096	73,198	85,238	104,048	98	6
East North-Central	212	146	69	66	31	122	65,543	56,024	65,737	71,964	141	6
West North-Central	118	60	51	58	49	47	60,425	53,236	58,190	69,934	59	6
South Atlantic	153	56	37	97	63	37	63,097	49,704	60,846	74,199	48	7
East South-Central	54	18	33	36	67	12	46,189	40,226	44,080	52,741	15	6
West South-Central	118	109	92	9	8	72	66,659	47,891	57,548	67,610	103	2
Mountain	52	14	27	38	73	7	61,480	57,011	61,903	65,881	13	4
Pacific Coast	137	62	45	75	55	56	83,479	72,529	80,772	91,085	59	11

average maximums are $90,096 for Mid-Atlantic and $83,479 for Pacific Coast jurisdictions. Cost of living is certainly a factor to consider. The median home prices in the central United States are much lower than they are on the East and West Coasts.

The longevity pay patterns for firefighters (Table 10–8) show that 58% of jurisdictions reported longevity pay for fire personnel, including 92% of jurisdictions in the West South-Central division (the high) and 34% of those in the East South-Central division (the low).

The average maximum salary with longevity pay for firefighters is $62,415. Among population groups, the two cities with populations over 1,000,000 show the highest average maximum salary with longevity pay ($75,180). Geographically, Pacific Coast jurisdictions show the highest average maximum salary with longevity pay ($79,124), and East South-Central communities again show the lowest ($44,250).

Overall, the length of service required for police and firefighters to receive longevity pay is six years for police and five for fire, which is almost identical to the numbers reported every year since 2006. However, the number of years varies somewhat within the classification categories. In the Pacific Coast division, for example, both groups of personnel serve a well-above-average number of years (10 for fire and 11 for police) to qualify for longevity pay.

Expenditures

Respondents were asked to provide expenditure (not budget) figures for their police and fire departments' most recently completed fiscal year. The items include salaries and wages for all department personnel, contributions for employee benefits, capital outlays, and all other departmental expenditures. Average expenditures are presented in Tables 10–9 through 10–16. Per capita expenditures are shown in

Table 10-8 Longevity Pay for Firefighters, January 1, 2011

		Personnel can receive longevity pay				Maximum salary including longevity pay					No. of years of service to receive longevity pay	
	No. of cities reporting	Yes		No								
Classification	(A)	No.	% of (A)	No.	% of (A)	No. of cities reporting	Mean ($)	First quartile ($)	Median ($)	Third quartile ($)	No. of cities reporting	Mean
Total	824	479	58	345	42	342	62,415	50,385	57,432	68,340	448	5
Population group												
Over 1,000,000	2	2	100	0	0	1	75,180	75,180	75,180	75,180	2	13
500,000-1,000,000	8	7	88	1	13	5	68,661	64,274	64,874	68,626	7	5
250,000-499,999	9	4	44	5	56	2	58,062	56,376	58,062	59,748	3	6
100,000-249,999	47	33	70	14	30	24	68,144	60,973	65,469	72,725	32	6
50,000-99,999	96	59	62	37	39	40	66,283	56,536	63,006	75,505	53	6
25,000-49,999	211	136	65	75	36	104	66,488	52,758	59,665	74,236	128	5
10,000-24,999	451	238	53	213	47	166	57,889	45,809	53,250	63,848	223	5
Geographic division												
New England	57	44	77	13	23	34	57,561	51,773	55,404	62,243	41	7
Mid-Atlantic	62	36	58	26	42	27	67,086	52,902	61,278	85,914	33	5
East North-Central	173	122	71	51	30	97	62,151	52,713	61,855	69,890	117	5
West North-Central	97	43	44	54	56	32	53,705	48,862	53,120	56,254	42	6
South Atlantic	126	52	41	74	59	33	61,414	48,432	55,770	67,527	42	6
East South-Central	53	18	34	35	66	12	44,250	38,714	42,618	50,724	14	6
West South-Central	115	106	92	9	8	66	64,693	44,676	55,124	63,664	102	2
Mountain	45	17	38	28	62	9	52,308	42,955	60,258	62,501	16	4
Pacific Coast	96	41	43	55	57	32	79,124	71,389	77,385	86,714	41	10

addition to average expenditures. Again, per capita presentations are useful because they normalize the information.

Salaries and Wages

Part of ICMA's process of reviewing survey results is to design logic checks that will identify problematic values. One logic check is that total expenditures for salaries and wages must be greater than the minimum salary for police (or fire) sworn personnel multiplied by the number of sworn personnel reported. For those jurisdictions reporting total expenditures for salaries and wages below that amount, the total amount of salary and wage expenditures amount was removed.

Table 10–9 shows that the average per capita expenditure for civilian and uniformed police personnel in 2011 was $170.14, a decrease from the 2010 average of $182.54. As population decreases, average per capita expenditures also generally decrease. So, too, do average salary and wage expenditures for police: from $227,176,628 for the two cities with populations over 1,000,000 to $2,667,469 for cities of 10,000–24,999 in population. The average expenditure decrease is more pronounced than the average per capita decrease among population groups, which is to be expected because, again, per capita amounts normalize the data.

Overall, the spread of average per capita salary and wage expenditures is greater for police departments than for fire departments. The average per capita police expenditures show a low of $160.98 in cities of 50,000–99,999 in population and a high of $241.40 in cities of 250,000–499,999 in population (Table 10–9). For firefighters, the average per capita expenditures range from a low of $96.45 in cities with populations of 10,000–24,999 to a high of $133.31 in cities with populations of 500,000–1,000,000.

Geographically, New England and Mid-Atlantic jurisdictions show the highest average per capita

Table 10-9 Expenditures for Salaries and Wages (Civilian and Uniformed), 2011

	Police			Fire		
Classification	No. of cities reporting	Mean ($)	Per capita ($)	No. of cities reporting	Mean ($)	Per capita ($)
Total	906	7,975,858	170.14	731	5,556,737	105.37
Population group						
Over 1,000,000	2	227,176,628	194.09	2	135,762,836	116.30
500,000-1,000,000	7	149,609,076	222.92	8	86,292,605	133.31
250,000-499,999	7	77,347,834	241.40	7	47,107,362	132.82
100,000-249,999	43	33,488,555	236.05	42	17,016,973	112.24
50,000-99,999	92	11,014,236	160.98	83	7,838,095	117.13
25,000-49,999	222	5,891,878	165.56	189	4,071,889	115.23
10,000-24,999	533	2,667,469	166.59	400	1,588,737	96.45
Geographic division						
New England	65	8,644,165	194.00	55	3,624,630	122.31
Mid-Atlantic	99	4,529,069	191.75	48	2,468,799	78.95
East North-Central	191	6,097,594	162.19	163	4,409,344	100.88
West North-Central	98	3,377,227	128.16	86	2,922,346	63.88
South Atlantic	140	6,472,896	186.52	115	4,585,927	123.41
East South-Central	45	7,464,087	153.83	43	4,529,733	111.95
West South-Central	105	14,729,742	161.85	101	10,084,457	113.62
Mountain	46	11,046,708	170.44	39	8,333,284	98.00
Pacific Coast	117	12,165,889	180.74	81	8,745,487	126.76

salary and wage expenditures for police personnel ($194.00 and $191.75, respectively), and Pacific Coast jurisdictions show the highest for firefighters ($126.76). Cities in the West North-Central division show the lowest for both police ($128.16) and fire ($63.88) personnel.

Social Security and Retirement Benefits

The average expenditures for municipal contributions to federal social security and other employee retirement programs are reported in Table 10–10. These expenditures are for both uniformed and civilian personnel. The table shows combined retirement and social security contributions because some states opt out of social security programs for local government employees, relying instead on employee-sponsored retirement programs. Zeros have been removed from the calculations because although zero is a legitimate answer, it skews the averages.

The average per capita expenditure for employee social security and retirement benefits for police in 2011 ($36.39) is up from the 2010 amount ($35.06). Among the population groups, the highest average police per capita expenditure for social security and retirement ($55.75) is in the 250,000–499,999 population group. Geographically, the highest average police department per capita expenditure for these benefits is found in the Pacific Coast division ($46.29); the lowest is in the West North-Central division ($21.79).

The average per capita expenditure for social security and retirement benefits for fire departments in 2011 was $23.09 (Table 10–10), compared with $23.45 in 2010. The per capita amounts fluctuate among the population groups. Among the geographic divisions, the highest average fire department per capita expenditure for social security and retirement benefits is again in the Pacific Coast cities ($30.35), followed closely by the South Atlantic ($29.54) cities, and the lowest is again in the West North-Central ($13.57) cities.

Health, Hospitalization, Disability, and Life Insurance

Table 10–11 shows the average total municipal contributions for health, hospitalization, disability, and

Table 10-10 Total Municipal Contributions to Social Security and State/City-Administered Employee Retirement Systems, 2011

	Police			Fire		
Classification	No. of cities reporting	Mean ($)	Per capita ($)	No. of cities reporting	Mean ($)	Per capita ($)
Total	860	1,732,925	36.39	684	1,266,553	23.09
Population group						
Over 1,000,000	2	59,951,782	51.16	2	34,504,036	29.49
500,000-1,000,000	7	28,655,647	41.44	8	17,454,055	26.26
250,000-499,999	6	17,537,388	55.75	6	11,938,673	33.54
100,000-249,999	43	6,473,449	44.34	42	3,721,465	25.21
50,000-99,999	89	2,505,475	36.22	81	1,778,034	26.41
25,000-49,999	214	1,300,548	36.17	178	900,388	25.35
10,000-24,999	499	571,013	35.48	367	341,848	20.74
Geographic division						
New England	43	789,361	27.73	35	520,683	17.49
Mid-Atlantic	92	971,173	40.91	37	654,558	21.09
East North-Central	181	1,386,753	36.42	153	1,170,230	23.77
West North-Central	96	608,427	21.79	82	630,655	13.57
South Atlantic	139	1,724,323	43.35	116	1,238,684	29.54
East South-Central	45	1,607,674	32.64	43	972,395	24.12
West South-Central	105	3,158,582	32.59	103	1,938,773	20.90
Mountain	45	2,204,480	32.53	36	1,564,556	17.71
Pacific Coast	114	2,760,833	46.29	79	1,919,019	30.35

life insurance programs. The mean per capita expenditures for 2011 show a slight increase to $30.82 for police and an increase to $19.42 for fire. In 2010, they were $30.46 for police and $18.54 for fire.

Total Personnel Expenditures

Table 10–12 shows the total personnel expenditures for civilian and uniformed employees for both police and fire services. These data represent total salaries and wages; contributions for federal social security and other retirement programs; and contributions to health, hospitalization, disability, and life insurance programs. To be included in this table, responding jurisdictions had to provide each of these expenditures. Those that reported an amount of zero were excluded from the table. Again, although zero is a legitimate amount, it negatively skews the average.

For fire services in particular, the workforce composition affects personnel expenditures. Departments that rely heavily on volunteers have significantly lower personnel expenditures than those that use paid staff.

The mean per capita personnel expenditure amounts are $230.68 for police and $141.38 for fire. For police departments, these amounts fluctuate among population groups, although the per capita figures are lower among smaller population groups. Among the geographic divisions, the high for police is in the Pacific Coast division ($259.25), followed by the Mid-Atlantic ($257.25) and South Atlantic ($257.13) divisions; the low is in the West North-Central division ($169.59).

For fire departments, the mean per capita personnel expenditures also vary among population groups. Geographically, the average per capita high is in the Pacific Coast division ($176.89), followed by the South Atlantic division ($167.44); the low is in the West North-Central ($90.43) and Mid-Atlantic ($95.63) divisions.

Overtime Expenditures

At the request of some local governments, a new survey question was added last year on overtime expenditures (Table 10–13). Per capita average overtime expenditures for police in 2011 were $12.24 and for fire, $9.38. Overtime expenditures for fire personnel

Table 10-11 Total Municipal Contributions for Health, Hospitalization, Disability, and Life Insurance Programs, 2011

	Police			Fire		
Classification	No. of cities reporting	Mean ($)	Per capita ($)	No. of cities reporting	Mean ($)	Per capita ($)
Total	824	1,338,965	30.82	666	958,649	19.42
Population group						
Over 1,000,000	2	32,847,204	28.32	2	10,020,015	8.58
500,000-1,000,000	7	23,027,556	33.98	8	15,383,459	24.08
250,000-499,999	6	12,138,231	36.08	6	7,587,788	20.18
100,000-249,999	42	4,133,149	27.86	41	2,506,120	16.56
50,000-99,999	85	1,997,068	28.91	78	1,274,200	18.82
25,000-49,999	203	1,110,220	31.49	171	837,352	23.69
10,000-24,999	479	490,339	31.04	360	290,279	17.78
Geographic division						
New England	37	901,323	31.79	30	840,017	27.80
Mid-Atlantic	86	873,313	40.61	40	450,332	17.24
East North-Central	172	1,308,008	31.14	149	958,879	19.83
West North-Central	95	566,287	22.51	80	635,498	14.63
South Atlantic	134	1,040,501	30.71	110	713,948	20.97
East South-Central	45	1,045,344	25.66	43	700,751	19.80
West South-Central	101	2,175,552	27.23	99	1,265,705	18.45
Mountain	44	1,838,337	29.63	36	1,808,344	17.61
Pacific Coast	110	2,081,754	35.53	79	1,296,988	21.05

show more variation than those for police among population groups, and both services show noticeable variation among the geographic divisions.

As with all police and fire expenditures, it is important to consider population density and other factors before making definitive comparisons. A community with high manufacturing activity may pose a higher risk for fire, resulting in more overtime, and high levels of gang activity may influence the need for police overtime. In addition, for some communities, paying overtime is less costly than hiring additional personnel.

Capital Outlays

Table 10-14 shows departmental expenditures for capital outlays. These outlays include the purchase and replacement of equipment, the purchase of land and existing structures, and the cost of construction. The amounts include the capital expenditures within individual departmental budgets as well as those expenditures included in citywide capital budgets designated for departmental programs or equipment.

Total capital outlay expenditures may fluctuate dramatically from one year to the next for both police and fire departments. This is because the cost of individual capital projects varies widely among communities as well as within the same community over time. Whereas the number of employees, which relates to population size, determines personnel expenditures, fire equipment such as pumpers will cost the same regardless of the size of the community. Thus, the per capita cost for the pumpers will necessarily be higher among cities with fewer people.

The 2011 average municipal capital outlay expenditures per capita were $10.56 for police, a decrease from the $11.56 shown in 2010, and $12.02 for fire, which is above the 2010 figure of $11.38. For police and fire services, the highest average capital outlay expenditures per capita ($11.64 and $16.41, respectively) are in the population group 10,000–24,999. Geographically, the highest average capital outlay expenditures per capita for police services are in the Mountain division cities ($17.78); for fire services, they are in the Pacific Coast division cities ($30.27).

Table 10-12 Total Personnel Expenditures, 2011

	Police			Fire		
Classification	No. of cities reporting	Mean ($)	Per capita ($)	No. of cities reporting	Mean ($)	Per capita ($)
Total	914	10,743,709	230.68	748	7,442,189	141.38
Population group						
Over 1,000,000	2	319,975,614	273.57	2	180,286,886	154.37
500,000-1,000,000	7	201,292,280	298.33	8	119,130,119	183.66
250,000-499,999	7	102,784,080	320.11	7	63,844,328	178.86
100,000-249,999	43	43,999,034	307.61	42	23,184,888	153.60
50,000-99,999	93	15,118,793	220.33	86	10,395,002	154.99
25,000-49,999	222	8,160,760	229.22	191	5,618,027	158.87
10,000-24,999	540	3,595,498	224.75	412	2,100,615	127.66
Geographic division						
New England	65	9,679,418	230.44	56	4,335,341	145.95
Mid-Atlantic	102	6,008,144	257.25	55	2,922,442	95.63
East North-Central	193	8,500,623	222.42	165	6,306,917	139.60
West North-Central	99	4,476,510	169.59	86	4,114,829	90.43
South Atlantic	141	9,115,699	257.13	119	6,299,186	167.44
East South-Central	45	10,117,105	212.13	44	6,061,905	152.34
West South-Central	105	19,980,997	220.64	103	13,043,967	150.05
Mountain	47	14,643,340	225.70	39	11,446,730	130.61
Pacific Coast	117	16,813,137	259.25	81	11,882,087	176.89

For police services, the lowest average capital outlay expenditures per capita are in New England and East North-Central division cities ($6.41 and $6.64, respectively); and for fire, they are in the Mountain division ($5.32).

Other Expenditures

Table 10–15 presents the data for all other departmental expenditures not accounted for in the previous tables. These include ongoing maintenance, utilities, fuel, supplies, and other miscellaneous items. The average per capita expenditures in 2011 were $39.75 for police, an increase from the $36.51 reported in 2010, and $23.69 for fire, which is virtually identical to the 2010 average.

Total Department Expenditures

Table 10–16 shows the combined personnel, capital outlay, and all other departmental expenditures. The average per capita figures for 2011 are $283.65 and $194.17 for police and fire, respectively—a stable figure for police personnel and an increase over the $177.25 reported for fire personnel in 2010.

Total expenditures are not included for those localities in which the sum of expenditures reported (salaries and wages, employee benefit contributions, capital outlay, and other expenses) differ from the amount reported for total expenditures by more than $100. Most of the variations were by thousands of dollars. This same logic has been applied each year for the analysis.

Not all cities include the same expenditures in their budgets. Of the 678 jurisdictions providing information about services included in the fire department budget, 50% cited ambulance personnel and 50% cited ambulance equipment (not shown). Emergency medical technicians (EMTs) were included by 90%, and EMT equipment was included by 92%. This does not necessarily mean, however, that these are the only jurisdictions that provide EMT and ambulance services; these are just the cities that reported having these services in the fire department budget.

Table 10-13 Total Overtime Expenditures, 2011

	Police			Fire		
Classification	No. of cities reporting	Mean ($)	Per capita ($)	No. of cities reporting	Mean ($)	Per capita ($)
Total	892	523,615	12.24	666	507,814	9.38
Population group						
Over 1,000,000	2	13,099,832	11.24	2	16,358,413	14.09
500,000-1,000,000	7	9,339,811	13.32	8	8,229,350	12.91
250,000-499,999	7	5,560,019	16.59	7	3,504,659	10.17
100,000-249,999	43	1,793,656	12.15	42	1,184,357	7.98
50,000-99,999	93	756,838	11.02	82	670,370	9.93
25,000-49,999	217	380,890	10.74	181	314,745	9.03
10,000-24,999	523	203,442	13.02	344	155,342	9.47
Geographic division						
New England	63	451,950	17.62	50	590,075	20.96
Mid-Atlantic	97	276,427	12.27	35	218,990	7.03
East North-Central	181	453,132	12.94	141	332,102	7.53
West North-Central	99	185,648	6.82	73	147,984	4.10
South Atlantic	138	421,397	15.08	113	227,796	8.44
East South-Central	45	381,427	9.80	44	266,230	8.08
West South-Central	102	865,538	8.84	97	814,490	6.64
Mountain	47	580,041	10.19	35	966,430	9.29
Pacific Coast	120	1,004,323	14.17	78	1,193,854	16.83

Conclusion

This report has examined the cross-sectional and longitudinal patterns found in the responses to ICMA's annual *Police and Fire Personnel, Salaries, and Expenditures* survey. Most of the changes over time in police and fire employment and expenditures have been small, incremental shifts. It is not uncommon for one year to show increases and the next to show decreases in average expenditures.

Although using per capita figures instead of absolute numbers reduces the skew of the data, any analysis of the reported changes must control for population size of the responding jurisdictions. Another influential factor is a significant difference in the number reporting in any population group. Any major increase or decrease in that number can affect the average.

Table 10-14 Municipal Expenditures for Capital Outlays, 2011

	Police			Fire		
Classification	No. of cities reporting	Mean ($)	Per capita ($)	No. of cities reporting	Mean ($)	Per capita ($)
Total	718	363,227	10.56	573	474,185	12.02
Population group						
Over 1,000,000	2	1,733,530	1.51	2	15,323,966	12.91
500,000-1,000,000	5	7,267,220	10.70	8	5,571,431	8.22
250,000-499,999	6	477,149	1.52	6	1,280,410	4.05
100,000-249,999	33	999,054	6.38	34	654,036	4.14
50,000-99,999	81	473,176	7.18	77	440,997	6.78
25,000-49,999	179	410,664	10.80	156	312,180	8.65
10,000-24,999	412	177,975	11.64	290	289,352	16.41
Geographic division						
New England	47	128,353	6.41	37	194,470	12.83
Mid-Atlantic	74	177,329	8.79	42	163,850	9.83
East North-Central	147	240,803	6.64	130	316,164	9.10
West North-Central	83	303,006	15.33	65	291,682	11.67
South Atlantic	122	400,532	13.69	87	296,883	10.21
East South-Central	40	258,693	9.62	32	282,488	9.35
West South-Central	86	441,381	9.41	80	947,997	8.31
Mountain	36	966,327	17.78	33	260,105	5.32
Pacific Coast	83	591,990	10.60	67	1,168,337	30.27

Table 10-15 All Other Department Expenditures, 2011

	Police			Fire		
Classification	No. of cities reporting	Mean ($)	Per capita ($)	No. of cities reporting	Mean ($)	Per capita ($)
Total	851	1,846,180	39.75	705	1,082,048	23.69
Population group						
Over 1,000,000	2	41,379,013	35.60	2	20,618,098	17.90
500,000-1,000,000	7	25,566,670	40.61	8	9,644,235	15.48
250,000-499,999	7	23,926,858	71.37	7	12,630,329	33.38
100,000-249,999	42	7,150,250	47.38	41	3,139,857	21.44
50,000-99,999	89	2,784,131	41.34	83	1,594,879	24.53
25,000-49,999	207	1,371,169	38.71	176	842,318	23.87
10,000-24,999	497	623,654	38.82	388	378,053	23.69
Geographic division						
New England	58	892,071	30.00	48	883,230	28.27
Mid-Atlantic	93	437,739	20.74	58	398,494	21.95
East North-Central	174	1,078,436	30.97	151	695,842	17.83
West North-Central	92	913,208	33.46	78	788,553	17.59
South Atlantic	136	2,145,249	56.27	113	1,236,305	31.03
East South-Central	42	1,458,199	33.42	41	627,502	16.47
West South-Central	101	2,944,331	33.67	101	1,483,789	21.48
Mountain	45	2,643,155	43.34	38	1,431,510	18.52
Pacific Coast	110	3,978,804	66.23	77	2,091,776	38.32

Table 10-16 Total Department Expenditures, 2011

	Police			Fire		
Classification	No. of cities reporting	Mean ($)	Per capita ($)	No. of cities reporting	Mean ($)	Per capita ($)
Total	496	13,453,166	283.65	471	7,702,145	194.17
Population group						
Over 1,000,000	2	376,187,991	321.91	1	222,071,424	194.01
500,000-1,000,000	4	245,230,888	366.97	3	161,008,091	227.49
250,000-499,999	5	117,481,470	352.28	5	68,259,218	207.18
100,000-249,999	21	46,559,110	322.71	18	24,498,745	169.19
50,000-99,999	49	18,441,807	274.39	45	12,018,392	184.91
25,000-49,999	113	10,109,904	293.63	106	6,026,339	173.81
10,000-24,999	302	4,398,193	276.21	293	3,278,912	203.92
Geographic division						
New England	44	5,782,087	220.34	40	5,234,005	196.05
Mid-Atlantic	57	7,951,380	327.67	45	2,352,820	86.66
East North-Central	114	11,290,841	279.26	106	9,229,250	265.27
West North-Central	44	5,077,860	209.06	49	2,915,539	98.60
South Atlantic	67	9,999,337	325.58	69	5,728,384	206.86
East South-Central	19	4,650,216	232.91	24	5,379,005	158.06
West South-Central	48	28,020,567	244.17	60	11,436,860	160.91
Mountain	30	22,234,472	303.60	24	8,371,779	156.17
Pacific Coast	73	23,071,466	331.74	54	14,441,151	283.16

Directories

1 Directory Tables

2 Professional, Special Assistance, and Educational Organizations Serving Local and State Governments

e • Innovations • Pensions • Health Insurance Pro

act Fee • 311/CRM Systems • Police and Fire • Di

ation • Innovations • Sustainability • CAO Compensatio

Pensions • CAOCompensation • Sustainability • Dire

s • Innovations • Police and Fire • Health Insurance Pro

Directories • Police and Fire • Pensions • CAO Compe

s • E-Government • Sustainability • Directorie

Insurance Programs • CAO Compensation • Pensi

ability • Development Impact Fees • 311/CRM Systems • H

nt • Sustainability • Police and Fire • Direct

ires • Innovations • Health Insurance Programs • Pen

s • 311/CRM Systems • Pensions • E-Government •

Sustainability • CAO Compensation • Health In

surance Programs • 311/CRM Systems • Pen

1

Directory Tables

Directory 1 in this section of the *Year Book* contains tables providing the names and websites of U.S. state municipal leagues; provincial and territorial associations and unions in Canada; state agencies for community affairs; provincial and territorial agencies for local affairs in Canada; U.S. municipal management associations; international municipal management associations; state associations of counties; and U.S. councils of governments recognized by ICMA. In all cases, where there is no website available, we have provided the name of the president/permanent officer/executive director and all contact information for that individual.

Information in Directory Tables 1–1 through 1–8 was obtained from the National League of Cities (1–1), the Federation of Canadian Municipalities (1–2), the Council of State Community Development Agencies (1–3), the Ontario Ministry of Municipal Affairs (1–4), ICMA files (1–5, 1–6, and 1–8), and the National Association of Counties (1–7), and is current as of January 19, 2012, unless otherwise indicated.

U.S. State Municipal Leagues

Directory Table 1–1 shows 49 state leagues of municipalities serving 49 states. (Hawaii does not have a league.) Information includes league address and website. State municipal leagues provide a wide range of research, consulting, training, publications, and legislative representation services for their clients.

Provincial and Territorial Associations and Unions in Canada

Directory 1–2 shows the websites of the 16 associations and unions serving the 12 provinces and territories of Canada.

State Agencies for Community Affairs

Directory 1–3 shows the names, addresses, and websites of 47 agencies for community affairs in the United States, as well as that for Puerto Rico. These agencies of state governments offer a variety of research, financial information, and coordination services for cities and other local governments.

Provincial and Territorial Agencies for Local Affairs in Canada

Directory 1–4 shows the names, addresses, phone numbers, fax numbers, and websites of the agencies for local affairs serving the 12 provinces and territories of Canada.

U.S. Municipal Management Associations

Directory 1–5 shows the names and websites of municipal management associations serving 47 of the United States. (The states of Wyoming, Idaho, Montana, North Dakota, and South Dakota are served by the Great Open Spaces City Management Association; Idaho and South Dakota are also served by their own associations; and neither Hawaii nor Louisiana has an association.)

International Municipal Management Associations

Directory 1–6 shows the names and websites (where available) of municipal management associations serving Canada and 22 other countries.

U.S. State Associations of Counties

Directory 1–7 shows the names and websites for 53 county associations serving 47 states. (Two associations serve the states of Arizona, South Dakota, Washington, and West Virginia; three associations serve the state of Illinois; and three states—Connecticut,

Rhode Island, and Vermont—do not have associations.) Like their municipal league counterparts, these associations provide a wide range of research, training, consulting, publications, and legislative representation services.

U.S. Councils of Governments Recognized by ICMA

Directory 1–8 gives the names and websites for 96 councils of governments recognized by ICMA.

Other Local Government Directories

The names of municipal officials not reported in the *Year Book* are available in many states through directories published by state municipal leagues, state municipal management associations, and state associations of counties. Names and websites of these leagues and associations are shown in Directories 1–1, 1–5, and 1–7. In some states, the secretary of state, the state agency for community affairs (Directory 1–3), or another state agency publishes a directory that includes municipal and county officials. In addition, several directories with national coverage are published for health officers, welfare workers, housing and urban renewal officials, and other professional groups.

Directory 1-1 U.S. State Municipal Leagues

Shown below are the state municipal leagues of municipalities serving 49 states. For each league the directory provides the address and website so that readers can go directly to the site to find additional information.

Alabama
Alabama League of Municipalities
P.O. Box 1270
Montgomery 36102
alalm.org

Alaska
Alaska Municipal League
217 Second Street, Suite 200
Juneau 99801
akml.org

Arizona
League of Arizona Cities and Towns
1820 West Washington Street
Phoenix 85007
azleague.org

Arkansas
Arkansas Municipal League
301 West Second Street
Box 38
North Little Rock 72115
arml.org

California
League of California Cities
1400 K Street, Suite 400
Sacramento 95814
cacities.org

Colorado
Colorado Municipal League
1144 Sherman Street
Denver 80203
cml.org

Connecticut
Connecticut Conference of Municipalities
900 Chapel Street, 9th Floor
New Haven 06510-2807
ccm-ct.org

Delaware
Delaware League of Local Governments
P.O. Box 484
Dover 19903-0484
dllg.org/about.html

Florida
Florida League of Cities
301 South Bronough Street, Suite 300
Tallahassee 32301
floridaleagueofcities.com

Georgia
Georgia Municipal Association
201 Pryor Street, S.W.
Atlanta 30303
gmanet.com/home

Idaho
Association of Idaho Cities
3100 South Vista Avenue, Suite 310
Boise 83705
idahocities.org

Illinois
Illinois Municipal League
500 East Capitol Avenue
Springfield 62701
iml.org

Indiana
Indiana Association of Cities and Towns
200 South Meridian Street, Suite 340
Indianapolis 46225
citiesandtowns.org

Iowa
Iowa League of Cities
317 Sixth Avenue, Suite 800
Des Moines 50309-4111
iowaleague.org

Kansas
League of Kansas Municipalities
300 S.W. Eighth Avenue
Topeka 66603
lkm.org

Kentucky

Kentucky League of Cities
100 East Vine Street, Suite 800
Lexington 40507
klc.org

Louisiana

Louisiana Municipal Association
700 North 10th Street
Baton Rouge 70802
lamunis.org

Maine

Maine Municipal Association
60 Community Drive
Augusta 04330
memun.org

Maryland

Maryland Municipal League
1212 West Street
Annapolis 21401
mdmunicipal.org

Massachusetts

Massachusetts Municipal Association
One Winthrop Square
Boston 02110
mma.org

Michigan

Michigan Municipal League
1675 Green Road
Ann Arbor 48105
mml.org

Minnesota

League of Minnesota Cities
145 University Avenue West
St. Paul 55103-2044
lmnc.org

Mississippi

Mississippi Municipal League
600 East Amite Street, Suite 104
Jackson 39201
mmlonline.com

Missouri

Missouri Municipal League
1727 Southridge Drive
Jefferson City 65109
mocities.com

Montana

Montana League of Cities and Towns
208 North Montana Avenue, Suite 106
Helena 59601
mlct.org

Nebraska

League of Nebraska Municipalities
1335 L Street
Lincoln 68508
lonm.org

Nevada

Nevada League of Cities and Municipalities
310 South Curry Street
Carson City 89703
nvleague.org

New Hampshire

New Hampshire Local Government Center
25 Triangle Park Drive
Concord 03301
nhlgc.org

New Jersey

New Jersey State League of Municipalities
222 West State Street
Trenton 08608
njslom.com

New Mexico

New Mexico Municipal League
1229 Paseo de Peralta
Santa Fe 87501
nmml.org

New York

New York State Conference of Mayors and Municipal Officials
119 Washington Avenue
Albany 12210
nycom.org

North Carolina

North Carolina League of Municipalities
215 North Dawson Street
Raleigh 27603
nclm.org

North Dakota

North Dakota League of Cities
410 East Front Avenue
Bismarck 58504
ndlc.org

Ohio

Ohio Municipal League
175 South Third Street, Suite 510
Columbus 43215
omlohio.org

Oklahoma

Oklahoma Municipal League
201 N.E. 23rd Street
Oklahoma City 73105
oml.org

Oregon

League of Oregon Cities
1201 Court Street, N.E., Suite 200
Salem 97301
orcities.org

Pennsylvania

Pennsylvania League of Cities and Municipalities
414 North Second Street
Harrisburg 17101
plcm.org

Rhode Island

Rhode Island League of Cities and Towns
One State Street, Suite 502
Providence 02908
rileague.org

South Carolina

Municipal Association of South Carolina
1411 Gervais Street
Columbia 29211
masc.sc

South Dakota

South Dakota Municipal League
208 Island Drive
Fort Pierre 57532
sdmunicipalleague.org

Tennessee

Tennessee Municipal League
226 Capitol Boulevard, Suite 710
Nashville 37219
tml1.org

Texas

Texas Municipal League
1821 Rutherford Lane, Suite 400
Austin 78754
tml.org

Utah

Utah League of Cities and Towns
50 South 600 East, Suite 150
Salt Lake City 84102
ulct.org

Vermont

Vermont League of Cities and Towns
89 Main Street, Suite 4
Montpelier 05602-2948
vlct.org

Virginia

Virginia Municipal League
13 East Franklin Street
Richmond 23219
vml.org

Washington

Association of Washington Cities
1076 Franklin Street, S.E.
Olympia 98501
awcnet.org

West Virginia

West Virginia Municipal League
2020 Kanawha Boulevard
Charleston 25311
wvml.org

Wisconsin

League of Wisconsin Municipalities
122 West Washington Avenue, Suite 300
Madison 53703-2715
lwm-info.org

Wyoming

Wyoming Association of Municipalities
315 West 27th Street
Cheyenne 82001
wyomuni.org

Directory 1-2 Provincial and Territorial Associations and Unions in Canada

Shown below are the associations and unions serving the provinces and territories of Canada. For each association the directory provides the website so that readers can go directly to the site to find additional information. Where there is no website available, we have provided the names of the president and permanent officer, along with all contact information for the latter.

Alberta

Alberta Association of Municipal Districts and Counties
aamdc.com

Alberta Urban Municipalities Association
munilink.net/live/

British Columbia

Union of British Columbia Municipalities
civicnet.bc.ca/ubcm

Manitoba

Association of Manitoba Municipalities
amm.mb.ca

New Brunswick

Association Francophone des Municipalités du Nouveau-Brunswick
afmnb.org

Cities of New Brunswick Association
Joel Richardson, president
Sandra Mark, executive director
P.O. Box 1421, Station A
Fredericton E3B 5E3
506-357-4242 (phone)
506-357-4243 (fax)
cities@rogers.com

Newfoundland and Labrador

Newfoundland and Labrador Federation of Municipalities
municipalitiesnl.ca

Northwest Territories

Northwest Territories Association of Communities
nwtac.com

Nova Scotia

Union of Nova Scotia Municipalities
unsm.ca

Ontario

Association of Municipalities of Ontario
amo.on.ca

Federation of Canadian Municipalities
fcm.ca

Prince Edward Island

Federation of Prince Edward Island Municipalities
fpeim.ca

Québec

Union des Municipalités du Québec
umq.qc.ca

Saskatchewan

Saskatchewan Association of Rural Municipalities
sarm.ca

Saskatchewan Urban Municipalities Association
suma.org

Yukon

Association of Yukon Communities
ayc.yk.ca

Directory 1-3 State Agencies for Community Affairs

Shown below are the agencies for community affairs for 47 states and Puerto Rico. For each agency the directory provides the name, address, and website so that readers can go directly to the site to find additional information.

Alabama

Department of Economic and Community Affairs
401 Adams Avenue
Montgomery 36104
adeca.state.al.us

Alaska

Department of Commerce, Community and Economic Development
P.O. Box 110800
Juneau 99811-0800
dced.state.ak.us

Arizona

Arizona Commerce Authority
333 North Central Avenue, Suite 1900
Phoenix 85004
azcommerce.com

Arkansas

Economic Development Commission
900 West Capitol Avenue
Little Rock 72201
1800arkansas.com

California

Department of Housing and Community Development
1800 Third Street
Sacramento 95811-6942
hcd.ca.gov

Colorado

Department of Local Affairs
1313 Sherman Street, Suite 518
Denver 80203
dola.state.co.us

Connecticut

Department of Economic and Community Development
505 Hudson Street
Hartford 06106-7106
ct.gov/ecd/site/default.asp

Delaware

Delaware State Housing Authority
18 The Green
Dover 19901
destatehousing.com/

Florida

Department of Economic Opportunity
107 East Madison Street
Caldwell Building
Tallahassee 32399-4120
dca.state.fl.us

Georgia

Department of Community Affairs
60 Executive Park South, N.E.
Atlanta 30329
dca.state.ga.us

Idaho

Idaho Department of Commerce
700 West State Street
Boise 83720-0093
commerce.idaho.gov

Illinois

Illinois Department of Commerce and Economic Opportunity
500 East Monroe
Springfield 62701
commerce.state.il.us/dceo

Indiana

Indiana Housing and Community Development Authority
30 South Meridian Street, Suite 1000
Indianapolis 46204
in.gov/ihfa

Iowa

Iowa Department of Economic Development
200 East Grand Avenue
Des Moines 50309
iowalifechanging.com

Kansas

Department of Commerce
Division of Community Development
1000 S.W. Jackson Street, Suite 100
Topeka 66612
kansascommerce.com/index.aspx?NID=98

Kentucky

Department for Local Government
1024 Capital Center Drive, Suite 340
Frankfort 40601
dlg.ky.gov/grants/

Louisiana

Office of Community Development
Division of Administration
1201 North Third Street
Claiborne Building, Suite 7-270
Baton Rouge 70802
doa.louisiana.gov/cdbg/cdbg.htm

Maine

Maine Department of Economic and Community Development
59 State House Station
Augusta 04333-0059
econdevmaine.com

Maryland

Department of Housing and Community Development
100 Community Place
Crownsville 21032
dhcd.state.md.us

Michigan

Michigan Economic Development Corporation
300 North Washington Square
Lansing 48913
medc.michigan.org

Minnesota

Department of Employment and Economic Development
First National Bank Building
332 Minnesota Street, Suite E-200
St. Paul 55101-1351
positivelyminnesota.com/

Mississippi

Mississippi Development Authority
501 North West Street
Jackson 39201
Mississippi.org

Missouri

Department of Economic Development
301 West High Street
P.O. Box 1157
Jefferson City 65102
ded.mo.gov

Montana

Department of Commerce
Local Government Assistance Division
301 South Park
P.O. Box 200501
Helena 59620-0501
commerce.mt.gov/

Nebraska

Nebraska Department of Economic Development
301 Centennial Mall South
P.O. Box 94666
Lincoln 68509-4666
neded.org

Nevada

Nevada Commission on Economic Development
808 West Nye Lane
Carson City 89703
http://www.diversifynevada.com/

New Hampshire

Office of Energy and Planning
Johnson Hall, 3rd Floor
107 Pleasant Street
Concord 03301
nh.gov/oep

New Jersey

Department of Community Affairs
101 South Broad Street
P.O. Box 800
Trenton 08625-0800
state.nj.us/dca

New Mexico

Department of Finance and Administration
Local Government Division
180 Bataan Memorial Building
Santa Fe, 87501
local.nmdfa.state.nm.us

New York

New York State Division of Housing and Community Renewal
Hampton Plaza, 38-40 State Street
Albany 12207
nysdhcr.gov/index.htm

North Carolina

Department of Commerce
301 North Wilmington Street
Raleigh 27601-1058
nccommerce.com/en

North Dakota

Department of Commerce
Division of Community Services
1600 East Century Avenue, Suite 2
P.O. Box 2057
Bismarck 58503-2057
state.nd.us/dcs

Ohio

Department of Development
77 South High Street
Columbus 43216-1001
odod.state.oh.us

Oklahoma

Department of Commerce
900 North Stiles Avenue
Oklahoma City 73104
okcommerce.gov

Oregon

Business Oregon
775 Summer Street, N.E., Suite 200
Salem 97301-1280
oregon4biz.com

Pennsylvania

Department of Community and Economic Development
Commonwealth Keystone Building
400 North Street, 4th Floor
Harrisburg 17120-0225
newpa.com/default.aspx?id=223

Puerto Rico

Office of the Commissioner of Municipal Affairs
P.O. Box 70167
San Juan 00936-8167
ocam.gobierno.pr

Rhode Island

Rhode Island Housing Resources Commission
One Capitol Hill, 3rd Floor
Providence 02908
hrc.ri.gov/index.php

South Carolina

Department of Commerce
1201 Main Street, Suite 1600
Columbia 29201-3200
sccommerce.com

South Dakota

Department of Tourism and State Development
711 East Wells Avenue
Pierre 57501-3369
tsd.sd.gov/index.asp

Tennessee

Tennessee Housing Development Agency
404 James Robertson Parkway, Suite 1200
Nashville 37243-0900
state.tn.us/thda

Texas

Texas Department of Housing and Community Affairs
221 East 11th Street
Austin 78701-2401
tdhca.state.tx.us

Utah

Utah Governor's Office of Economic Development
324 South State Street, Suite 500
Salt Lake City 84111
goed.utah.gov

Utah Department of Community and Culture
324 South State Street, Suite 500
Salt Lake City 84111
community.utah.gov

Vermont

Vermont Department of Housing and Community Affairs
National Life Drive, 6th Floor
One National Life Drive
Montpelier 05620
dhca.state.vt.us/

Virginia

Virginia Department of Housing and Community Development
Main Street Centre
600 East Main Street, Suite 300
Richmond 23219
dhcd.virginia.gov

Washington

Department of Commerce
1011 Plum Street S.E.
P.O. Box 42525
Olympia 98504-2525
cted.wa.gov

West Virginia

West Virginia Department of Commerce
Capitol Complex, Building 6, Room 525
1900 Kanawha Boulevard East
Charleston 25305-0311
wvcommerce.org/business/business_external/default.aspx

Wisconsin

Wisconsin Department of Commerce
201 West Washington Avenue
Madison 53703
commerce.state.wi.us

Directory 1-4 Provincial and Territorial Agencies for Local Affairs in Canada

Shown below are the agencies for local affairs serving the provinces and territories of Canada. For each agency the directory provides the address and website for the ministry so that readers can go directly to the site to find additional information.

Alberta

Alberta Municipal Affairs
Communications Branch
Commerce Place, 18th Floor
10155-102 Street
Edmonton T5J 4L4
municipalaffairs.gov.ab.ca

British Columbia

Ministry of Community, Sport and Cultural Development
P.O. Box 9490
Station Provincial Government
Victoria V8W 9N7
gov.bc.ca/cserv/index.html

Manitoba

Manitoba Aboriginal and Northern Affairs
344-450 Broadway
Winnipeg R3C 0V8
gov.mb.ca/ana

New Brunswick

Aboriginal Affairs Secretariat
Kings Place
P.O. Box 6000
Fredericton E3B 5H1
www2.gnb.ca/content/gnb/en/departments/aboriginal_affairs.html

Newfoundland and Labrador

Department of Municipal Affairs
Confederation Building, 4th Floor (West Block)
P.O. Box 8700
St. John's A1B 4J6
ma.gov.nl.ca/ma

Northwest Territories

Department of Education, Culture and Employment
P.O. Box 1320
Yellowknife X1A 2L9
ece.gov.nt.ca

Nova Scotia

Service Nova Scotia and Municipal Relations
Mail Room, 8 South, Maritime Centre
1505 Barrington Street
Halifax B3J 3K5
gov.ns.ca/snsmr/

Ontario

Ministry of Municipal Affairs and Housing
777 Bay Street, 17th Floor
Toronto M5G 2E5
mah.gov.on.ca/

Prince Edward Island

Department of Finance and Municipal Affairs
Shaw Building, Second Floor South
95 Rochford Street
P.O. Box 2000
Charlottetown C1A 7N8
gov.pe.ca/finance/index.php3

Québec

Affaires Municipales, Régions et Occupation du territoire
(Ministry of Municipal Affairs, Regions and Land Occupancy)
mamrot.gouv.qc.ca/

Saskatchewan

Public Service Commission
2350 Albert Street
Regina S4P 4A6
psc.gov.sk.ca

Yukon

Department of Community Services
Yukon Government Administration Building
2071 Second Avenue
P.O. Box 2703
Whitehorse Y1A 1B2
community.gov.yk.ca/

Directory 1-5 U.S. Municipal Management Associations

Shown below are the names of the 47 municipal management associations in the United States. For each association the directory provides the website so that readers can go directly to the site to find additional information. Where there is no website available, we have provided the name, address, and all contact information for the association president (current as of January 19, 2012).

Alabama

Alabama City/County Management Association
accma-online.org/

Alaska

Alaska Municipal Management Association
alaskamanagers.org/

Arizona

Arizona City/County Management Association
azmanagement.org/

Arkansas

Arkansas City/County Management Association
Lance B. Hudnell (as of May 2012)
City Manager
City of Hot Springs
P.O. Box 700
Hot Springs 71902-0700
501-321-6810 (phone)
501-321-6809 (fax)
lhudnell@cityhs.net

California

City Manager's Department, League of California Cities
cacities.org

Cal-ICMA
icma.org/en/ca/home

Colorado

Colorado City and County Management Association
coloradoccma.org

Connecticut

Connecticut Town and City Management Association
cttcma.govoffice3.com/

Delaware

City Management Association of Delaware
Kyle R. Sonnenberg (through October 2012)
City Manager
City of Newark
220 Elkton Road
Newark 19711-4594
302-366-7020 (phone)
302-366-7035 (fax)
ksonnenberg@newark.de.us

Florida

Florida City and County Management Association
fccma.org/

Georgia

Georgia City-County Management Association
gccma.com

Idaho

Idaho City/County Management Association
See Wyoming

Illinois

Illinois City/County Management Association
ilcma.org/

Indiana

Indiana Municipal Management Association
citiesandtowns.org

Iowa

Iowa City/County Management Association
Iacma.net

Kansas

Kansas Association of City/County Management
kacm.us/

Kentucky

Kentucky City/County Management Association
kccma.org/

Maine

Maine Town and City Management Association
mtcma.org

Maryland

Maryland City County Management Association
icma.org/en/md/home

Massachusetts

Massachusetts Municipal Management Association
massmanagers.org

Michigan

Michigan Local Government Management Association
mlgma.org

Minnesota

Minnesota City/County Management Association
mncma.org

Mississippi

Mississippi City and County Management Association
Mary Ann Hess (through December 2012)
Finance Director/City Clerk
City of Laurel
P.O. Box 647
Laurel 39441-0647
maryannhess@laurelms.com
601-428-6430 (phone)
601-428-6415 (fax)

Missouri

Missouri City/County Management Association
momanagers.org

Montana

See Wyoming

Nebraska

Nebraska City/County Management Association
nebraskacma.org

Nevada

Local Government Managers Association of Nevada
nevadalogman.org/

New Hampshire

New Hampshire Municipal Management Association
nhmunicipal.org

New Jersey

New Jersey Municipal Management Association
njmma.org/

New Mexico

New Mexico City Management Association
James C. Jimenez (through September 2012)
City Manager
City of Rio Rancho
3200 Civic Center Circle, Suite 400
Rio Rancho 87144-4501
505-891-5002 (phone)
jjimenez@ci.rio-rancho.nm.us

New York

New York State City/County Management Association
nyscma.govoffice.com/

North Carolina

North Carolina City and County Management Association
ncmanagers.org/

North Dakota

See Wyoming

Ohio

Ohio City/County Management Association
ocmaohio.org/

Oklahoma

City Management Association of Oklahoma
cmao-ok.org/

Oregon

Oregon City/County Management Association
occma.org

Pennsylvania

Association for Pennsylvania Municipal Management
apmm.net

Rhode Island

Rhode Island City and Town Management Association
William Sequino Jr. (through August 2012)
Town Manager
Town of East Greenwich
P.O. Box 111
East Greenwich 02818-0111
401-886-8665 (phone)
401-886-8623 (fax)
wsequino@eastgreenwichri.com

South Carolina

South Carolina City and County Management Association
icma.org/en/sc/home

South Dakota

South Dakota City Management Association
sdmunicipalleague.org (Go to "Affiliate Organizations" and then to "City Management")

Tennessee

Tennessee City Management Association
tncma.org/

Texas

Texas City Management Association
tcma.org/

Utah

Utah City Management Association
ucma-utah.org/

Vermont

Vermont Town and City Management Association
Kathleen S. Ramsay (through May 2012)
Assistant Town Manager
Town of Middlebury
P.O. Box 429
Killington 05751
802-388-8100, ext 201 (phone)
802-388-4364 (fax)
kramsay@townofmiddlebury.org

Virginia

Virginia Local Government Management Association
vlgma.org

Washington

Washington City/County Management Association
wccma.org

West Virginia

West Virginia City Management Association
wvmanagers.org/

Wisconsin

Wisconsin City/County Management Association
wcma-wi.org

Wyoming, Idaho, Montana, North Dakota, and South Dakota

Great Open Spaces City Management Association
icma.org/en/go/home

Directory 1-6 International Municipal Management Associations

Shown below are the names of 25 international municipal management associations. For each association the directory provides the website so that readers can go directly to the site to find additional information. Where there is no website available, we have provided the name, address, and all contact information for the president of the association (current as of January 19, 2012).

Australia

Local Government Managers Australia (LGMA)
lgma.org.au

Canada

Canadian Association of Municipal Administrators (CAMA)
camacam.ca

Denmark

National Association of Chief Executives in Danish Municipalities (KOMDIR)
komdir.dk

Georgia

Municipal Service Providers' Association (Georgia)
mspa.ge/

Hungary

Partnership of Hungarian Local Government Associations
kisvarosok.hu

India

City Managers' Association, Gujarat
cmag-india.com

City Managers' Association, Karnataka (CMAK)
cmakarnataka.com/

City Managers' Association, Orissa
cmao.nic.in

Indonesia

All-Indonesia Association of City Government (APEKSI)
apeksi.or.id

Ireland

County and City Managers' Association
Ċaitríona Ní Mhurchú
Executive Administrator
Office for Local Authority Management
Local Government Management Services Board
Local Government House
35-39 Ushers Quay
Dublin 8
353-1-643-8400 (phone)
cnimhurchu@lgma.ie

Israel

Union of Local Authorities in Israel (ULAI)
masham.org.il/English/Pages/default.aspx

Mexico

Mexican Association of Municipalities (AMMAC)
ammac.org.mx

Nepal

Municipal Association of Nepal (MuAN)
muannepal.org.np/

Netherlands

Dutch City Managers Association
gemeentesecretaris.nl

New Zealand

New Zealand Society of Local Government Managers
solgm.org.nz

Norway

Norwegian Forum of Municipal Executives
Finn Brevig
Executive Director
Norsk Radmannsforum
Box 354
2001 Lillestrom
f.c.brevig@radmann.no
472-150-2020

Russia

Russian National Congress of Municipalities
www.rncm.ru (no English version)

Slovakia

Slovak City Managers' Association
apums.sk

South Africa

Institute for Local Government Management of South Africa
ilgm.co.za

South Korea

Korean Urban Management Association
kruma.org

Spain

L'Union des Dirigeants Territoriaux de l'Europe (U.Di.T.E.)
udite.eu

Sri Lanka

Federation of Sri Lankan Local Government Authorities (FSLGA)
fslga.wordpress.com

Sweden

Association of Swedish City Managers
Anna Sandborgh
Chair
Karlstads kommun
Kommunledningskontoret
651 84 Karlstad
anna.sandborgh@karlstad.se
46-5-429-5102

United Kingdom

Society of Local Authority Chief Executives (SOLACE)
solace.org.uk

Viet Nam

Association of Cities of Viet Nam
acvn.vn

Directory 1-7 U.S. State Associations of Counties

Shown below are the names of the 53 state associations of counties in the United States. For each association the directory provides the address and website so that readers can go directly to the site to find additional information. Where there is no website available, we have provided the name and phone number for the executive director (current as of January 19, 2012).

Alabama

Association of County Commissions of Alabama
100 North Jackson Street
Montgomery 36104
acca-online.org

Alaska

Alaska Municipal League
217 Second Street, Suite 200
Juneau 99801
akml.org

Arizona

Arizona Association of Counties
1910 West Jefferson, Suite 1
Phoenix 85009
azcounties.org

County Supervisors Association of Arizona
1905 West Washington Street, Suite 100
Phoenix 85009
countysupervisors.org

Arkansas

Association of Arkansas Counties
1415 West Third Street
Little Rock 72201
arcounties.org

California

California State Association of Counties
1100 K Street, Suite 101
Sacramento 95814
csac.counties.org

Colorado

Colorado Counties, Inc.
800 Grant Street, Suite 500
Denver 80203
ccionline.org

Delaware

Delaware Association of Counties
Richard Cecil
Executive Director
12 North Washington Avenue
Lewes 19958-1806
302-645-0432 (phone)
302-645-2232 (fax)
dick_cecil@yahoo.com

Florida

Florida Association of Counties
P.O. Box 549
Tallahassee 32302
fl-counties.com

Georgia

Association County Commissioners of Georgia
50 Hurt Plaza, Suite 1000
Atlanta 30303
accg.org

Hawaii

Hawaii State Association of Counties
4396 Rice Street, Suite 206
Lihue 96766
808-270-7760 (phone)
808-270-7639 (fax)

Idaho

Idaho Association of Counties
700 West Washington
P.O. Box 1623
Boise 83701
idcounties.org

Illinois

Illinois Association of County Board Members
413 West Monroe Street, 2nd Floor
Springfield 62704
ilcounty.org/

Metro Counties of Illinois
Dwight Magalis
Executive Director
1303 Brandywine Road
Libertyville 60048-3000
847-816-0889 (phone)
847-247-9915 (fax)
magalisike@msn.com

United Counties Council of Illinois
W. Michael McCreery
Executive Director
217 East Monroe, Suite 101
Springfield 62701-1743
217-544-5585 (phone)
217-544-5571 (fax)
mike@mmccreery.com

Indiana

Association of Indiana Counties
101 West Ohio Street, Suite 1575
Indianapolis 46204
indianacounties.org

Iowa

Iowa State Association of Counties
5500 Westown Parkway, Suite 190
West Des Moines 50266
iowacounties.org

Kansas

Kansas Association of Counties
300 S.W. Eighth Street, 3rd Floor
Topeka 66603
kansascounties.org

Kentucky

Kentucky Association of Counties
400 Englewood Drive
Frankfort 40601
kaco.org

Louisiana

Police Jury Association of Louisiana
707 North Seventh Street
Baton Rouge 70802
lpgov.org

Maine

Maine County Commissioners Association
11 Columbia Street
Augusta 04330
mainecounties.org

Maryland

Maryland Association of Counties
169 Conduit Street
Annapolis 21401
mdcounties.org

Massachusetts

Massachusetts Association of County Commissioners
Peter Collins
Executive Director
614 High Street
Dedham 02027-0310
781-461-6105 (phone)
781-326-6480 (fax)

Michigan

Michigan Association of Counties
935 North Washington Avenue
Lansing 48906
micounties.org

Minnesota

Association of Minnesota Counties
125 Charles Avenue
St. Paul 55103-2108
mncounties.org

Mississippi

Mississippi Association of Supervisors
793 North President Street
Jackson 39202
masnetwork.org

Missouri

Missouri Association of Counties
516 East Capitol Avenue
P.O. Box 234
Jefferson City 65102-0234
mocounties.com

Montana

Montana Association of Counties
2715 Skyway Drive
Helena 59602-1213
maco.cog.mt.us

Nebraska

Nebraska Association of County Officials
625 South 14th Street
Lincoln 68508
nacone.org

Nevada

Nevada Association of Counties
304 South Minnesota Street
Carson City 89703
nvnaco.org

New Hampshire

New Hampshire Association of Counties
Bow Brook Place
46 Donovan Street, Suite 2
Concord 03301-2624
nhcounties.org

New Jersey

New Jersey Association of Counties
150 West State Street
Trenton 08608
njac.org

New Mexico

New Mexico Association of Counties
613 Old Santa Fe Trail
Santa Fe 87505
nmcounties.org

New York

New York State Association of Counties
540 Broadway, 5th Floor
Albany 12207
nysac.org

North Carolina

North Carolina Association of County Commissioners
215 North Dawson Street
Raleigh 27603
ncacc.org

North Dakota

North Dakota Association of Counties
1661 Capitol Way
P.O. Box 877
Bismarck 58502-0877
ndaco.org

Ohio

County Commissioners Association of Ohio
209 East State Street
Columbus 43215-4309
ccao.org

Oklahoma

Association of County Commissioners of Oklahoma City
429 N.E. 50th Street
Oklahoma City 73105
okacco.com

Oregon

Association of Oregon Counties
P.O. Box 12729
Salem 97309
aocweb.org

Pennsylvania

County Commissioners Association of Pennsylvania
P.O. Box 60769
Harrisburg 17106-0769
pacounties.org

South Carolina

South Carolina Association of Counties
1919 Thurmond Mall
Columbia 29201
sccounties.org

South Dakota

South Dakota Association of County Officials
300 East Capitol Avenue, Suite 2
Pierre 57501
sdcounties.org

South Dakota Association of County Commissioners
222 East Capitol Avenue, Suite 1
Pierre 57501
sdcc.govoffice2.com

Tennessee

Tennessee County Services Association
226 Capitol Boulevard, Suite 700
Nashville 37219-1896
tncounties.org

Texas

Texas Association of Counties
1210 San Antonio Street
Austin 78701
county.org

Utah

Utah Association of Counties
5397 South Vine Street
Salt Lake City 84107
uacnet.org

Virginia

Virginia Association of Counties
1207 East Main Street, Suite 300
Richmond 23219-3627
vaco.org

Washington

Washington Association of County Officials
206 Tenth Avenue, S.E.
Olympia 98501
wacounties.org/waco

Washington State Association of Counties
206 Tenth Avenue, S.E.
Olympia 98501
wacounties.org/wsac

West Virginia

County Commissioners' Association of West Virginia
2309 Washington Street, East
Charleston 25311
polsci.wvu.edu/wv

West Virginia Association of Counties
2211 Washington Street East
Charleston 25311-2118
wvcounties.org

Wisconsin

Wisconsin Counties Association
22 East Mifflin Street, Suite 900
Madison 53703
wicounties.org

Wyoming

Wyoming County Commissioners Association
409 West 24th Street
P.O. Box 86
Cheyenne 82003
wyo-wcca.org

Directory 1-8 U.S. Councils of Governments Recognized by ICMA

Shown below are the names and websites of the 96 U.S. councils of government recognized by ICMA state associations of counties in the United States. Where there is no website available, we have provided the phone number for the council office.

ALABAMA-4

Central Alabama Regional Planning and Development Commission
carpdc.com

East Alabama Regional Planning & Development Commission
earpdc.org

Regional Planning Commission of Greater Birmingham
rpcgb.org

South Central Alabama Development Commission
scadc.net

ARIZONA-2

Maricopa Association of Governments
azmag.gov

Pima Association of Governments
pagnet.org

ARKANSAS-3

Metroplan
metroplan.org

Northwest Arkansas Regional Planning Commission
nwarpc.org

White River Planning & Development District
wrpdd.org

CALIFORNIA-9

Association of Bay Area Governments
abag.ca.gov

Fresno Council of Governments
fresnocog.org

Sacramento Area Council of Governments
sacog.org

San Bernardino Associated Governments
sanbag.ca.gov

San Diego Association of Governments
sandag.org

Santa Barbara County Association of Governments
sbcag.org

Southern California Association of Governments
scag.ca.gov

Stanislaus Council of Governments
stancog.org

Western Riverside Council of Governments
wrcog.cog.ca.us

COLORADO-1

Denver Regional Council of Governments
drcog.org

DISTRICT OF COLUMBIA-1

Metropolitan Washington Council of Governments
mwcog.org

FLORIDA-2

Solid Waste Authority of Palm Beach County
swa.org

Tampa Bay Regional Planning Council
tbrpc.org

GEORGIA-3

Atlanta Regional Commission
atlantaregional.com

Middle Georgia Regional Commission
middlegeorgiarc.org

Southern Georgia Regional Commission
sgrdc.com

IDAHO-1

Panhandle Area Council
pacni.org

ILLINOIS-9

Bi-State Regional Commission
bistateonline.org

Champaign County Regional Planning Commission
ccrpc.org

DuPage Mayors and Managers Conference
dmmc-cog.org

Lake County Municipal League
lakecountyleague.org

North Central Illinois Council of Governments
ncicg.org

Northwest Municipal Conference
nwmc-cog.org

South Central Illinois Regional Planning and Development Commission
scirpdc.com

Southwestern Illinois Metropolitan and Regional Planning Commission
618 344-4250

Tri-County Regional Planning Commission
tricountyrpc.org

IOWA-1

Midas Council of Governments
midascog.net

KENTUCKY-4

Barren River Area Development District
bradd.org

Big Sandy Area Development District
bigsandy.org

Lincoln Trail Area Development District
ltadd.org

Northern Kentucky Area Development District
nkadd.org

MARYLAND-2

Baltimore Metropolitan Council
baltometro.org

Tri-County Council For Southern Maryland
tccsmd.org

MICHIGAN-1

Southeast Michigan Council of Governments
semcog.org

MISSISSIPPI-1

Central Mississippi Planning & Development District
cmpdd.org

MISSOURI-3

East-West Gateway Council of Governments
ewgateway.org

Mid-America Regional Council
marc.org

South Central Ozark Council of Governments
scocog.org

NEW MEXICO-2

Mid-Region Council of Governments
mrcog-nm.gov

Southwest New Mexico Council of Governments
swnmcog.org

NEW YORK-1

Capital District Regional Planning Commission
cdrpc.org

NORTH CAROLINA-5

Centralina Council of Governments
centralina.org

Eastern Carolina Council of Governments
eccog.org

Lumber River Council of Governments
lumberrivercog.org

Piedmont Triad Council of Governments
ptcog.org

Upper Coastal Plain Council of Governments
ucpcog.org

OHIO-4

Miami Valley Regional Planning Commission
mvrpc.org

Ohio-Kentucky-Indiana Regional Council of Governments
oki.org

Ohio Mid-Eastern Governments Association
omegadistrict.org

Toledo Metropolitan Area Council of Governments
tmacog.org

OKLAHOMA-2

Association of Central Oklahoma Governments
acogok.org

Central Oklahoma Economic Development District
coedd.org

OREGON-4

Lane Council of Governments
lcog.org

Mid-Columbia Economic Development District
mcedd.org

Mid-Willamette Valley Council of Governments
mwvcog.org

Oregon Cascades West Council of Governments
ocwcog.org

SOUTH CAROLINA-3

Central Midlands Council of Governments
centralmidlands.org

South Carolina Appalachian Council of Governments
scacog.org

Upper Savannah Council of Governments
uppersavannah.com

SOUTH DAKOTA-2

Northeast Council of Governments
necog.org

Planning and Development District III
districtiii.org

TEXAS-15

Alamo Area Council of Governments
aacog.dst.tx.us

Ark-Tex Council of Governments
atcog.org

Capital Area Planning Council
capcog.org

Central Texas Council of Governments
ctcog.org

Coastal Bend Council of Governments
cbcog98.org

Concho Valley Council of Governments
cvcog.org

Deep East Texas Council of Governments
detcog.org

Heart of Texas Council of Governments
hotcog.org

Houston-Galveston Area Council
h-gac.com

Nortex Regional Planning Commission
nortexrpc.org

North Central Texas Council of Governments
nctcog.org

Panhandle Regional Planning Commission
theprpc.org

South Plains Association of Governments
spag.org

Texoma Council of Governments
texoma.cog.tx.us

West Central Texas Council of Governments
wctcog.org

UTAH-1

Five County Association of Governments
fcaog.state.ut.us

VIRGINIA-5

Crater Planning District Commission
craterpdc.org

Hampton Roads Planning District Commission
hrpdc.org

Northern Neck Planning District Commission
nnpdc.org

Northern Virginia Planning District Commission
novaregion.org

West Piedmont Planning District Commission
wppdc.org

WASHINGTON-1

Benton-Franklin Regional Council
bfcog.us

WEST VIRGINIA-3

Bel-O-Mar Regional Council
belomar.org

Mid-Ohio Valley Regional Council
movrc.org

Region One Planning & Development Council
regiononepdc.org

WISCONSIN-1

East Central Wisconsin Regional Planning Commission
eastcentralrpc.org

2

Professional, Special Assistance, and Educational Organizations Serving Local and State Governments

This article briefly describes 79 organizations that provide services of particular importance to cities, counties, and other local and state governments. Most of the organizations are membership groups for school administrators, health officers, city planners, city managers, public works directors, city attorneys, and other administrators who are appointed rather than elected. Several are general service and representational organizations for states, cities, counties, and administrators and citizens. Some organizations provide distinctive research, technological, consulting, and educational programs on a cost-of-service basis and have been established to meet specific needs of state and local governments. The others support educational activities and conduct research in urban affairs or government administration, thereby indirectly strengthening professionalism in government administration.

The assistance available through the secretariats of these national organizations provides an excellent method of obtaining expert advice and actual information on specific problems. The information secured in this way enables local and state officials to improve administrative practices, organization, and methods and thus improve the quality of services rendered. Many of these organizations also are active in raising the professional standards of their members through in-service training, special conferences and seminars, and other kinds of professional development.

Research on current problems is a continuing activity of many of these groups, and all issue a variety of publications ranging from newsletters and occasional bulletins to diversified books, monographs, research papers, conference proceedings, and regular and special reports.

These organizations provide many of the services that in other countries would be the responsibility of the national government. They arrange annual conferences, answer inquiries, provide in-service training and other kinds of professional development, provide placement services for members, and develop service and cost standards for various activities. Most of the organizations listed have individual memberships, and several also have agency or institutional memberships. Some of these organizations have service memberships that may be based on the population of the jurisdiction, the annual revenue of the jurisdiction or agency, or other criteria that roughly measure the costs of providing service. In addition to these kinds of membership fees, some of the organizations provide specialized consulting, training, and information services both by annual subscription and by charges for specific projects.

Listing of Organizations

Airports Council International–North America (ACI-NA)

1775 K Street, N.W., Suite 500
Washington, D.C. 20006
202-293-8500; fax: 202-331-1362

Website: aci-na.org

President: Greg Principato

Major publications: *Airport Highlights;* studies, surveys, reports

Purpose: To promote sound policies dealing with the financing, construction, management, operations, and development of airports; to provide reference and resource facilities and information for airport operators; and to act as the "voice" of airports to governmental agencies, officials, and the public on problems and solutions concerning airport operations. Established 1948.

American Association of Airport Executives (AAAE)

601 Madison Street, Suite 400
Alexandria, Virginia 22314
703-824-0500; fax: 703-820-1395

Website: aaae.org

President: Charles M. Barclay

Major publications: *Airport Report; Airport Magazine; Airport Report Express*

Purpose: To assist airport managers in performing their complex and diverse responsibilities through an airport management reference library; a consulting service; publications containing technical, administrative, legal, and operational information; an electronic bulletin board system; a professional accreditation program for airport executives; and Aviation News and Training Network, a private satellite broadcast network for airport employee training and news. Established 1928.

American Association of Port Authorities (AAPA)

1010 Duke Street
Alexandria, Virginia 22314-3589
703-684-5700; fax: 703-684-6321

E-mail: info@aapa-ports.org

Website: aapa-ports.org

President: Kurt J. Nagle

Major publications: *Alert Newsletter*; *AAPA Directory–Seaports of the Americas*; *Seaport Magazine*

Purpose: To promote the common interests of the port community and provide leadership on trade, transportation, environmental, and other issues related to port development and operations. As the alliance of ports of the Western Hemisphere, AAPA furthers public understanding of the essential role fulfilled by ports within the global transportation system. It also serves as a resource to help members accomplish their professional responsibilities. Established 1912.

American Association of School Administrators (AASA)

801 North Quincy Street, Suite 700
Arlington, Virginia 22203
703-528-0700; fax: 703-841-1543

Website: aasa.org

Executive director: Daniel A. Domenech

Major publications: *The School Administrator*; Critical Issues Series

Purpose: To develop qualified educational leaders and support excellence in educational administration; to initiate and support laws, policies, research, and practices that will improve education; to promote programs and activities that focus on leadership for learning and excellence in education; and to cultivate a climate in which quality education can thrive. Established 1865.

American College of Healthcare Executives (ACHE)

One North Franklin Street, Suite 1700
Chicago, Illinois 60606-3529
312-424-2800; fax: 312-424-0023

Website: ache.org

President/CEO: Thomas C. Dolan, PhD, FACHE, CAE

Major publications: *Journal of Healthcare Management*; *Healthcare Executive*; *Frontiers of Health Services Management*; miscellaneous studies and task force, committee, and seminar reports

Purpose: To be the premier professional society for health care executives who are dedicated to improving health care delivery and to advancing health care management excellence. Established 1933.

American Institute of Architects (AIA)

1735 New York Avenue, N.W.
Washington, D.C. 20006
202-626-7300; fax: 202-626-7547
800-242-3837

Website: aia.org

President: Clark Manus

Major publication: *AIArchitect*

Purpose: To organize and unite in fellowship the members of the architectural profession; to promote the aesthetic, scientific, and practical efficiency of the profession; to advance the science and art of planning and building by advancing the standards of architectural education, training, and practice; to coordinate the efforts of the building industry and the profession of architecture to ensure the advancement of living standards for people through improved environment; and to make the profession of architecture one of ever-increasing service to society. Established 1857.

American Library Association (ALA)

50 East Huron Street
Chicago, Illinois 60611
312-944-6780; fax: 312-440-9374
800-545-2433
Also at 1615 New Hampshire Avenue, N.W.
Washington, D.C. 20009-2520
202-628-8410; fax: 202-628-8419
800-941-8478

Website: www.ala.org

Executive director: Keith Michael Fiels

Major publications: *American Libraries; Booklist, Book Links, Smart Libraries Newsletter; Library Technology Reports;* Guide to Reference (a subscription database); and the websites ALA TechSource and RDA [Research Description and Access] Toolkit.

Purpose: To assist libraries and librarians in promoting and improving library service and librarianship. Established 1876.

American Planning Association (APA), and its professional institute, the American Institute of Certified Planners (AICP)

1030 15th Street, N.W.
Washington, D.C. 20005-1503
202-872-0611; fax: 202-872-0643
Also at 205 North Michigan Avenue, Suite 1200
Chicago, Illinois 60601
312-431-9100; fax: 312-786-6700

Website: planning.org

Executive director/CEO: W. Paul Farmer, FAICP

Major publications: *Journal of the APA; Planning; Planning and Environmental Law; Zoning Practice; The Commissioner; Practicing Planner; Interact; APA Advocate;* Planning Advisory Service (PAS) Reports

Purpose: To encourage planning that will meet the needs of people and society more effectively. APA is a nonprofit public interest and research organization representing 43,000 practicing planners, officials, and citizens involved with urban and rural planning issues. Sixty-five percent of its members work for state and local government agencies and are involved, on a day-to-day basis, in formulating planning policies and preparing land use regulations. AICP is APA's professional institute, providing recognized leadership nationwide in the certification of professional planners, ethics, professional development, planning education, and the standards of planning practice. APA resulted from a consolidation of the American Institute of Planners, founded in 1917, and the American Society of Planning Officials, established in 1934.

American Public Gas Association (APGA)

201 Massachusetts Avenue, N.E., Suite C-4
Washington, D.C. 20002
202-464-2742; fax: 202-464-0246

E-mail: bkalisch@apga.org

Website: apga.org

President/CEO: Bert Kalisch

Major publications: *Public Gas News* (bi-weekly newsletter); *Publicly Owned Natural Gas System Directory* (annual); *The Source* (quarterly magazine)

Purpose: To be an advocate for publicly owned natural gas distribution systems, and effectively educate and communicate with members to promote safety, awareness, performance, and competitiveness. Established 1961.

American Public Health Association (APHA)

800-I Street, N.W.
Washington, D.C. 20001-3710
202-777-2742; fax: 202-777-2534

Website: apha.org

Executive director: Georges Benjamin, MD

Major publications: *American Journal of Public Health; The Nation's Health*

Purpose: To protect the health of the public through the maintenance of standards for scientific procedures, legislative education, and practical application of innovative health programs. Established 1872.

American Public Human Services Association (APHSA)

1133 19th Street, N.W., Suite 400
Washington, D.C. 20036
202-682-0100; fax: 202-289-6555

Website: aphsa.org

Executive director: Tracy Wareing

Major publications: *Policy and Practice* magazine; *Public Human Services Directory; This Week in Health; This Week in Washington; W-Memo; Working for Tomorrow*

Purpose: To develop and promote policies and practices that improve the health and well-being of families, children, and adults. Established 1930.

American Public Power Association (APPA)

1875 Connecticut Avenue, N.W., Suite 1200
Washington, D.C. 20009
202-467-2900; fax: 202-467-2910

Website: publicpower.org

President/CEO: Mark Crisson

Major publications: *Public Power* (magazine); *Public Power Weekly* (newsletter); *Public Power Daily*

Purpose: To promote the efficiency and benefits of publicly owned electric systems; to achieve cooperation among public systems; to protect the interests of publicly owned utilities; and to provide service in the fields of management and operation, energy conservation, consumer services, public relations, engineering, design, construction, research, and accounting practice. APPA represents more than 2,000 community-owned electric utilities and provides services in the areas of government relations, engineering and operations, accounting and finance, energy research and development, management, customer relations, and public communications. The association represents public power interests before Congress, federal agencies, and the courts; provides educational programs and energy planning services in technical and management areas; and collects, analyzes, and disseminates information on public power and the electric utility industry. APPA publishes a weekly newsletter, a magazine, and many specialized publications; funds energy research and development projects; recognizes utilities and individuals for excellence in management and operations; and serves as a resource for federal, state, and local policy makers and officials, news reporters, public interest and other organizations, and the general public on public power and energy issues. Established 1940.

American Public Transportation Association (APTA)

1666 K Street, N.W., Suite 1100
Washington, D.C. 20006
202-496-4800; fax: 202-496-4324

Website: apta.com

President: Gary C. Thomas

Major publications: *Passenger Transport; Public Transportation Fact Book*

Purpose: To represent the operators of and suppliers to public transit; to provide a medium for discussion, exchange of experiences, and comparative study of industry affairs; and to research and investigate methods to improve public transit. The association also assists public transit entities with special issues, and collects and makes available public transit-related data and information. Established 1882.

American Public Works Association (APWA)

2345 Grand Boulevard, Suite 700
Kansas City, Missouri 64108-2625
816-472-6100; fax: 816-472-1610
Also at 1275 K Street, N.W., Suite 750
Washington, D.C. 20005-4083
202-408-9541; fax: 202-408-9542

Website: apwa.net

Executive director: Peter B. King

Major publications: *APWA Reporter* (12 issues), research reports, technical publications and manuals

Purpose: To develop and support the people, agencies, and organizations that plan, build, maintain, and improve our communities. Established 1894.

American Society for Public Administration (ASPA)

1301 Pennsylvania Avenue, N.W., Suite 700
Washington, D.C. 20004
202-393-7878; fax: 202-638-4952

Website: aspanet.org

Executive director: Antoinette A. Samuel

Major publications: *Public Administration Review; PA Times*

Purpose: To improve the management of public service at all levels of government; to advocate on behalf of public service; to advance the science, processes, and art of public administration; and to disseminate information and facilitate the exchange of knowledge among persons interested in the practice or teaching of public administration. Established 1939.

American Water Works Association (AWWA)

6666 West Quincy Avenue
Denver, Colorado 80235
303-794-7711; fax: 303-347-0804

Website: awwa.org

Executive director: David B. LaFrance

Major publications: *AWWA Journal; MainStream; OpFlow; WaterWeek*

Purpose: To promote public health and welfare in the provision of drinking water of unquestionable and sufficient quality. Founded 1881.

Association of Public-Safety Communications Officials–International, Inc.

351 North Williamson Boulevard
Daytona Beach, Florida 32114-1112
386-322-2500; fax: 386-322-2501
Also at 1426 Prince Street
Alexandria, Virginia 22314-2815
571-312-4400; fax: 571-312-4419

Website: apcointl.org

Interim executive director: Mark Cannon

Major publications: *APCO BULLETIN; The Journal of Public Safety Communications; Public Safety Operating Procedures Manual;* APCO training courses

Purpose: To promote the development and progress of public safety telecommunications through research, planning, and training; to promote cooperation among public safety agencies; to perform frequency coordination for radio services administered by the Federal Communications Commission; and to act as a liaison with federal regulatory bodies. Established 1935.

Association of Public Treasurers (APT)

962 Wayne Avenue, Suite 910
Silver Spring, Maryland 20910
301-495-5560; fax: 301-495-5561

Website: aptusc.org

Executive director: Lindsey Dively

Major publications: *Technical Topics; Treasury Notes*

Purpose: To enhance local treasury management by providing educational training, technical assistance, legislative services, and a forum for treasurers to exchange ideas and develop policy papers and positions. Established 1965.

Canadian Association of Municipal Administrators (CAMA)

P.O. Box 128, Station A
Fredericton, New Brunswick E3B 4Y2
866-771-2262; fax: 506-460-2134

Website: camacam.ca

Executive director: Jennifer Goodine

Purpose: To achieve greater communication and cooperation among municipal managers across Canada, and to focus the talents of its members on the preservation and advancement of municipal government by enhancing the quality of municipal management in Canada. Established 1972.

Center for State and Local Government Excellence (SLGE)

777 North Capitol Street, N.E., Suite 500
Washington, D.C. 20002-4201
202-682-6100; fax: 202-962-3604

Website: slge.org

President and CEO: Elizabeth Kellar

Recent research reports: *The Funding of State and Local Pensions: 2013; Comparing Compensation: State-Local versus Private Sector Workers; How Local Governments Are Addressing Retiree Health Care Funding; State and Local Government Workforce: 2011 Realities;* and case studies on public sector pensions and retiree health, wellness and chronic care management programs, and other health care reform issues.

Purpose: To help state and local governments become knowledgeable and competitive employers so that they can attract and retain talented, committed, and well-prepared individuals to public service. Research areas include workforce analyses and implications of changing demographics, competitive employment practices, compensation analyses, state and local government retirement plans, postemployment and retiree health care benefits, and financial wellness and retirement planning. Public Plans Database, developed in partnership with the Center for Retirement Research at Boston College, provides comprehensive financial, governance, and plan design information for more than 120 state and local defined benefit plans. Established 2006.

Council of State Community Development Agencies (COSCDA)

1825 K Street, Suite 515
Washington, D.C. 20006
202-293-5820; fax: 202-293-2820

Website: coscda.org

Executive director: Dianne Taylor

Major publications: *The National Line; StateLine; Member Update; Annual Report*

Purpose: To promote the value and importance of state involvement in community development, economic development, affordable housing, and homelessness programs. For over 30 years, COSCDA has positioned itself as the premier national association charged with advocating and enhancing the leadership role of states in these issue areas, which it accomplishes through information sharing and a variety of technical assistance programs. COSCDA seeks to support, facilitate, and communicate states' priorities to its membership, as well as to elected and appointed officials and to state and federal policy makers. Its Training Academy offers basic and advanced courses on community development block grants and an introductory course on housing programs. COSCDA also holds an annual training conference in the fall and a program managers' conference in the spring. Established 1974.

Council of State Governments (CSG)

2760 Research Park Drive
Lexington, Kentucky 40511
859-244-8000; fax: 859-244-8001

Website: csg.org

Executive director/CEO: David Adkins

Major publications: *Book of the States; Capitol Ideas* magazine; *CSG State Directories*

Purpose: To prepare states for the future by interpreting changing national and international trends and conditions; to promote the sovereignty of the states and their role in the American federal system; to advocate multistate problem solving and partnerships; and to build leadership skills to improve decision making. CSG is a multibranch and regionally focused association of the states, U.S. territories, and commonwealths. Established 1933.

Federation of Canadian Municipalities (FCM)

24 Clarence Street
Ottawa, Ontario K1N 5P3
613-241-5221; fax: 613-241-7440

E-mail: ceo@fcm.ca

Website: fcm.ca

CEO: Brock Carlton

Major publications: *Forum* (national magazine); *Crossroads: The Newsletter for FCM International*

Purpose: To represent the interests of all municipalities on policy and program matters within federal jurisdictions. Policy and program priorities are determined by FCM's board of directors, standing committees, and task forces. Issues include payments in lieu of taxes, goods and service taxes, economic development, municipal infrastructure, environment, transportation, community safety and crime prevention, quality-of-life social indicators, housing, race relations, and international trade and aid. FCM members include Canada's largest cities, small urban and rural communities, and the 18 major provincial and territorial municipal associations, which together represent more than 20 million Canadians. Established 1937.

Government Finance Officers Association (GFOA)

203 North LaSalle Street, Suite 2700
Chicago, Illinois 60601-1210
312-977-9700; fax: 312-977-4806
Also at 1301 Pennsylvania Avenue, N.W., Suite 309
Washington, D.C. 20004
202-393-8020; fax: 202-393-0780

Website: gfoa.org

Executive director/CEO: Jeffrey L. Esser

Major publications: GFOA *Newsletter; Government Finance Review Magazine; Public Investor; GAAFR Review; Pension & Benefits Update; Governmental Accounting, Auditing, and Financial Reporting; Investing Public Funds; Elected Official's Series*

Purpose: To enhance and promote the professional management of governmental financial resources by identifying, developing, and advancing fiscal strategies, policies, and practices for the public benefit. Established 1906.

Government Management Information Sciences Users Group (GMIS)

P.O. Box 27923
Austin, Texas 78755
877-963-4647; fax: 512-857-7711

Website: gmis.org

GMIS listserv: Headquarters@GMIS.org

Executive director: Johnny A. Walton

Purpose: To provide a forum for the exchange of ideas, information, and techniques; and to foster enhancements in hardware, software, and communication developments as they relate to government activities. State and local government agencies are members represented by their top computer or information technology professionals. The GMIS Annual Educational Conference promotes sharing of ideas and the latest technology. GMIS sponsors an annual "Professional of the Year" program, publishes a newsletter, and provides organizational support to 19 state chapters. State chapters enable member agencies within a geographical area to develop close relationships and to foster the spirit and intent of GMIS through cooperation, assistance, and mutual support. GMIS is affiliated with KommITS, a sister organization of local governments in Sweden; SOCITM in the United Kingdom; ALGIM in New Zealand; VIAG in The Netherlands; MISA/ASIM in Ontario, Canada; LOLA-International (Linked Organisation of Local Authority ICT Societies); and V-ICT-OR in Belgium. Established 1971.

Governmental Accounting Standards Board (GASB)

401 Merritt 7
P.O. Box 5116
Norwalk, Connecticut 06856-5116
203-847-0700; fax: 203-849-9714

Website: gasb.org

Chairman: Robert Attmore

Major publications: Governmental Accounting Standards Series; Codification of Standards; implementation guides; Suggested Guidelines for Voluntary Reporting; exposure drafts; Preliminary Views documents; *The GASB Report* (monthly newsletter); plain-language user guides

Purpose: To establish and improve standards of financial accounting and reporting for state and local governmental entities. GASB standards guide the preparation of those entities' external financial reports so that users of the reports can obtain the state and local government financial information needed to make economic, social, and political decisions. Interested parties are encouraged to read and comment on discussion documents of proposed standards, which can be downloaded free of charge from the GASB website. Final standards, guides to implementing standards and using government financial reports, and subscriptions to the GASB's publications can be ordered through the website as well. GASB's website also provides up-to-date information about current projects, forms for submitting technical questions and signing up for e-mail news alerts, a section devoted to financial report users, and a link to its Performance Measurement for Government website. The GASB is overseen by the Financial Accounting Foundation's Board of Trustees. Established 1984.

Governmental Research Association (GRA)

P.O. Box 292300
402 Samford Hall
Samford University
Birmingham, Alabama 35229
585-327-7054

Website: graonline.org

President: Kent Garder

Major publications: *Directory of Organizations and Individuals Professionally Engaged in Governmental Research and Related Activities* (annual); *GRA Reporter* (quarterly)

Purpose: To promote and coordinate the activities of governmental research agencies; to encourage the development of effective organization and methods for the administration and operation of government; to encourage the development of common standards for the appraisal of results; to facilitate the exchange of ideas and experiences; and to serve as a clearinghouse. Established 1914.

ICMA

777 North Capitol Street, N.E., Suite 500
Washington, D.C. 20002-4201
202-289-4262; fax: 202-962-3500

Website: icma.org

Executive director: Robert J. O'Neill Jr.

Major publications: *Homeland Security: Best Practices for Local Government; Statistics for Public Administration: Practical Uses for Better Decision Making; Economic Development: Strategies for State and Local Practice* (2nd ed.); *Capital Budgeting and Finance: A Guide for Local Governments* (2nd ed.); *Human Resource Management in Local Government: An Essential Guide* (3rd ed.); *Managing Local Government: Cases in Effectiveness; Effective Supervisory Practices* (4th ed.); *Leading Your Community: A Guide for Local Elected Leaders; Budgeting: A Guide for Local Governments; A Revenue Guide for Local Government*; "Green" Books, *The Municipal Year Book, Public Management (PM)* magazine, *In Focus* (formerly *IQ Reports*), *ICMA Newsletter;* self-study courses, training packages

Purpose: To create excellence in local governance by developing and advocating professional management of local government worldwide. ICMA provides member support; publications, data, and information; peer and results-oriented assistance; and training and professional development to more than 9,000 city, town, and county experts and other individuals throughout the world. The management decisions made by ICMA's members affect 185 million individuals living in thousands of communities, from small villages and towns to large metropolitan areas. Established 1914.

ICMA Retirement Corporation (ICMA-RC)

777 North Capitol Street, N.E., Suite 600
Washington, D.C. 20002
202-962-4600; fax: 202-962-4601
800-669-7400

Website: www.icmarc.org

President/CEO: Joan McCallen

Purpose: To provide retirement plans and related services for more than 920,000 public employees in over 9,000 retirement plans. An independent financial services corporation focused on the retirement savings needs of the public sector, ICMA-RC is dedicated to helping build retirement security for public employees by providing investment tools, financial education, and other retirement-related services. The corporation also works to ease the administrative responsibility of local, city, and state governments that offer these benefits to their employees. Established 1972.

Institute of Internal Auditors, Inc., (The IIA)

247 Maitland Avenue
Altamonte Springs, Florida 32701-4201
407-937-1111; fax: 407-937-1101

Website: theiia.org

Chairman of the Board: Dennis K. Beran

Major publications: *Internal Auditor; Tone at the Top* (quarterly corporate governance newsletter)

Purpose: To provide comprehensive professional development and standards for the practice of internal auditing; and to research, disseminate, and promote education in internal auditing and internal control. The IIA offers the Certified Government Auditing Professional (CGAP) to distinguish leaders in public sector auditing. In addition to offering quality assessment services, the IIA performs custom on-site seminars for government auditors and offers educational products that address issues pertaining to government auditing. An international professional association with global headquarters in Altamonte Springs, Florida, The IIA has more than 140,000 members in internal auditing, governance, internal control, information technology audit, education, and security. With representation from more than 165 countries, The IIA is the internal audit profession's global voice, recognized authority, acknowledged leader, chief advocate, and principal educator worldwide. Established 1941.

Institute for Public Administration (IPA)

180 Graham Hall
University of Delaware
Newark, Delaware 19716-7380
302-831-8971; fax: 302-831-3488

Website: ipa.udel.edu

Director: Jerome R. Lewis

Major publications: IPA Reports, available at dspace.udel.edu:8080/dspace/handle/19716/7

Purpose: To address the policy, planning, and management needs of its partners through the integration of applied research, professional development, and the education of tomorrow's leaders. IPA provides direct staff assistance, research, policy analysis, training, and forums while contributing to the scholarly body of knowledge in public administration. Established 1973.

Institute of Transportation Engineers (ITE)

1627 Eye Street, N.W., Suite 600
Washington, D.C. 20006
202-785-0060; fax: 202-785-0609

Website: ite.org

Executive director: Thomas W. Brahms

Major publications: *Trip Generation, Parking Generation; Innovative Bicycle Treatments; Transportation and Land Use Development; Transportation Engineering Handbook; Transportation Planning Handbook; Manual of Transportation Engineering Studies; Traffic Safety Toolbox, A Primer on Traffic Safety; Manual of Uniform Traffic Control Devices, 2009; Traffic Control Devices Handbook; ITE Journal*

Purpose: To promote professional development in the field through education, research, development of public awareness, and exchange of information. Established 1930.

International Association of Assessing Officers (IAAO)

314 West 10th Street
Kansas City, Missouri 64105
816-701-8100; fax: 816-701-8149

Website: iaao.org

Executive director: Lisa J. Daniels

Major publications: *Journal of Property Tax Assessment and Administration; Property Appraisal and Assessment Administration; Property Assessment Valuation* (3rd ed., 2010); *Mass Appraisal of Real Property* (1999); *GIS Guidelines for Assessors* (2nd ed., with URISA, 1999); Assessment Standards

Purpose: To provide leadership in accurate property valuation, property tax administration, and property tax policy throughout the world. Established 1934.

International Association of Chiefs of Police (IACP)

515 North Washington Street
Alexandria, Virginia 22314-2357
703-836-6767; fax: 703-836-4543
800-THE IACP

Website: theiacp.org

Executive director: Daniel N. Rosenblatt

Major publications: *Police Chief; Training Keys*

Purpose: To advance the art of police science through the development and dissemination of improved administrative, technical, and operational practices, and to promote the use of such practices in police work. Fosters police cooperation through the exchange of information among police administrators, and encourages all police officers to adhere to high standards of performance and conduct. Established 1893.

International Association of Fire Chiefs (IAFC)

4025 Fair Ridge Drive, Suite 300
Fairfax, Virginia 22033-2868
703-273-0911; fax: 703-273-9363

Website: iafc.org

Executive director/CEO: Mark Light, CAE

Major publication: *On Scene* (twice-monthly newsletter)

Purpose: To enhance the professionalism and capabilities of career and volunteer fire chiefs, chief fire officers, and managers of emergency service organizations throughout the international community through vision, services, information, education, and representation. Established 1873.

International Association of Venue Managers (IAVM)

635 Fritz Drive, Suite 100
Coppell, Texas 75019-4442
972-906-7441; fax: 972-906-7418

Website: iavm.org

President/CEO: Vicki Hawarden, CMP

Major publications: *Facility Manager; IAVM Guide to Members and Services; IAVM E-News*

Purpose: To educate, advocate for, and inspire public assembly venue professionals worldwide. Established 1925.

International Code Council

500 New Jersey Avenue, N.W., 6th Floor
Washington, D.C. 20001-2070
888-422-7233; fax: 202-783-2348

Website: iccsafe.org

CEO: Richard P. Weiland

Major publication: *The International Codes*

Purpose: To build safety and fire prevention by developing the codes used to construct residential and commercial buildings, including homes and schools. Most U.S. cities, counties, and states that adopt codes choose the international codes developed by the ICC, a membership association. Established 1994.

International Economic Development Council (IEDC)

734 15th Street, N.W., Suite 900
Washington, D.C. 20005
202-223-7800; fax: 202-223-4745

Website: iedconline.org

President/CEO: Jeffrey A. Finkle, CEcD

Major publications: *Economic Development Journal; Economic Development Now; Economic Development America; Federal Directory; Federal Review; Budget Overview*

Purpose: To help economic development professionals improve the quality of life in their communities. With more than 4,000 members, IEDC represents all levels of government, academia, and private industry, providing a broad range of member services that includes research, advisory services, conferences, professional certification, professional development, publications, and legislative tracking. Established 2001.

International Institute of Municipal Clerks (IIMC)

8331 Utica Avenue, Suite 200
Rancho Cucamonga, California 91730
909-944-4162; fax: 909-944-8545
800-251-1639

Website: iimc.com

Executive director: Chris Shalby

Major publications: *IIMC News Digest; The Language of Local Government; Meeting Administration Handbook; Parliamentary Procedures in Local Government; Role Call: Strategy for a Professional Clerk;* "Partners in Democracy" video, case study packets, technical bulletins

Purpose: To promote continuing education and certification through university and college-based institutes, and provide networking solutions, services, and benefits to its members worldwide. Established 1947.

International Municipal Lawyers Association (IMLA)

7910 Woodmont Avenue, Suite 1440
Bethesda, Maryland 20814
202-466-5424; fax: 202-785-0152

E-mail: info@imla.org

Website: imla.org

General counsel/executive director: Chuck Thompson

Major publications: *The IMLA Model Ordinance Service; Municipal Lawyer*

Purpose: To provide continuing legal education events, publications, research, legal advocacy assistance, and excellent networking opportunities for the local government legal community. IMLA is a membership organization of U.S. and Canadian city and county attorneys. Established 1935.

International Public Management Association for Human Resources (IPMA-HR)

1617 Duke Street
Alexandria, Virginia 22314
703-549-7100; fax: 703-684-0948

Website: ipma-hr.org

Executive director: Neil E. Reichenberg

Major publications: *Public Personnel Management; HR Bulletin; IPMA-HR News*

Purpose: To improve service to the public by promoting quality human resource management in the public sector. Established 1973.

League of Women Voters of the United States (LWVUS)

1730 M Street, N.W., Suite 1000
Washington, D.C. 20036-4508
202-429-1965; fax: 202-429-0854

Website: lwv.org

Executive director: Nancy Tate

Major publications: *Choosing the President 2008: A Citizen's Guide to the Electoral Process;* voters' reference guides and brochures in English and Spanish

Purpose: To encourage informed and active participation in government and to influence public policy through education and advocacy. The league's current advocacy priorities are health care reform, climate change, election reform, a fair judiciary, immigration, openness in government, redistricting reform, campaign finance, lobbying, and election reform. The League of Women Voters Education Fund, a separate but complementary organization, provides research and public education services to the public to encourage and enable citizen participation in government. Current public education programs include voter outreach and education, the Vote 411.org website, election reform, judicial independence, and international forms and exchange activities. The league is a nonpartisan political organization. Established 1920.

National Animal Control Association (NACA)

P.O. Box 480851
Kansas City, Missouri 64148-0851
913-768-1319; fax: 913-768-1378

Website: nacanet.org

President: Todd Stosvy

Major publications: *The NACA News; The NACA Training Guide*

Purpose: To provide training for animal control personnel; consultation and guidance for local governments on animal control ordinances, animal shelter design, budget and program planning, and staff training; and public education. Established 1978.

National Association of Counties (NACo)

25 Massachusetts Avenue, N.W., Suite 500
Washington, D.C. 20001-1431
202-393-6226; fax: 202-393-2630

Website: naco.org

Executive director: Larry Naake

Major publications: *County News; NACo e-News*

Purpose: To provide essential services to the nation's 2,995 counties. The only national organization that represents county governments in the United States, NACo advances issues with a unified voice before the federal government; improves the public's understanding of county government, assists counties in finding and sharing innovative solutions through education and research, and provides value-added services to save counties and taxpayers money. Established 1935.

National Association of County and City Health Officials (NACCHO)

1100 17th Street, N.W., 7th Floor
Washington, D.C. 20036
202-783-5550; fax: 202-783-1583

Website: naccho.org

Executive director: Robert M. Pestronk, MPH

Major publications: *National Profile of Local Health Departments* (annual); *Public Health Dispatch* (newsletter); *NACCHO Exchange* (quarterly); research briefs and videos

Purpose: To support efforts that protect and improve the health of all people and all communities by promoting national policy, developing resources and programs, seeking health equity, and supporting effective local public health practice and systems. Established 1960s.

National Association for County Community and Economic Development (NACCED)

2025 M Street, N.W., Suite 800
Washington, D.C. 20036-3309
202-367-1149; fax: 202-367-2149

Website: nacced.org

Executive director: John Murphy

Purpose: To help develop the technical capacity of county agencies in administering community development, economic development, and affordable housing programs. Created as an affiliate of the National Association of Counties (NACo), NACCED is a nonprofit national organization that also serves as a voice within NACo to articulate the needs, concerns, and interests of county agencies. Established 1978.

National Association of Development Organizations (NADO)

400 North Capitol Street, N.W., Suite 390
Washington, D.C. 20001
202-624-7806; fax: 202-624-8813

Website: nado.org

Executive director: Matthew Chase

Major publications: *EDFS Reporter; NADO News; Regional Development Digest*

Purpose: To provide training, information, and representation for regional development organizations serving small metropolitan and rural America. Building on nearly four decades of experience, the association offers its members exclusive access to a variety of services and benefits—all of which are crafted to enhance the activities, programs, and prospects of regional development organizations. Established 1970s.

National Association of Housing and Redevelopment Officials (NAHRO)

630 Eye Street, N.W.
Washington, D.C. 20001
202-289-3500; fax: 202-289-8181
877-866-2476

Website: nahro.org

CEO: Saul N. Ramirez

Major publications: *Journal of Housing and Community Development; NAHRO Monitor; Directory of Local Agencies; The NAHRO Public Relations Handbook; Commissioners Handbook*

Purpose: To serve as a professional membership organization representing local housing authorities; community development agencies; and professionals in the housing, community development, and redevelopment fields. Divided into eight regions and 43 chapters, NAHRO works to provide decent and affordable housing for low- and moderate-income persons. It provides its 20,000 members with information on federal policy, legislation, regulations, and funding. It also provides professional development and training programs in all phases of agency operations, including management, maintenance, and procurement. In addition, NAHRO sponsors a legislative conference, a summer conference, and a national conference and exhibition every year. Established 1933.

National Association of Regional Councils (NARC)

1666 Connecticut Avenue, N.W., Suite 300
Washington, D.C. 20009-1038
202-986-1032; fax: 202-986-1038

Website: narc.org

Executive director: Fred Abousleman

Purpose: To promote regional approaches and collaboration in addressing diverse development challenges. A nonprofit membership organization, NARC has represented the interests of its members and has advanced regional cooperation through effective interaction and advocacy with Congress, federal officials, and other related agencies and interest groups for more than 40 years. Its member organizations are composed of multiple local government units, such as regional councils and metropolitan planning organizations, that work together to serve American communities, large and small, urban and rural. Among the issues it addresses are transportation, homeland security and regional preparedness, economic and community development, the environment, and a variety of community concerns of interest to member organizations. NARC provides its members with valuable information and research on key national policy issues, federal policy developments, and best practices; in addition, it conducts enriching training sessions, conferences, and workshops. Established 1967.

National Association of Schools of Public Affairs and Administration (NASPAA)

1029 Vermont Avenue, N.W., Suite 1100
Washington, D.C. 20005
202-628-8965; fax: 202-626-4978

E-mail: naspaa@naspaa.org

Websites: naspaa.org; globalmpa.org; and publicservicecareers.org

Executive director: Laurel McFarland

Major publications: *Journal of Public Affairs Education (J-PAE)*; Newsletter; *MPA Accreditation Standards*; MPA/MPP Brochure; peer review and accreditation documents

Purpose: To serve as a national and international center for information about programs and developments in the area of public affairs and administration; to foster goals and standards of educational excellence; to represent members' concerns and interests in the formulation and support of national, state, and local policies for public affairs education and research; and to serve as a specialized accrediting agency for MPA/MPP degrees. Established 1970.

National Association of State Chief Information Officers (NASCIO)

c/o AMR Management Services
201 East Main Street, Suite 1405
Lexington, Kentucky 40507
859-514-9156; fax: 859-514-9166

Website: nascio.org

Executive director: Doug Robinson

Major publications: *State CIO Top Ten Policy and Technology Priorities for 2012; 2011 Best Practices in the Use of Information Technology in State Government; The 2011 State CIO Survey; State Cyber Security Resource Guide: Awareness, Education, and Training Initiatives; Capitals in the Clouds–The Case for Cloud Computing in State Government, Parts I-III; CIO Leadership for State Governments: Emerging Trends and Practices; On the Fence: IT Implications of the Health Benefit Exchanges; State IT Workforce: Under Pressure; State Governments at Risk: A Call to Secure Citizen Data and Inspire Public Trust; Friends, Followers, and Feeds: A National Survey of Social Media Use in State Government; The Heart of the Matter: A Core Services Taxonomy for State IT Security Programs; NASCIO Connections* (newsletter)

Purpose: To be the premier network and resource for state chief information officers (CIOs) and a leading advocate for information technology (IT) policy at all levels of government. NASCIO represents state CIOs and IT executives from the states, territories, and the District of Columbia. Its primary state government members are senior officials who have executive-level and statewide responsibility for IT leadership. State officials who are involved in agency-level IT management may participate as state members; representatives from other public sector and nonprofit organizations may participate as associate members. Private sector firms may join as corporate members and participate in the Corporate Leadership Council. Established 1969.

National Association of Towns and Townships (NATaT)

1130 Connecticut Avenue, N.W., Suite 300
Washington, D.C. 20036
202-454-3950; fax: 202-331-1598

Website: natat.org

Federal director: Jennifer Imo

Major publication: *Washington Report*

Purpose: To strengthen the effectiveness of town and township government by educating lawmakers and public policy officials about how small-town governments operate and by advocating policies on their behalf in Washington, D.C. Established 1976.

National Career Development Association (NCDA)

305 North Beech Circle
Broken Arrow, Oklahoma 74012
918-663-7060; fax: 918-663-7058

Website: ncda.org

Executive director: Deneen Pennington

Major publications: *A Counselor's Guide to Career Assessments; The Internet: A Tool for Career Planning; Career Developments* magazine

Purpose: To promote career development of all people throughout the lifespan. A division of the American Counseling Association, NCDA provides services to the public and to professionals involved with or interested in career development; services include professional development activities, publications, research, public information, professional standards, advocacy, and recognition for achievement and service. Established 1913.

National Civic League (NCL)

1889 York Street
Denver, Colorado 80206
303-571-4343; fax: 888-314-6053

E-mail: ncl@ncl.org

Website: ncl.org

Blog: allamericacityaward.com

President: Gloria Rubio-Cortés

Major publications: *The Community Visioning and Strategic Planning Handbook; Model County Charter; National Civic Review; 8th Edition of the Model City Charter; New Civic Index; The Guide for Charter Commission*

Purpose: To strengthen democracy by increasing the capacity of our nation's people to fully participate in and build healthy and prosperous communities across America. NCL facilitates community-wide strategic planning in fiscal sustainability and comprehensive plans. Good at the science of local government and the art of public engagement, NCL leads and celebrates the progress that can be achieved when people work together. NCL is the home of the All-America City Award, now in its 63rd year. The year 2011 was the *National Civic Review*'s 100th year of publishing; the yearlong theme was "What's Working in American Communities." Established 1894.

National Community Development Association (NCDA)

522 21st Street, N.W., #120
Washington, D.C. 20006
202-293-7587; fax: 202-887-5546

Website: ncdaonline.org

Executive director: Cardell Cooper

Purpose: To serve as a national clearinghouse of ideas for local government officials and federal policy makers on pertinent national issues affecting America's communities. NCDA is a national nonprofit organization comprising more than 550 local governments across the country that administer federally supported community and economic development, housing, and human service programs, including those of the U.S. Department of Housing and Urban Development (HUD), the Community Development Block Grant program, and HOME Investment Partnerships. NCDA provides timely, direct information and technical support to its members in their efforts to secure effective and responsive housing and community development programs. Established 1968.

National Conference of State Legislatures (NCSL)

7700 East First Place
Denver, Colorado 80230
303-364-7700; fax: 303-364-7800
Also at 444 North Capitol Street, N.W., Suite 515
Washington, D.C. 20001-1201
202-624-5400; fax: 202-737-1069

Website: ncsl.org

Executive director: William T. Pound

Major publications: *Capitol to Capitol, Federal Update, State Legislatures*

Purpose: To improve the quality and effectiveness of state legislatures; to ensure that states have a strong, cohesive voice in the federal decision-making process; and to foster interstate communication and cooperation. A bipartisan organization that serves the legislators and staffs of the nation's states, commonwealths, and territories, NCSL provides research, technical assistance, and opportunities for policy makers to exchange ideas on the most pressing state issues. Established 1975.

National Environmental Health Association (NEHA)

720 South Colorado Boulevard, Suite 1000-N
Denver, Colorado 80246
303-756-9090; fax: 303-691-9490

E-mail: staff@neha.org

Website: neha.org

Executive director: Nelson E. Fabian

Major publications: *2009 H1N1 Pandemic Influenza Planning Manual; Microbial Safety of Fresh Produce; Planet Water: Investing in the World's Most Valuable Resource; Environmental Toxicants: Human Exposures and Their Health Effects; Resolving Messy Policy Problems; Journal of Environmental Health*

Purpose: To advance the professional in the environmental field through education, professional meetings, and the dissemination of information. NEHA also publishes information relating to environmental health and protection and promotes professionalism in the field. Established 1937.

National Fire Protection Association (NFPA)

One Batterymarch Park
Quincy, Massachusetts 02169-7471
617-770-3000; fax: 617-770-0700

Website: nfpa.org

President/CEO: James M. Shannon

Major publications: *Fire Protection Handbook; Fire Technology; NFPA Journal; National Electrical Code®; National Fire Codes®; Life Safety Code®; Risk Watch?; Learn Not to Burn? Curriculum;* and textbooks, manuals, training packages, detailed analyses of important fires, and fire officers guides

Purpose: To reduce the worldwide burden of fire and other hazards on the quality of life by providing and advocating scientifically based consensus codes and standards, research, training, and education. Established 1896.

National Governors Association (NGA)

Hall of the States
444 North Capitol Street, Suite 267
Washington, D.C. 20001-1512
202-624-5300; fax: 202-624-5313

Website: nga.org

Executive director: Dan Crippen

Major publications: *The Fiscal Survey of States; Policy Positions;* reports on a wide range of state issues

Purpose: To act as a liaison between the states and the federal government, and to serve as a clearinghouse for information and ideas on state and national issues. Established 1908.

National Housing Conference (NHC)

1900 M Street, N.W., Suite 200
Washington, D.C. 20036
202-466-2121; fax: 202-466-2122

Website: nhc.org

Interim president/CEO: Jeanne Engel

Major publications: *New Century Housing; NHC at Work; NHC Affordable Housing Policy Review; Washington Wire*

Purpose: To promote better communities and affordable housing for Americans through education and advocacy. Established 1931.

National League of Cities (NLC)

1301 Pennsylvania Avenue, N.W., Suite 550
Washington, D.C. 20004-1763
202-626-3000; fax: 202-626-3043

Website: nlc.org

Executive director: Donald J. Borut

President: Ted Ellis

Major publications: *Nation's Cities Weekly*, guide books, directories, and research reports

Purpose: To strengthen and promote cities as centers of opportunity, leadership, and governance; to serve as an advocate for its members in Washington in the legislative, administrative, and judicial processes that affect them; to offer training, technical assistance, and information to local government and state league officials to help them improve the quality of local government; and to research and analyze policy issues of importance to cities and towns in America. Established 1924.

National Public Employer Labor Relations Association (NPELRA)

1012 South Coast Highway, Suite M
Oceanside, California 92054
760-433-1686; fax: 760-433-1687

E-mail: info@npelra.org

Website: npelra.org

Executive director: Michael T. Kolb

Purpose: To provide its members with high-quality, progressive labor relations professional development that balances the needs of management, employees, and the public. The premier organization for public sector labor relations and human resource professionals, NPELRA is a network of state and regional affiliates. Its more than 3,000 members around the country represent public employers in a wide range of areas, from employee-management contract negotiations to arbitration under grievance and arbitration procedures. NPELRA also works to promote the interests of public sector management in the judicial and legislative arenas, and to provide opportunities for networking among members by establishing state and regional organizations throughout the country. The governmental agencies represented in NPELRA employ more than 4 million workers in federal, state, and local government.

National Recreation and Park Association (NRPA)

22377 Belmont Ridge Road
Ashburn, Virginia 20148
800-626-6772; fax: 703-858-0794

Website: nrpa.org

CEO: Barbara Tulipane

Major publication: *Parks & Recreation Magazine*

Purpose: To advance parks, recreation, and environmental conservation efforts that enhance the quality of life for all people. Established 1965.

National School Boards Association (NSBA)

1680 Duke Street
Alexandria, Virginia 22314-3493
703-838-6722; fax: 703-683-7590

Website: nsba.org

Executive director: Anne L. Bryant

Major publications: *American School Board Journal;* ASBK.com; *Inquiry and Analysis; Leadership Insider; School Board News*

Purpose: To work with and through all our state associations to advocate for excellence and equity in public education through school board leadership. Established 1940.

NIGP: The Institute for Public Procurement

151 Spring Street
Herndon, Virginia 20170-5223
703-736-8900; fax: 703-736-2818
800-FOR NIGP (800-367-6447)

Website: nigp.org

CEO: Rick Grimm, CPPO, CPPB

Major publications: *GoPro: Government Procurement* magazine, a bimonthly publication distributed to NIGP members and procurement professionals; *2011 Compensation Survey Report,* a biennial study that provides comparative compensation information to assist in classifying public procurement positions and determining appropriate salary ranges; *2011 NIGP Vision Map for Public Procurement,* which provides a strategic planning roadmap for public entities and identifies current and future issues with recommendations; *2011 Survey on the Use of Procurement Software in the Public Sector,* which provides a benchmark of measuring changes and growth in the adoption of procurement software; NIGP *Sector Spotlight* edition of *BuyWeekly*, published electronically at the beginning of the month to NIGP members with procurement-related news briefs that affect the procurement community; NIGP's *BuyWeekly,* electronic newsletter, distributed midmonth, a quick overview of current highlights in the profession and at NIGP; the *NIGP Online Dictionary of Purchasing Terms;* access to the *VAULT*, an active repository with the latest analysis and sector insights from research partner, Aberdeen Group; NIGP MEASURE, an online tool that records and reports procurement-generated savings; and an online supplier directory to over 2,000 government suppliers in the United States and Canada.

Purpose: To develop, support, and promote the public procurement profession through premier educational and research programs, professional support, technical services, and advocacy initiatives that have benefited members and constituents since 1944. With over 2,400 member agencies representing over 15,000 professionals across the United States, Canada, and countries outside of North America, NIGP is international in its reach. Its goal is recognition and esteem for the government procurement profession and its dedicated practitioners. NIGP led the way in developing Values and Guiding Principles of Public Procurement, which have been adopted or supported by over 70 organizations and over 50 NIGP chapters. Its Learning Central offers traditional face-to-face courses, independent and interactive online courses, and no-travel webinars that address current industry issues and trends affecting the way governments do business. All NIGP education experiences qualify toward achieving certification from the Universal Public Procurement Certification Council (UPPCC). NIGP hosts an annual Forum and Products Exposition, the largest gathering of public procurement officials in North America. It offers fixed-price NIGP Consulting Services, which evaluate policies and procedures, contract administration, and pcard program practices; establish relevant benchmark measures; and identify best practices. A strategic partnership between Spikes Cavell and NIGP brings a proven spend analysis solution to the U.S. public sector. The NIGP Observatory is a spend-and-supplier management solution that delivers the data, tools, and intelligence required to give procurement the insight it needs to reduce cost, realize cooperative opportunities, improve contract compliance, and drive continuous improvements in spend-and-supplier management. NIGP's technology partner, Periscope Holdings, supports the ongoing development of the NIGP Code and the 1,400-plus agencies that already use the code, a universal taxonomy for identifying commodities and services in their procurement systems. NIGP is a cofounding sponsor of U.S. Communities and its affiliate, Canadian Communities, demonstrating its conviction to fully support the practice of cooperative purchasing for the efficiencies it achieves for public entities and the tremendous savings cooperative programs realize for the taxpayer. It is also a cofounding supporter of the UPPCC and its two-level certification program for public procurement personnel. Established 1944.

Police Executive Research Forum (PERF)

1120 Connecticut Avenue, N.W., Suite 930
Washington, D.C. 20036
202-466-7820; fax: 202-466-7826

Website: policeforum.org

Executive director: Chuck Wexler

Major publication: *Subject to Debate* (bimonthly newsletter)

Purpose: To improve policing and advance professionalism through research and involvement in public policy debate. PERF is a national membership organization of progressive police executives from the largest city, county, and state law enforcement agencies. It conducts research and convenes national meetings of police executives and other stakeholders to identify best practices and policies on issues such as police use of force, crime reduction strategies, community and problem-oriented policing, and racial bias, as well as on organizational issues in policing. Incorporated 1977.

Police Foundation

1201 Connecticut Avenue, N.W.
Washington, D.C. 20036-2636
202-833-1460; fax: 202-659-9149

E-mail: pfinfo@policefoundation.org

Website: policefoundation.org

President: Hubert Williams

Major publications: *Ideas in American Policing* series; research and technical reports on a wide range of law enforcement and public safety issues

Purpose: To improve policing through research, evaluation, field experimentation, training, technical assistance, technology, and information. Objective, nonpartisan, and nonprofit, the Police Foundation helps national, state, and local governments, both in the United States and abroad, to improve performance, service delivery, accountability, and community satisfaction with police services. The foundation offers a wide range of services and specializations, including research, evaluation, surveys, management and operational reviews, climate and culture assessment, training and technical assistance, early-warning and intervention systems, community police collaboration, accountability and ethics, community policing strategies, performance management, racial profiling/biased policing, professional and leadership development. Motivating all its efforts is the goal of efficient, effective, humane policing that operates within the framework of democratic principles. Established in 1970.

Public Risk Management Association (PRIMA)

700 South Washington Street, Suite 218
Alexandria, Virginia 22314-1516
703-528-7701; fax: 703-739-0200

E-mail: info@primacentral.org

Website: primacentral.org

Executive director: Mark G. Doherty

Major publications: *Public Risk Magazine; Public Sector Risk Management Manual; Cost of Risk Evaluation in State and Local Government; 1998 Tort Liability Today: A Guide for State and Local Governments; Shaping a Secure Future* (video)

Purpose: To promote effective risk management in the public interest as an essential component of administration. Established 1978.

Public Technology Institute (PTI)

1426 Prince Street
Alexandria, Virginia 22314
202-626-2400; fax: 202-626-2498

E-mail: dbowen@pti.org

Website: pti.org

Executive director: Alan R. Shark

Major publications: *CIO Leadership for Cities & Counties; Local Energy Assurance Planning Guide; Beyond e-Government & e-Democracy: A Global Perspective; Measuring Up 2.0; Performance Is the Best Politics; Roads Less Traveled: ITS for Sustainable Communities; Sustainable Building Technical Manual; Mission Possible: Strong Governance Structures for the Integration of Justice Information Systems; E-Government: Factors Affecting ROI; E-Government: A Strategic Planning Guide for Local Officials; Why Not Do It Ourselves? A Resource Guide for Local Government Officials and Citizens Regarding Public Ownership of Utility Systems; Online* magazine (www.prismonline.org); *Winning Solutions* (annual); numerous case studies on energy and environmental technology development and sustainable management

Purpose: To identify and test technologies and management approaches that help all local governments provide the best possible services to citizens and business communities. With ICMA, NLC, and NACo, PTI works with progressive member cities and counties to (1) make communities "well-connected" by advancing communication capabilities; (2) develop tools and processes for wise decision making; and (3) promote sustainable approaches that ensure a balance between economic development and a clean, quality environment. PTI's member program engages cities and counties as laboratories for research, development, and public enterprise to advance technology applications in telecommunications, energy, the environment, transportation, and public safety. To disseminate member research, PTI provides print and electronic resources, and peer consultation and networking. Through partnerships with private vendors, PTI offers several technology products and services that help local governments save money by bypassing rigorist RFP requirements as they are competitively bid and chosen for superior quality and competitive pricing. PTI's research and development division continues to examine information and Internet technology, public safety, geographic information systems (GIS), energy-conserving technologies, sustainable management, and intelligent transportation systems. Established 1971.

Sister Cities International (SCI)

915 15th Street, N.W., 4th Floor
Washington DC 20005
202-347-8630; fax 202-393-6524

E-mail: info@sister-cities.org

Website: sister-cities.org

Executive vice president and interim CEO: Jim Doumas

Major publication: Sister Cities International Membership Directory

Purpose: To build global cooperation at the municipal level, promote cultural understanding, and stimulate economic development. SCI is a nonprofit citizen diplomacy network that creates and strengthens partnerships between U.S. and international communities. With its international headquarters in Washington, D.C., SCI promotes sustainable development, youth involvement, cultural understanding, and humanitarian assistance. As an international membership organization, SCI officially certifies, represents, and supports partnerships between U.S. cities, counties, and states and similar jurisdictions in other countries to ensure their continued commitment and success. The SCI network represents nearly 2,000 partnerships in 136 countries. Established 1956.

Solid Waste Association of North America (SWANA)

1100 Wayne Avenue, Suite 700
Silver Spring, Maryland 20907-7219
301-585-2898; fax: 301-589-7068
800-467-9262

E-mail: info@swana.org

Website: swana.org

Executive director: John H. Skinner, PhD

Purpose: To advance the practice of environmentally and economically sound municipal solid-waste management in North America. Established 1961.

Special Libraries Association (SLA)

331 South Patrick Street
Alexandria, Virginia 22314-3501
703-647-4900; fax: 703-647-4901

E-mail: sla@sla.org

Website: sla.org

CEO: Janice R. Lachance

Major publication: *Information Outlook*

Purpose: To further the professional growth and success of its membership. The international association representing the interests of thousands of information professionals in 84 countries, SLA offers a variety of programs and services designed to help its members serve their customers more effectively and succeed in an increasingly challenging global information arena. Established 1909.

State and Local Legal Center

Hall of States
444 N Capitol Street, N.W., Suite 500
Washington, D.C. 20001

Website: statelocallc.org

Chief consult: Lisa Sorenson

Publication list: Available on request

Purpose: The State and Local Legal Center files amicus briefs in the U.S. Supreme Court in support of states and local governments, conducts moot courts for attorneys arguing in the Supreme Court, and provides other assistance to states and local governments in connection with Supreme Court litigation.

Universal Public Procurement Certification Council (UPPCC)

151 Spring Street
Herndon, Virginia 20170
800-367-6447; fax: 703-796-9611

E-mail: certification@uppcc.org

Website: uppcc.org

Director: Ann Peshoff, CAE, CMP

Purpose: To identify and establish a standard of competency for the public procurement profession; establish and monitor eligibility requirements of those interested in achieving certification; and further the cause of certification in the public sector. The UPPCC certification programs have been established to meet the requirements of all public procurement personnel in federal, state, and local governments. Certification, which reflects established standards and competencies for those engaged in governmental procurement and attests to the purchaser's ability to obtain maximum value for the taxpayer's dollar, is applicable to all public and governmental organizations, regardless of size. The council offers two credentials: the Certified Professional Public Buyer (CPPB), which applies to individuals who have demonstrated prescribed levels of professional competency as buyers in governmental procurement, and the Certified Public Procurement Officer (CPPO), which applies to similar individuals who also assume managerial functions within their jurisdictions or agencies. As the trend in governmental procurement is for mandatory certification of procurement professionals, these credentials communicate to the taxpayer that the public employee who manages tax dollars has reached a level of education and practical experience within government procurement to be recognized by the UPPCC. Established 1978.

Urban Affairs Association (UAA)

University of Wisconsin–Milwaukee
P.O. Box 413
Milwaukee, Wisconsin 53201-0413
414-229-3025

Website: urbanaffairsassociation.org

Executive director: Dr. Margaret Wilder

Major publications: *Journal of Urban Affairs; Urban Affairs* (a newsletter)

Purpose: To encourage the dissemination of information and research findings about urbanism and urbanization; to support the development of university education, research, and service programs in urban affairs; and to foster the development of urban affairs as a professional and academic field. Established 1969.

Urban Institute (UI)

2100 M Street, N.W.
Washington, D.C. 20037
202-833-7200

Website: urban.org

President: Robert D. Reischauer

Publications: Research papers, policy briefs, events, podcasts, web modules, and books on social and economic issues, including health care, welfare reform, immigration policy, tax reform, prisoner reentry, housing policy, retirement, charitable giving, school accountability, economic development, and community revitalization; all publications available online except books

Purpose: To respond to needs for objective analyses and basic information on the social and economic challenges confronting the nation, and for nonpartisan evaluation of the government policies and programs designed to alleviate such problems. Established 1968.

Urban and Regional Information Systems Association (URISA)

701 Lee Street, Suite 680
Des Plaines, Illinois 60016
847-824-6300; fax: 847-824-6363

Website: urisa.org

Executive director: Wendy Nelson

Major publications: *URISA Journal; The GIS Professional;* Quick Studies, books and compendiums, salary surveys, conference proceedings, videos

Purpose: To promote the effective and ethical use of spatial information and information technologies for the understanding and management of urban and regional systems. URISA is a nonprofit professional, educational, and multidisciplinary association where professionals from all parts of the spatial data community can come together and share concerns and ideas. It is the professional home of choice for public sector GIS and information technology executives throughout the United States, Canada, and other countries worldwide. Established 1963.

U.S. Conference of Mayors (USCM)

1620 Eye Street, N.W.
Washington, D.C. 20006
202-293-7330; fax: 202-293-2352

E-mail: info@usmayors.org

Website: usmayors.org

Executive director/CEO: Tom Cochran

Major publications: *U.S. Mayor; Mayors of America's Principal Cities*

Purpose: To act as the official nonpartisan organization of cities with populations of 30,000 or more; to aid the development of effective national urban policy; to ensure that federal policy meets urban needs; and to provide mayors with leadership and management tools. Each city is represented in the conference by its mayor. Established 1932.

Water Environment Federation (WEF)

601 Wythe Street
Alexandria, Virginia 22314-1994
703-684-2430; fax: 703-684-2492
800-666-0206

Websites: wef.org, weftec.org

Executive director: Jeff Eger

Major publications: *Water Environment Research; Water Practice; Water Environment and Technology; Operations Forum; Water Environment Regulation Watch; Biosolids Technical Bulletin; Utility Executive Technical Bulletin;* series of Manuals of Practice

Purpose: To develop and disseminate technical information concerning the preservation and enhancement of the global water environment. As an integral component of its mandate, the federation has pledged to act as a source of education to the general public as well as to individuals engaged in the field of water pollution control. Established 1928.

Authors and Contributors

ic • Innovations • Pensions • Health Insurance Pro

pact Fees • 311/CRM Systems • Police and Fire • D

ation • Innovations • Sustainability • CAO Compensatio

Pensions • CAO Compensation • Sustainability • Dire

ls • Innovations • Police and Fire • Health Insurance Pro

Directories • Police and Fire • Pensions • CAO Compen

s • E-Government • Sustainability • Directorie

Insurance Programs • CAO Compensation • Pensio

sation • Development Impact Fees • 311/CRM Systems • H

nt • Sustainability • Police and Fire • Directo

ries • Innovations • Health Insurance Programs • Pen

ns • 311/CRM Systems • Pensions • E-Government •

Sustainability • CAO Compensation • Health I

surance Programs • 311/CRM Systems • Pens

Authors and Contributors

Jeffrey Amell is the strategy and marketing officer for CIGNA. His primary focus is on the government and education sector, including state and local government, education, and higher education markets. He has been in the financial services sector for over 10 years and previously ran the Group Retiree Medical business at The Hartford. Prior to that, his professional experience included vice president of marketing for Diageo in the United Kingdom and brand manager of Jose Cuervo tequila in the United States; he was also in brand management at Procter & Gamble in their food/beverage division. Mr. Amell holds a chemical engineering degree from Clarkson University and a master's of business administration from the University of Chicago.

Ron Carlee is ICMA's chief operating officer and adjunct professor at the Trachtenberg School of Public Policy and Public Administration at the George Washington University. Prior to joining ICMA in 2009, he had held several positions in Arlington, Virginia, including county manager, director of health and human services, director of parks and recreation, and director of information services. Before that, he was assistant to the mayor in Birmingham, Alabama. Dr. Carlee is a Fellow in the National Academy for Public Administration. He holds a bachelor's degree from the University of Montevallo, a master's degree from the University of Alabama–Birmingham, and doctorate in public administration from George Mason University.

David Eichenthal is a director and senior managing consultant with Public Financial Management (PFM). Prior to joining PFM, he served for six and a half years as president and CEO of the Ochs Center for Metropolitan Studies in Chattanooga, Tennessee. As city finance officer and director of performance review in Chattanooga, he oversaw the launch of the city's 311 system and implementation of chattanoogaRESULTS. He has also spent more than a dozen years in senior management positions with the city of New York. Mr. Eichenthal is the author of two chapters in *Urban Politics New York Style* (H. E. Sharpe, 1990) and coauthor of a chapter in *Innovations in E-Government* (Rowman & Littlefield, 2005), and he has published articles in the *New York Daily News, New York Newsday, The Chattanooga Times Free Press, Justice Quarterly, and The Prison Journal.* He has taught public administration and public policy at New York University, Baruch College, the University of Tennessee at Chattanooga, and Georgia State University. He earned a degree in public policy from the University of Chicago and a law degree from New York University.

Cory Fleming served as the project director for the ICMA National Study of 311 and Customer Service Technology, funded by the Alfred P. Sloan Foundation, from 2006 to 2011 and now oversees ICMA's technical assistance services in 311/CRM technology. She is currently assisting the city of Philadelphia in the selection of a new CRM application for Philly311. For over a decade, Ms. Fleming worked with local governments, community groups, and nonprofit organizations on a variety of development issues at the Iowa Department of Economic Development. Just prior to joining ICMA, she was at the Center on Nonprofits and Philanthropy at the Urban Institute, where she conducted research on the building capacity of nonprofit organizations.

She also edited *The GIS Guide for Local Government Officials,* a joint publication produced by ESRI and ICMA and released in 2005, and she is currently working on a follow-up publication, *The Elected Official's Guide to GIS.*

George C. Homsy is a PhD candidate in Cornell University's Department of City and Regional Planning, where he focuses on sustainability in small communities as well as on property rights, family-friendly cities, and local decision making, and he also teaches an undergraduate course titled "Sustainability in the City." He began his investigation of cities and their environmental impacts as a journalist with the public radio newsmagazine *Living on Earth,* which he cofounded and coproduced. Subsequently, as a freelance journalist, he wrote for *Planning* and *Tomorrow* magazines as well as for National Public Radio, CBS Radio's *Osgood Files,* and *The Boston Globe.* Realizing that his journalistic inquiries were driven by an interest in how urban planning addresses environmental, economic, and social issues, he earned a master's degree from Cornell and then spent five years as a planning consultant helping small- to medium-sized communities create environmentally and economically sustainable communities.

Elizabeth K. Kellar is the president/CEO of the Center for State and Local Government Excellence. She speaks and writes on a variety of issues, including ethics, workforce challenges, retirement and health plans, and intergovernmental relations. She is a Fellow in the National Academy of Public Administration (NAPA) and has served as chair for NAPA's Standing Panel on the Federal System. She also serves as ICMA's deputy executive director, overseeing public policy and representing the association at White House and congressional meetings. She serves on the advisory council of the American University School of Public Affairs and has completed two terms on the Montgomery County (Maryland) Ethics Commission, serving as the chair for three years. Her publications include *Managing with Less: A Book of Readings; Ethical Insight, Ethical Action;* and *Ethos.* Prior to joining ICMA, she was responsible for community relations for the city of Sunnyvale, California. She has a master's degree in journalism and political science from Ohio State University.

Larry L. Lawhon, PhD, AICP, is an associate professor in the Regional and Community Planning program at Kansas State University's College of Architecture, Planning and Design, where he joined the faculty in 1998. His areas of specialization are housing and community growth management. He also has approximately 12 years of experience as a local government planner. He is a member of the American Planning Association, the American Institute of Certified Planners, and the Society for American City and Regional Planning History. He received his doctorate in urban planning from Texas A&M University.

Evelina R. Moulder, director of ICMA's survey research, is responsible for the development of survey instruments, design of the sample, design of logic checks, quality control, and analysis of survey results. Among the surveys conducted by ICMA under her supervision are economic development, e-government, financing infrastructure, homeland security, labor-management relations, parks and recreation, police and fire personnel and expenditures, service delivery, technology, and SARA Title III. She has also directed several survey projects funded by other organizations. With more than 20 years of experience in local government survey research, Ms. Moulder has collaborated extensively with government agencies, professors, the private sector, and other researchers in survey development, and she has played a key role in ICMA's homeland security and emergency response initiatives, including concept and proposal development.

Donald F. Norris is professor and chair of the Department of Public Policy, and director of the Maryland Institute for Policy Analysis and Research at the University of Maryland, Baltimore County. He is a specialist in public management; urban politics; and the application, uses, and impacts of information technology (including e-government) on public organizations. He holds a BS in history from the University of Memphis and both an MA and a PhD in government from the University of Virginia.

Martha Perego is the director of ICMA's ethics program. In that capacity, she provides advice, guidance, and training to ICMA members on applying the principles of the ICMA Code of Ethics to the local government profession; administers the ethics enforcement process and provides support to the ICMA Committee on Professional Conduct; consults with local governments on the development of ethics policies and codes; and conducts training programs for local government staff and elected officials on ethical issues. She is also the author of a monthly column "Ethics Matter!" for ICMA's *PM* magazine. Prior to joining ICMA in 1998, Ms. Perego worked in local government for 17 years as a municipal manager, assistant manager, finance director, and budget analyst. She holds an undergraduate degree in public service from Pennsylvania State University and an MPA from the University of North Carolina at Chapel Hill, and she is an ICMA Credentialed Manager.

Christopher G. Reddick is an associate professor and chair of the Department of Public Administration at the University of Texas at San Antonio. His research and teaching interests are in information technology and public sector organizations. Some of his publications can be found in *Government Information Quarterly, Electronic Government*, and the *International Journal of Electronic Government Research*. Dr. Reddick recently edited the two-volume *Handbook of Research on Strategies for Local E-Government Adoption and Implementation: Comparative Studies*. He is also author of *Homeland Security Preparedness and Information Systems*, which deals with the impact of information technology on homeland security preparedness. Dr. Reddick received his BA, MA, and MBA at the University of Guelph in Ontario, Canada, and his PhD at the University of Sheffield in the United Kingdom.

James H. Svara is a professor of public affairs at Arizona State University and the director of the Center for Urban Innovation. He specializes in local government leadership, innovation, and management. He is a Fellow of the National Academy of Public Administration, a member of the board of the Alliance for Innovation, and an honorary member of ICMA, and he has served on the ICMA Strategic Planning Committee. He is currently involved in research projects on sustainability in local government and codes of ethics in associations of public professionals.

Karen Thoreson is president/chief operating officer for the Alliance for Innovation. Prior to working for the Alliance, she was economic development director for the city of Glendale, Arizona. She also served as assistant city manager of Tucson and as director of the community services department. Ms. Thoreson began her career in local government in Boulder, Colorado; since then, she has been a trainer and a speaker on public-private partnerships, community revitalization, innovation, and strategic planning. She has a bachelor's degree from the University of Minnesota and a master's degree in public administration from the University of Northern Colorado.

Mildred Warner is a professor in the City and Regional Planning Department at Cornell University, where her work is primarily on the role of local government in community development. Her research focuses on devolution, privatization, and their implications for local government service delivery. She also studies economic development and the role of local services. She publishes widely in the public administration, planning, and economic development literature. Dr. Warner received her BA from Oberlin College and her MA and PhD from Cornell.

Cumulative Index, 2008-2012

re • Innovations • Pensions • Health Insurance Pr

pact Fees • 311/CRM Systems • Police and Fire • D

ation • Innovations • Sustainability • CAO Compensatio

• Pensions • CAO Compensation • Sustainability • Dire

ns • Innovations • Police and Fire • Health Insurance Pro

Directories • Police and Fire • Pensions • CAO Compe

s • E-Government • Sustainability • Directori

Insurance Programs • CAO Compensation • Pensi

sation • Development Impact Fees • 311/CRM Systems • I

ent • Sustainability • Police and Fire • Direct

Fire • Innovations • Health Insurance Programs • Pen

ns • 311/CRM Systems • Pensions • E-Government

Sustainability • CAO Compensation • Health I

nsurance Programs • 311/CRM Systems • Pen

Cumulative Index, 2008-2012

The cumulative index comprises the years 2008 through 2012 of *The Municipal Year Book*. Entries prior to 2008 are found in earlier editions.

How to Use This Index. Entries run in chronological order, starting with 2008. The **year** is in **boldface** numerals, followed by a colon (e.g., **08:**); the relevant page numbers follow. Years are separated by semicolons.